CONSCIENCE AND JUNG'S MORAL VISION

CONSCIENCE AND JUNG'S MORAL VISION

From Id to Thou

by

David W. Robinson

Paulist Press
New York/Mahwah, N.J.

Excerpts from Jung, C. G.; *The Collected Works of C. G. Jung*. 1977 Princeton University Press. Reprinted by permission of Princeton University Press.

Cover Photo by David W. Robinson
Cover design by Sharyn Banks
Book design by Lynn Else

Library of Congress Cataloging-in-Publication Data

Robinson, David W.
    Conscience and Jung's moral vision : from id to thou / by David W. Robinson.
        p. cm.—(Jung and spirituality)
    Includes bibliographical references (p.   ) and index.
    ISBN 0-8091-4340-2 (alk. paper)
    1. Conscience. 2. Jung, C. G. (Carl Gustav), 1875–1961—Ethics. I. Title. II. Series.
    BJ1471.R63 2005
    150.19'54'092—dc22

                                                            2005005978

Published by Paulist Press
997 Macarthur Boulevard
Mahwah, New Jersey, 07430

www.paulistpress.com

Printed and bound in the
United States of America

CONTENTS

Contents

ACKNOWLEDGMENTS

(Dear Reader, the joys of scholarship—at least for this author—are a case of feast and famine. Long, long hunger, then a feasting such that the famine is all but forgotten. Oasis in the desert! Bones come alive! The writing of these Acknowledgments is a moment of feasting. The expositions, the propositions, the analyses: they will all come in abundance in the following pages, be assured. I too value them. But in this brief space, please permit me unguarded gratitude.)

In any work such as this—one that has occupied many years of a person's life, and in ways defines those years—the number of persons owed a debt of gratitude by the author is beyond recounting. I can only hope that those who have known me and have helped me, in ways large and small, will know that my gratitude is real and imperishable. Many of you have helped in ways that you do not even know. My mind's eye recalls countless gestures of kindness and generosity, not all easy, but all good. These acts of yours tipped the balance forward toward "yes" and moved the pen to paper, making real what could have disappeared. And to the nameless stranger who helped, I raise my hand in greeting. May the gift be reciprocal!

To Rod Hunter, a true scholastic warrior, whose mind is an analytical sword wielded in the service of what is true and good, I say: your patience and your fierceness saw me through. To Robert Moore, a man of great *gravitas* and a huge heart of compassion, I say: I sought you out, and you pointed the way (onward).

To Father and Mother, both of you, your unconditional support then and now is the root of my strength. To Steve Meizlish, you have journeyed with me (literally!) the whole of the way. Thank you for the freedom to travel. Ever onward! To Christopher Holgate, you are my brother, and I am yours. Though ofttimes maddening, your classical virtues inspire through example, and elevate the lives of all who know you. *In Hoc.* To Robert Mattingly, our shared discernment of the journey has spoken to me from a place of wisdom, yielding a certitude that gives fortitude. To Jennifer, you helped me to believe—priceless. Your heart of gold, amidst the suffering, taught me. To Lucinda, much is, and always will be, a mystery to me. But in this mystery much has been given, and more will be revealed! And to X, your life is a testimony to the supremacy of wisdom over youth. Love ya, bro.

To the Hermans, Father Gooley, Sister Sylvia, my brothers in Taiwan (especially James and David—Abeano, where are you?!), Robert J., Hank and Alice, Coop and Jess, beloved sister Susan, Zekey, and all others who have given of house and home—you fed and sheltered my body, and for that my heart is grateful. And to Tinapple, place of great nourishment, though no more, your image lives on!

And, believing as I do, I also wish to acknowledge the great chain of thinking, pondering, and wondering souls to whom I owe so much: Jung, of course, and also, Thoreau, Merton, Tillich, James, Otto, Blake, Campbell, Eliade, Nietzsche, Kierkegaard, Weiner, Kohák, Olney, and, the dancing and ecstatic great ones, Rumi and Eckhart and all those who now share your joy.

David W. Robinson
Columbus, Ohio
Spring, 2005

SERIES EDITORS' INTRODUCTION

ABOUT THE
JUNG AND SPIRITUALITY SERIES

The Jung and Spirituality Series was founded in 1987 in order to facilitate the utilization of Jungian psychoanalysis as a resource for in-depth interdisciplinary, multicultural, and interreligious communication and dialogue. It is a project of the Institute for Psychoanalysis, Culture and Spirituality. We are indebted to Paulist Press for its collaboration in this challenging enterprise.

The dialogue between psychoanalysis, philosophy, and spirituality has never been more important than in our time, as we attempt to face radical pluralism without losing our psychological and spiritual bearings. We believe that interdisciplinary Jungian studies offer one of the most powerful vessels for enabling the human species to become more conscious of the archetypal forces in the collective unconscious, which fuel objectifying and depreciating caricatures of the scientific, cultural, and religious "other." As a science of the soul, Jungian psychoanalysis gives us hope that we may make progress in integrative understanding of the deep foundations in the collective unconscious that we share as a species even as our lack of awareness issues in fragmenting tribalism in scientific, cultural, and spiritual endeavors. It is our hope that Jung's legacy can enable us to mature in our scientific, spiritual, and psychological development as a species. This series has been dedicated to that vision.

Since 1987, many volumes have been published by the series addressing the challenges described above. These volumes have included the dialogue between religions, the dialogue between Jungian psychoanalysis and philosophy, and the utilization of Jungian thought to improve the theory and practice of spiritual direction.

This new addition to the series, *Conscience and Jung's Moral Vision: From Id to Thou* by David Robinson, is an outstanding contribution to the goals of the series. We hope that you will find it as helpful as we have.

Margaret Shanahan, Psy.D.
Robert Moore, Ph.D.
Series Editors

The Institute for Psychoanalysis, Culture and Spirituality is a nonprofit institution (501C3) dedicated to psychoanalytic research, education, and publication. In addition to its publication series, the Institute offers education and training experiences including courses, seminars, lectures, and workshops. IPCS gives particular attention to the ways in which psychoanalytic knowledge can help us understand the interaction of personality, culture, and spirituality. IPCS offers consultation, education, and training experiences including courses, lectures, and workshops. Clinical research and training seminars are offered through the clinical research and training division, the Institute for the Science of Psychoanalysis. ISP is a Neo-Jungian Institute dedicated to carrying forward Jung's legacy of the quest for an integrative science of psychoanalysis adequate to the multidimensional complexity of human experience in personality, culture, and spirituality.

Programs by IPCS and ISP are announced at www.robertmoore-phd.com. Dr. Margaret Shanahan is Director of Studies. Dr. Robert Moore is Director of Research.

All of the activities of IPCS and ISP are dedicated to the facilitation of the psychological, moral, and spiritual maturation of our species. Contributions to the work of the Institute are tax deductible and may be sent to: IPCS/ISP, 1415 E. 54th Street, Chicago, IL 60615-5414.

FOREWORD

To the best of my knowledge, this is the first book to make explicit that a moral vision informed C. G. Jung's effort to understand and befriend the unconscious. Many have recognized that Jung sought to teach people how to integrate the autonomous psyche so that they could apply it to ethical decision making—not only in their own lives but also in the way they care for the world around them. Why then has Jungian Studies been so reticent as a field to expose this goal at the heart of Jung's alchemical endeavor? Hermetically bringing seemingly incommensurate entities—unconsciousness and consciousness—together, analytical psychology has concealed the fact that its ends and its methods inescapably implicate the conscience.

Jung himself gives us part of the reason. In a foreword written in 1949 for a book that was groundbreaking to the Jungians of its time, Erich Neumann's *Depth Psychology and a New Ethic*, Jung wrote "it is only as an empiricist, and never as a philosopher, that I have been concerned with depth psychology, and cannot boast of ever having tried my hand at formulating ethical principles" (p. 11). In other words, Jung thought it might sound presumptuous to claim to derive an ethical standpoint from the analysis of the unconscious. Even though his psychology, in its reach, is both philosophical and religious, Jung did not want to be caught posing as a philosopher, nor did he care to be seen mounting a minister's pulpit. Because of his interest in topics that were normally relegated to theology, he was already being labeled a mystic. Because expressing his own deepest standpoint and reactions was part of his analytic technique, he was ever vulnerable to the mis-

understanding that he was simply practicing his personal prejudices. Jung's writings on psychotherapy make it clear that he
understood analysis as dialogic intersubjectivity aiming at an ethical position with the help of an intervening "third," the objectivity of the psyche itself; but his anxiety as to how this might look
to the world made him sometimes speak as if the process were an
objective, empirical investigation of the "unconscious." This
defensive turn to the persona of a scientist has undercut his actual
contribution to science, having the unfortunate effect of making
the unconscious seem like a clinical object, and the Jungian school
just one more way of looking at it from the privileged distance of
a theory.

Another reason for the denial of the centrality of conscience
in Jungian work among contemporary students of analytical psychology might lie in the way Jungian analysts are trained. Even
today, most analytic institutes do not offer courses in the exchange
of values as a process in analytical psychotherapy. And those of us
who would like to develop just this discourse have found that it is
a very hard thing to talk about. I still recall the first seminar I gave
at the Jung Institute of San Francisco, entitled "Integrity in the
Analytic Relationship." The candidates and I were talking about
something we felt deeply but could barely articulate. We did not
have a language for the process involved.

A third reason some of us have been skittish about getting
into the ethical implications of our discipline goes beyond Jung
and the traditions of Jungian training. Dialogue between the
Jungian intellectual community and the academy, where moral
philosophers and moral psychologists work and publish, is still in
an embryonic stage. Broad-based prejudices against Jung, based
on a misreading of his personal and political history, still color the
attitude of those who are asked to entertain the moral implications of his thought.

The three parts of the answer to why Jungians have not been
very bold in exposing the moral ambition at the heart of Jung's
thought suggest the structure of a double bind: you can't do this,
you can't do that, and you can't get out of the paralyzing field of
the paradox. Fortunately, members of my own generation of
Jungian scholars have begun to shake off the spell and have started

in unembarrassed earnest to explore the ethical implications of Jungian thought. I think of Andrew Samuels, who told us we could walk in this area in his essay "Original Morality in a Depressed Culture," and his later book *The Political Psyche;* Hester Solomon, whose paper "The Ethical Attitude" served to keynote an international conference on ethics in analytical psychology; Robert Bosnak, who has argued that analysis works to release ethical instincts; and Murray Stein, who was the first I know to recognize that Jung was developing a Swiss Protestant conscience tradition in his writings and made his own contribution to that tradition with *Solar Conscience/Lunar Conscience: An Essay on the Psychological Foundations of Morality, Lawfulness, and the Sense of Justice.*

Some of these authors and their books are mentioned in this one, for they are in a sense its forebears. But this book makes it clear that none of us has looked as closely as we might have at the way Jung himself framed the problem of conscience. Late in his life, he packed a lifetime of struggle with the problem of conscience in the suitcase of a traditional Western ethical understanding of a conflict of duties. It is the complex vision inside that David Robinson unpacks in this book. Unpacks and reveals its surprising serviceability, for he discovers a sturdy set of moral clothes fully able to hold their own beside the more fashionable ethical wardrobes of Nietzsche and Buber. It will be up to the reader of this book to try on Jung's ideas about the role of individual conscience in achieving a moral standpoint. Not everyone who pursues the arguments in this book will find a good fit. But readers who allow the pages that follow to shape their perception of Jung will learn to recognize the moral genius of a thinker who in dark times, by investigating the conscience with the conscience, revived an all-but-forgotten method of moral discernment and established an unsuspected ground for the ethical.

John Beebe

INTRODUCTION

Chapter 1

———❦———

CONSCIENCE: BACKGROUND, PROBLEMS, AND PROPOSITION

A FORAY

If one attempts to better understand a particular psychological phenomenon by tracing its conceptual development through the history of Western thought, it quickly becomes apparent that while certain concepts are perennially present, such as *soul*, or *mind*, or *the good*, the precise meaning of these terms changes with the spirit of the age and the demands of its people, those who have lived and died by such words. Though this fluidity of meaning presents certain difficulties for the investigator, it also suggests that these concepts point to vital elements of experience, complex in themselves, that have been necessary to account for and include in any adequate worldview. In the beginning was the experience, from which was born the word.

Sociologically, these primordial words support plausibility structures, facilitating the social contract. Psychologically, these concepts and their attendant images denote what is most significant, because most compelling, for the inward life. Philosophically, in either austere singularity, or complex unison, or in conflicted tension, these terms comprise our "ultimate concern."[1] And, theologically, these expressions point like fingers to the sky, toward—a people's God. These fundamental concepts are thus enjoined to fulfill many tasks and are, of necessity, multivalent in their suggestive possibilities. Therefore, if we examine these

3

words with a curious and critical mind we may expect rich, multi-layered meanings that convey ideal depictions of human nature, orienting "frameworks of strong valuation,"[2] and "root metaphors of ultimacy."[3] Or, poetically speaking, we may perceive in these primary concepts something like William Blake's grain of sand, revealing world upon world through their particular utterance.[4] *Conscience* is such a word—perennially present, ever generating new vectors of meaning from its experiential root.

In this project I seek to examine how one twentieth-century thinker, Carl Jung, a Swiss psychiatrist, understood the meaning of this word *conscience* and the significance of the phenomena toward which the term points. Anticipating my conclusions, one may say that, for Jung, conscience is that singular dimension of experience which is most definitive of our humanity, emerging in that moment when awareness of responsible and creative agency begins, when the merely "it is" becomes "I ought." Moreover, in its most decisive form conscience entails an encounter with an "other," a "knowing with," such that where there was once only *id* there shall now be a *thou.*

Thus conceived, the dynamics and dictates of conscience assume a central role in Jung's portrayal, both descriptively and prescriptively, of the human life lived well. It will be argued that the goal of individuation is not to be realized in a rarefied and cultivated private consciousness—as it is so often portrayed—but rather in deliberate engagement with the ever-present ethical decisions and actions that constitute the relational life. From this investigation a distinctive rendering of conscience will emerge, marked by desire, risk, and grace, complementing, if not superseding, the conscience of guilt, authority, and law.[5]

Finally, it will be recognized that although words are derived from experience, language and its symbolic exponents do indeed beget and give currency to subsequent acts and interpretations of experience. Thus, while Jung himself believed in the generative powers of the psyche to reestablish for the apostate a viable *Weltanschauung,* he also viewed the current collapse of cultural myths as potentially catastrophic if they are not restored on a basis of new understanding. Conscience, as primordial and perennial word, is part of our collective mythic heritage thus imperiled. It will therefore be argued that if the concept of conscience is further eroded in our culture's prevailing views—believed to be, in the end, insubstantial, introjected, or merely functional—we are threatened with a diminished mythic framework from which we may live and choose to die. For as psyche is that which turns mere event into experience, so conscience is that which transforms experience into drama, specifically, the human drama.[6]

THE PROBLEM OF CONSCIENCE

As alluded to above, the etymology of *conscience* may be traced to the Latin word *conscientia*, meaning "to know with,"[7] and is a term used widely by the Stoics and other moral philosophers in the early common era. The basic sense of the word *conscience*—that is, provisionally stated, "an inward dialogue of a moral nature"—may be traced back even further in the West through both its Hebraic and Hellenistic roots.[8] Yet this ancient lineage has bequeathed to us neither consensus nor clarity; rather, conscience has assumed in our day an awkward, anomalistic status. Conscience, once an intelligible concept with meaningful specificity, has become increasingly problematic in theory. And yet, in our actual practice, the experience of and reliance on conscience have assumed an ever-greater role as heteronomous sources of moral guidance continue to decline in plausibility, authority, and efficacy.[9] In sum, our theory is inadequate to our practice.

We risk, not only within the academic world but in the broader culture as well, what may be described as a performative self-contradiction on a grand scale. We act, *de facto*, inescapably, from and through our conscience, and yet we have great difficulty understanding and justifying this fact, which serves to estrange us from both ourselves and each other as we live lives of diminished certitude. Were this contradiction of theory and practice about matters inconsequential, indifference would be defensible. But that is not the case, for we speak here about our conscience, or, broadly, our lived sense of significance as creative and responsible moral agents.

THESES AND METHOD OF DEMONSTRATION

This disjunction between our thoughts and our deeds provides the impetus and rationale for this study and informs its fundamental aim: to contribute to the reconciliation of the theory and practice of conscience. In order to achieve this, I advance the following theory, stated in the form of two theses:

1. Jung's theory of conscience, despite complexities in his own presentation and distorted readings of him by advocates and detractors alike, is sound and significant, and may be successfully employed in refuting predominant criticisms of conscience as a plausible and consequential phenomenon.
2. Moreover, Jung's theory of conscience—once made explicit—provides a hermeneutical lens, both optimal and necessary, for understanding the character and significance of Jung's thought as a whole.

These two theses interrelate and support each other. Appreciating the theoretical force and relevance of Jung's theory of conscience by engaging the concept in a critical dialogue illuminates the significance of the whole of his thought. And a reassessment of the whole then sheds light on the nature of conscience, broadening and complexifying its character. It is this interrelated embeddedness of Jung's theory of conscience with the very fabric of his thought that determines the following method and logical structure of this work.

Demonstrating these claims will require three sequential steps: (1) describing the broad framework of Jung's psychology of moral experience and practice with attention to its underlying presuppositions and rationale, their relation to the totality of Jung's psychology, and its contrast to prevailing popular assumptions about Jung's psychology, namely, that it entails (a) other-worldly mysticism, (b) uncritical optimism, and (c) solipsistic individualism; (2) showing that the essential features of Jung's moral psychology of conscience are superior to, and can be defended successfully against, the major psychological theories of conscience in the modern and postmodern world, namely, (a) the reduction of conscience to socialization or biological determinism, and (b) the perspectival theory of all knowledge, including the moral claims of conscience; and (3) critically assessing how the resulting "ontic" theory of conscience illuminates key problems regarding the appeal of Jung's thought in contributing to a contemporary moral psychology. This method of demonstration informs the three-part structure of this study, which generally moves from exposition (chapters 2–4), to critical and comparative analysis (chapters 5–6), to constructive assessment (chapter 7).

METHODOLOGICAL PARAMETERS

In addition to statements of what this study *is*, it should be acknowledged at the outset what this project is *not*. This study is *not* an amplification of Jung's thought into a generalized theory of ethics. Nor is it an exhaustive and comprehensive exposition of Jungian thought. Even this more confined task is too vast for any single author, for his or her expertise would need to encompass psychology, cultural history, philosophy, theology, comparative religious studies, ethics, anthropology, paleontology, linguistics, and physics. Rather, my interests here are circumscribed by the element of the moral in Jung's thought and are focused on his theory of conscience. My method is not systematic exposition but instead a pointed extraction, focused analysis, and a very directed critical assessment.

Neither is this study biographical *per se*. This task has been executed by many others—by Jung's friends and foes alike—with the avowed aim of shedding light on Jung the man, demonstrating how the personal factor shaped the development of Jung's psychology, and I will not attempt to repeat this biographical work. One reason is simply practical. Most published biographies demonstrate far greater access to direct, personal sources than those currently available to me. Therefore, it would be unlikely that new insights or biographical facts would be generated through my secondary research into the life and work of Jung.

Further, while the relationship between biography and theory is possibly important, particularly when dealing with a psychological theorist, it is not necessarily decisive. I certainly acknowledge that there is always a context and personal element to the expression of any idea. A spectrum of psychic, linguistic, and cultural forms is always present and integral. Therefore, by looking to the biographical genesis of a theory we may indeed gain some insight into the particular forms of expression, character of its biases, and range of application. Yet it is my sense that the objective referents of a person's ideas may in fact extend the applicability and relevance of their ideas beyond the constraints of biography. It is this aspect of Jung's theory of conscience—its external referents and claims to general applicability—that I find potentially most important in contributing to contemporary moral theory. Therefore, in this study the ideas of Jung will be largely discussed of their own accord and without extended reference to biographical context. I adopt this methodological position not because I find Jung's life uninteresting, or somehow incommensurable with his ideas, but rather as a means of focusing the scope of this study.

HISTORICAL BACKGROUND

Traditional heteronomous sources of moral guidance and authority—for example, divinely ordained monarchies, the church, scriptures, and natural law—have been increasingly subjected to rational criticisms during the modern period and have gradually declined in their practical efficacy.[10] During this period—roughly the last seven to eight hundred years—conscience has undergone various transvaluations.[11] The status of conscience was "elevated" within Christendom following the Fourth Lateran Council of 1215, which required, at a minimum, annual confession by all Christians, thereby implying the individual possession of responsible moral agency. Conscience, casuistry, and the cure of souls became regulated through the institution of the Court of Conscience and the affiliated practice of confessional penance.[12] It should be noted that within this ecclesial context, conscience was neither "unencumbered" nor "transmoral" as we might conceive it today, but was instead ultimately constrained by the imperatives of revelation, canon law, and natural law as mediated by directors of conscience.

However, concurrent with this tripartite complex of conscience, casuistry, and the cure of souls—practiced by all members of the church—was the monastic practice of meditation and its emphasis upon the transformation of the soul via purgation, illumination, and, as cherished goal, mystical union with Christ. Within this disciplined practice—which was undertaken only by the "professional religious"—the moral conscience, conceived as a faculty capable of applying principles of natural law to issues of volition and overt behavior, became subordinated to concerns of a more purely religious or spiritual nature. Within this monastic institution and its practices lay the seeds of an "illumined transmoral conscience" that would revolt against the whole cultural complex of the forensic conscience, casuistry, and the mediated care of souls. This "illumined conscience" was also, via the concept of the divine scintilla, or "spark," a basis of the Reformation's "Inner Light" and the Enlightenment concept of "Reason."[13]

Luther, often depicted simplistically as the "champion of conscience," was in fact a fierce critic of conscience as it had been portrayed, promulgated, and enforced through the system of casuistry regnant in his day. It was precisely this "negative conscience"[14] that Luther associated with a "theology of works," and from which he sought to be delivered via faith through grace. Driven to despair by this legalistic, punitive conscience, Luther found acceptance through God's acceptance, resulting in a "good" conscience, as gift, before God.[15] This distinction—between the moral and the religious spheres and their associated forms of conscience—resulted in a strict Lutheran dualism between the political and the private, the former being the realm of obedience to earthly rulers and the latter the sphere of freedom of conscience. This distinction between the public and the personal may be seen as an example of the human tendency to formulate a dualistic "solution" to the problem of conscience, a tendency that will be observed in different contexts throughout this work.

Following Luther, conscience was often turned to by theologians of the Reformation and certain philosophers and politicians of the Enlightenment[16] as an alternative source of moral truth to those from which they had recently liberated themselves. Conscience—often allied with Reason—was understood variously

9

as the *vox Dei* or "genius of man." During this period of reform and revolution, conscience was often accorded a central place in prevailing anthropologies, being understood in some sense as a superior, if not near-divine faculty that both ennobled the individual and made possible the various "experiments" in autonomous and democratic governance then under way. Conscience, understood as innate proponent of what is just and good, was seen as both the precipitator of rebellion and a bulwark against antinomianism as the monarchies of church and state were deposed.

Yet, following this period of intense foment, conscience itself proved vulnerable to many of the criticisms that were previously brought to bear against traditional moral sources "outside" the individual. These various rational criticisms, though taking many specific forms, may each be traced to one or more of several broad-based theoretical developments shaping our modern and postmodern *Weltanschauungen*. What I consider to be the most significant of these theoretical arguments against conscience I have coalesced into two polemical points that structure the second part of this work: "the naturalization of conscience" and "the relativity of conscience." I will reserve extended discussion of these criticisms for that portion of this work where they will be engaged as a means of clarifying Jung's own concept of conscience.

"TRADITIONAL" AND "PROFANE" VIEWS OF CONSCIENCE

As I stated at the outset of this chapter, the specific meaning of the term *conscience* has been fluid and variable throughout the history of Western culture. Therefore, in order to clarify our discussion of Jung's concept of conscience, I offer the following brief portrayals of two antithetical views of conscience, what I have termed the "traditional" and the "profane" senses of conscience. These two terms designate generalized "types" of conscience that are characteristic of the worldviews they support. I will argue that Jung's theory of conscience overcomes the inadequacies of both these forms.

Conscience was traditionally conceived as an interior faculty capable of discerning moral truth and invested with an authority that one was obligated to act on. It was described variously as one's daemon, genius, guardian angel, heart, spark of celestial fire, or, most potently, the voice of God.[17] Though operating through multitudinous singular expressions, this "traditional conscience" was believed to possess a unity and consistency of purpose directed toward a common good. Yet this traditional conscience, as a "voice," was recognized as often being hard to hear and thus difficult to discern—so much so that intercourse with its promptings was generally recognized as potentially fallible.[18] More precisely, the human capacity to discern the "true conscience" was as fallible as human nature itself. This fallibility provided something of an "epistemic escape clause"[19]—when confronted with the obvious depravity of the world, as well as the immediate fact of contradictory claims of conscience between two individuals—for those who argued that one's true conscience was to be the final moral authority.

It is important to note, however, that although conscience was conceived of in some sense as an internal faculty, its authority and plausibility rested on the belief in a cosmic or natural moral order upon which, and from which, conscience conveyed its promptings. In other words, the claims of conscience were not conceived of as *sui generis* but were seen as manifesting one's relationship to this transpersonal moral order. It was the "voice" of conscience that expressed—or revealed—in a most immediate, intimate manner the reality of one's rapport with this moral source "beyond" one's own conscious personality. This foundational moral order "outside" the individual could be, and was, conceived in a perplexing plethora of forms by theologians and philosophers throughout history, ranging in orientation from Manicheism to pantheism. One prominent example is the natural law tradition in ethics, which expressed the belief in an objective moral order in terms of its manifestation within and through the natural realm. Natural law theory held that innate and universal moral principles could be discerned by natural reason alone (i.e., unaided by grace or special revelation) and were the basis of our judgments of good and bad. That which is in accord with natural law facilitates natural ends of fulfillment. In short, fulfilling these natural ends is good, and the good is that which is natural. The obverse is true for what is deemed bad and evil. Within this tradition, the judgments of conscience were seen as grounded on perception of the natural laws; and as the laws are universally present, so too is the faculty of conscience available to all.[20]

Yet during the last half millennium, these moral foundations of the traditional conscience, however conceived, have undergone radical criticism. One after another, the possible bases of moral certitude have been undermined for large segments of the population, whether this displaced cornerstone was a Heavenly Father, the Good Book, natural law, or a *consensus gentium*. This steady process of criticism has come to fruition in the last century, culminating in a state today where it is widely acknowledged among ethicists that it is no longer possible to reach general agreement among diverse individuals—even within the same culture—regarding rationally demonstrated, specific ethical norms.[21] Conscience, as a subcategory of ethical theory, has been radically recast within this critical climate. I say "recast" and not, for example, "refuted" or "exorcised," precisely because we still have experiences that we refer to as "conscience," although now perceived and understood through the kaleidoscopic lens of contemporary culture. The result is what I term the "profane conscience."

This profane conscience may be described in stark contrast to the traditional conscience. While the traditional conscience was seen as a point of contact, if not communion, with an objective moral order (and perhaps dynamic will of the divine), the profane conscience is understood to be wholly autonomous and subjective in character. Severed from its sacred roots, the source of this profane conscience is now to be sought elsewhere. Our scientific fingers thus point readily to forces of socialization (the family and culture), or those of nature (selection and survival) that are common to all and reducible to impersonal, collective forces.

Through the lenses of critical philosophy and scientific method, the profane conscience is now often viewed not even neutrally, but rather skeptically as being unfairly punitive and false, something to be liberated from, not listened or assented to. The result is a view of conscience devoid of oracular profundity, moral authority, or even individual authenticity. Philip Rieff captures something of the ethos behind this profane conscience when he writes that "the new anti-culture aims merely at an eternal interim ethic of release from the inherited controls," wherein humans "feel freer to live their lives with a minimum of pretense to anything more grand than sweetening the time."[22] In chapters 5 and 6 I will examine at some length the basic critical paradigms of contemporary culture—naturalistic reductionism and epistemological relativism—that have effected the transition from the traditional to the profane conscience. I will challenge the adequacy of these critical perspectives through the concepts and perspectives of Jung's thought, demonstrating the superiority of the latter for addressing the needs of the current moral climate. The outcome of this engagement will not be a claimed return to the traditional sense of conscience, for this is neither possible nor desirable. Rather, a third option based on Jung's thought is argued for in this study. In order to lead into the discussion of Jung's theory of conscience, a few remarks follow about the more general concept of "the moral in Jung's psychology."

THE MORAL IN JUNG'S PSYCHOLOGY

In some ways it is surprising that moral experience has been given so little attention within the field of Jungian scholarship. Jung himself stated that "the chief causes of neurosis are conflicts of conscience and difficult moral problems that require an answer."[23] Elsewhere he writes, "The *opus* consists of three parts: insight, endurance, and action. Psychology is needed only in the first part, but in the second and third parts moral strength plays the predominant role."[24] Given these statements—clear and unequivocal—and many others throughout Jung's writings that place great importance on the moral factor in both the etiology of neuroses and the realization of the self, it would seem likely that the moral dimension of experience would have received prominent attention.[25] Yet this is not the case.

In many notable studies of Jung, by both detractors and advocates, the term *conscience* is nowhere to be found—it is missing not only from the tables of contents and indices but from the extended discussions of the texts themselves.[26] Further, to date there have been published only three books of significance that focus on issues of Jungian ethics: Erich Neumann's *Depth Psychology and a New Ethic*, Ira Progoff's *Jung's Psychology and Its Social Meaning*, and Murray Stein's *Solar Conscience/Lunar Conscience*. Although each of these books contributes insights into certain ethical issues, they are also marked by significant limitations.

Erich Neumann, for example, writing from Tel Aviv in the chaotic years immediately following World War II, seeks in his book to develop a positive basis for ethical living by advocating a psychological disposition devoted to conscious avoidance of repression and the related effects of projecting and scapegoating. According to Neumann, conscience is the accrued and internalized exponent of collective values and is to be replaced (for the "moral man") by the "Voice," the individual expression of psychic truth. While these suggestions have compelling relative merit, his project is weakened by failure to discuss issues of discernment of the Voice, the adjudication of relative and conflicting claims of value embodied in the individual and others, and whether the collective mores may in fact express and perpetuate an original utterance of this Voice. Yet perhaps the most fundamental limitation to Neumann's treatise is its narrow circumscription of the problem, which he grounds in concerns of individual psychological transformation (and, to a lesser degree, sociology) while ignoring what may be called the mythic, spiritual, and religious dimensions of ethical experience. For example, he locates the source of evil (without qualification) in the human drive of aggression and destruction,[27] and he equates (without remainder) the collective unconscious with the "universal human unconscious."[28] This is no small matter, for these terms are central to his argument, and the manner in which they are conceived and described has far-reaching implications. Perhaps Neumann was simply being loose with his terminology, since he was focused on the pressing need to respond somehow to the Holocaust. Or perhaps he felt no obligation to use Jungian terms in a Jungian sense—even a cursory reading of the *Collected Works* indicates that, for Jung, the horizons of the collective unconscious extend deeper and farther than human culture alone.

The reasons for this neglect of the moral in Jung are severalfold. The relative absence of explicit ethical discourse in Jung's own work is perhaps the most basic of reasons. His most extended discussion of conscience is found in the relatively short (eighteen-page) essay "A Psychological View of Conscience," written only several years before his death.[29] This essay, though reflecting his mature thought, is little more than an introduction to the issues involved, begging many questions and containing in only germinal form some of the issues I will attempt to elucidate further in this study. Likewise, the essay "Good and Evil in Analytical Psychology," a thirteen-page transcript of an extemporaneous address, may be considered rich in suggestive content, particularly as it pertains to Jung's practical engagement with his patients' struggles with their "shadows," but short on exposition and clarification of broader issues of concern to a wider audience.[30] For example, what precisely does Jung mean when he says in this address, "Principles, when reduced to their ultimates, are simply aspects of God"?[31]

Beyond these two short essays, Jung's reflections on ethics are wholly nonsystematic and are found widely distributed throughout his writings. Statements that explicitly broach the realm of the ethical—and there are many—are typically embedded in essays of seemingly remote relevance to what I normally consider moral issues. For example, in the essay "The Psychology of the Transference," at the end of a paragraph devoted to a discussion of the reciprocal relationship between unconscious contents and conscious states, Jung adds the parenthetical afterthought: "(Hence the very common combination of extreme neglect of duty and a compulsion neurosis)."[32] This passage remains entirely undeveloped, leaving unexplored varied and significant questions about the impact of the moral factor on mental health and patterns of behavior or, conversely, the possibility of seeing symptoms as signs with a moral etiology.

More often, however, ethical problems are approached even more circumspectly by Jung than the example cited above. He engages ethical problems only vicariously through the language, concepts, and clinical concerns of analytical psychology proper, and thus one may easily overlook the moral content if focused on a different set of concerns. Jung's use of the term *shadow* illustrates this point. The concept of the *shadow* is used throughout his writings to refer to aspects of oneself likely to be repressed because they are in conflict with one's conscious self-image. The *shadow* is typically discussed under the general rubric of "self-knowledge" within the context of the therapeutic relationship and, specifically, the encounter with the personal unconscious within the process of individuation. These discussions of the shadow tend to focus on psychodynamic issues, for example, projection, the autonomy of complexes, resistances, adaptation, symptoms, and conscious integration. Yet looked at through the lens of ethical theory, the shadow is rich with implications, far beyond those of the socialized *persona*, suggesting nothing less than the locus of the moral problem itself, that is, provisionally stated, the *acceptance of oneself and its discerned, differentiated expression*. Therefore, in consideration of this dispersed, somewhat "veiled" engagement with ethical matters in Jung's writings, it will be necessary in this exposition to "distill" his works, looking for hidden resources, extracting the relevant ethical material before giving it concrete shape and explicit expression. The concept of conscience will serve as the pivotal category of this constructive exposition of Jung's thought.

Another reason for the relative neglect of the moral factor in analytical psychology is that Jung's portrayal of the interior landscape—its cast of characters and its boundless stage—is itself so alluring or, if one objects to its depiction, so absurd and offensive, that reflection upon the implications of his dramatic view of human nature has generally not progressed beyond first-generation studies still focused on psycho-cartography. In short, debate about Jung's psychology has largely centered on the ontology of our psychic world—the "What is there?" and "Is it for real?"— while ignoring or bracketing sustained ethical reflection on its implications. I do not criticize this prioritization of ontological problems, for upon these issues the durability of Jung's ideas must stand or fall.[33] (I myself will explore the relevance of these ontological issues throughout this book, specifically in chapters 2 and 5.) Yet the tone and tempo of Jungian discourse have gone flat through repetition and endless irresolution, and questions about Jung's relevance to real-life problems—beyond the confines of the consulting room or meditation cube—now beg to be engaged.

JUNG'S THEORY OF CONSCIENCE

One of the challenges of explicating Jung's theory of conscience is the fact that he treats the subject in an atypical, distinctly Jungian fashion. He did not, for example, rigorously engage the concept of conscience in the terms of classical moral philosophy, that is, defining, analyzing, and critiquing moral principles and tenets. Nor did Jung engage in ethics *per se*, for example, by focusing on standards of character, conduct, and moral values by which we may make ethical judgments through which to live. Nor did he formally pursue any of the various approaches of developmental psychologists, for example, the measuring, describing, and classifying of various forms, factors, and behaviors that constitute one's evolving moral capacities.

Rather than through these approaches—which are, in spite of their varied permutations, relatively direct and circumscribed in nature—Jung discussed conscience in the context of a dynamic psychology that, in the terms of Don Browning, had an extensively developed "metaphorical" superstructure.[34] That is, Jung used his psychological hermeneutic to develop a general theory not only of the psyche proper, but of a vast range of the psyche's manifestations in culture and history, resulting in a framework that transcended simple disciplinary boundaries. In fact, Jung's psychological theories had, by the end of his life, evolved into an interpretive worldview of such breadth that it could serve as a "myth of meaning" for Jung's adherents.[35]

Jung's conception of conscience was derived from, and was deeply embedded in, this broader theoretical framework. Therefore, to understand the Jungian conscience it must first be located in its assumptive and metaphorical surroundings. This work of contextualization will be pursued in the following chapters (2–4), where I focus on explicating Jung's root premises about the moral nature of the psyche and the cosmos of which it is a part. In order to give this discussion a point of reference, however, I provide below an initial expository statement outlining Jung's theory of conscience.

Jung conceived of conscience as a moral judgment that arises outside of one's consciousness and confronts the ego with claims that challenge the ego's narrow self-interest. Or, more accurately, conscience challenges on a moral basis the ego's self-perception of what constitutes its genuine self-interest. Conscience has this effect by compelling an examination not only of one's overt behavior but of one's motives for acts both real and imagined. Thus, not only does conscience impact one's social conduct, but it serves to effect an inward change in both one's sense of self and the self's locus of interest. "Self-interest" may be seen in this context as a bi-polar word and Jung conceived of conscience as affecting both poles.

Jung portrayed conscience as both the psychological agency behind the moral judgment and the form of knowledge that emerges out of the ego's encounter with this inner agency. As an *agency*, conscience is experienced as an inner imperative that arises spontaneously and is, at most, only partly controllable by the subject's will. Jung spoke of conscience as "a demand that asserts itself in spite of the subject."[36] The "demands" of this inner agency take the form of moral judgments that are generally experienced as "opposing" one's "subjective intentions" and, if persistent—or persistently denied—as forcing "disagreeable decisions." The judgments of conscience may "anticipate, accompany, or follow" any experience that has moral implications, though the moral quality of a situation or act may not be immediately evident to the ego.[37] The autonomous and seemingly intentional nature of conscience led Jung to describe it as bearing the qualities of an "unconscious personality"[38] capable of "unconscious acts."[39] Jung, acknowledging that the notion of an "unconscious personality" is potentially problematic at various levels—for example, raising claims that this "personality" is "the *vox Dei*"—suggested that we speak of the phenomena of conscience in terms of archetypal theory, "for this at least is understandable and accessible to investigation."[40] Thus, conscience, as inner agency, was conceived by Jung as a "numinous archetype."[41]

As a *form of knowledge*, Jung described conscience as a moral judgment that has entered consciousness in the form of a pronouncement arising from the unconscious.[42] It is, simply, "consciousness of a [psychological] factor" that either condemns or affirms one's decisions or acts.[43] Conscience as a form of knowing is fundamentally different from intellectual understanding arrived at through rational reflection and logical analysis: the former is comprised of value judgments reflecting a subjective point of view, while the latter claims an objectivity that is referential to a shared, public reality.[44] This "subjective point of view" of conscience yields an awareness that includes and implicates oneself as a responsible moral agent. Conscience implicates the ego by conveying some form of moral judgment upon its motivations and behavior. "Conscience as a form of knowledge" thus means the emergence into consciousness of a self-reflective moral evaluation originating from an interior source experienced as somehow "other than" the ego.

As this brief introduction suggests, the Jungian conscience is a "complex phenomenon." In one formulation Jung described it as comprised of elementary acts of the will, value judgments based on feelings, and rational reflections on the moral quality of one's motives for imagined or actual acts.[45] It was within this complex framing of the concept that Jung described conscience in *dialectic* terms, that is, as an example of the *transcendent function*, a "discursive cooperation" between the ego and the unconscious.[46] Describing conscience in this manner reflected Jung's viewpoint that there is, as a most basic psychological structure, a mutual dependency between the ego and the unconscious. Conscience, as dialectic—as a "knowing with"—was conceived of as a particular form of this dynamic relationship. In summary, Jung recognized three aspects of, or ways of seeing conscience: as an inner agency outside of the ego's sphere, as an intrapsychic dialectic between the ego and this unconscious agency, and as the form of knowledge that results from this dialogue.

Jung did not attempt to provide a scientific theory regarding the phylogenetic origin of conscience, presumably because he believed it to be—like the essential nature of the archetypes and consciousness itself—a metaphysical question outside the bounds of strict empirical inquiry.[47] Yet Jung did recognize the role of socialization in forming the particular contents of the individual conscience,[48] stating that the "great majority of cases of conscience" simply arise in response to "deviations from the moral code."[49] That is, in most cases conscience is nothing more complex than the "recollection of the moral code"[50] as it has been received within one's particular context. In these cases conscience serves a largely conservative function and simply reflects "the primitive fear of anything unusual, not customary, and hence 'immoral.'"[51]

Yet, according to Jung, conscience is not fully reducible to socialization. Conscience expresses as well what Jung considered to be an innate, and potentially creative, moral disposition of the psyche. This form of conscience was understood by him as being comprised of a "moral reaction"[52] arising from the unconscious (via the "inner agency" discussed above), in conjunction with the rational scrutiny that this "moral reaction" prompts and, in a sense, necessitates. Jung conceived of this "moral reaction" as a universal factor of the human psyche, "found at every level of human culture.[53] Jung contended that this inherited "moral reaction" is the primordial driving force of our moral behavior, which, through historical and cultural processes, has gradually precipitated into the existing moral codes.[54]

The claim that moral codes are derivative of customary behavior, which, in turn, is an expression of a primary "moral reaction," is most significant if one is to understand Jung's view that conscience is not simply reducible to a reflexive conformity with one's group mores. Jung acknowledged that it may *appear* that conscience is simply the product of socialization as long as one's practical life can be accommodated within the parameters of the moral code—when this conformity prevails, then one's conscience does indeed mirror the moral code (and vice versa). Yet when a conflict of duty arises, that is, a choice between two ethical goods, the autonomy of conscience becomes apparent in the face of the moral code's inability to foresee—and adjudicate—this particular, individual conflict. Jung made these points in the following manner:

> Our moral reactions exemplify the original behavior of the psyche, while moral laws are a late concomitant of moral behavior, congealed into precepts. In consequence, they appear to be identical with the moral reaction, that is, with conscience. This delusion becomes obvious the moment a conflict of duty makes clear the difference between conscience and the moral code. It will then be decided which is

the stronger: tradition and conventional morality, or conscience.[55]

To help make the distinction between moral experience governed primarily by the individual's instinct to conform to social mores and that which is impelled by a generative, autonomous inner agency, Jung differentiated, respectively, between the "moral" conscience and the "ethical" conscience. Jung described the "moral" form of conscience as that which "appears when the conscious mind leaves the path of custom or suddenly recollects it." In these cases, "the moral" is synonymous with "the mores," and conscience reflects primarily an instinctive desire to conform to the norms and expectations of one's social group and a corresponding aversion to whatever is new. Such expressions of conscience are accorded the designation of "moral conscience."[56]

Jung held in higher regard, however, what he termed the "ethical" form of conscience. This form of conscience may arise when "reflective, conscious scrutiny" has been brought to bear upon a choice between two ways of deciding or acting, "both affirmed to be moral [by one's regnant moral code] and therefore regarded as 'duties.'"[57] Jung described such situations as *"conflicts of duty,"*[58] which are characterized by "a fundamental doubt between two possible modes of moral behavior."[59] Jung described this dilemma, and the typical reaction to it, in the following manner:

> A situation like this can be "solved" only by suppressing one moral reaction, upon which one has not reflected till now, in favour of another. In this case the moral code will be invoked in vain, and the judging intellect finds itself in the position of Buridan's ass between two bundles of hay.[60]

Yet such suppression is not absolutely necessary and, in Jung's view, certainly not desirable, for "if one is sufficiently conscientious and the conflict is endured to the end," the creation of a "third standpoint" may emerge that represents a "creative solution" to the conflict of duties.[61] This solution, if "genuine," emerges from a "discursive co-operation of conscious and unconscious factors," that is, from the ethical conscience, and expresses the "deepest foundations" and "wholeness" of the personality.[62]

Jung held that the real driving force behind conscience, in both its moral and ethical forms, is the "emotional component" and attendant feelings.[63] It is the emotional dynamism of conscience that makes it effective by forcing the ego, through internal discord or a sense of longing, to consider and confront problems that it may otherwise choose to deny or postpone. The feelings associated with conscience may convey both negative, punitive restrictions and positive, generative demands. It is important to realize that Jung used the concept of "feelings" in a particular way and did *not* equate the feeling function with either nebulous moods or physical sensations. Rather, Jung considered feelings to be "rational" in the sense of being evaluative in nature (as opposed to "irrational" and receptive in nature, like the functions of sensation and intuition). For Jung, "feeling is a kind of *judgment*, differing from intellectual judgment in that its aim is not to establish conceptual relations but to set up a subjective criterion of acceptance or rejection."[64] This rational characterization of our feelings enabled Jung to accord them a positive, cooperative function in our moral life, representing and conveying ethical judgments that are meaningful and compatible with cognitive understandings.

Jung said little explicitly about the direct effects of conscience on either the individual or society. Yet if his theory of conscience is placed in the context of his broader theories—which I will do in the following chapters—inferences may be drawn. The Jungian conscience may be understood as facilitating a changed self-identity in which one's egocentricity is mitigated through a heightened sense of one's contextual location amid other moral beings. This "changed self-identity" may emerge through encounters with conscience because it is—or *may be* in its most decisive forms—experienced as an exponent of a transpersonal order that claims and conveys moral authority. Experiences of a "numinous other" within the depths of one's own psyche have the potential to profoundly alter a person's fundamental attitude toward their own interiority. By this I mean: the aggregate of desires, feelings, and impulses that can be lumped together and ascribed to that primal, amoral *id* of psychoanalytic theory, may, through encounters with one's conscience, become complexified

22

in nature and expressive of new meanings. Through experiences of the ethical conscience one's relationship with one's own interiority may be (re-)personalized,[65] even (re-)sacralized. One's desires become, potentially, more than blind libido. One's desires may come to assume moral significance in dialogue with this demanding "other" within. In short, through encounters with conscience, where there was once an *id* there shall now be a *thou*.

This changed relationship with one's own interiority is paradoxical in nature. On one hand, the ego suffers an apparent "defeat" by recognizing its own contingency in relation to an "inner agency" in a realm—the psyche—that it previously considered its own exclusive province. Yet, on the other hand, this recognition of contingency may serve to elevate the self-perceived significance of the individual life as it recognizes its participation in a dramatic moral context in which it finds its being. Jung describes this paradoxical effect in the general context of individuation in the following manner:

> Only consciousness of our narrow confinement in the self forms the link to the limitlessness of the unconscious. In such awareness we experience ourselves concurrently as limited and eternal, as both one and the other. In knowing ourselves to be unique in our personal combination—that is, ultimately limited—we possess also the capacity for becoming conscious of the infinite. But only then![66]

I will argue in this study that Jung conceives of conscience as effecting this realization—of the limits and relational reaches of the individual—in a dynamic and potent manner.

Jung's theory of conscience, however, is more complex than the outline above suggests. Indeed, if the summary above expressed the whole of his theory, then it could be understood as simply advocating that one "rely wholly on conscience" to make moral decisions. One's moral life would be that clear and simple. Yet the depth and perplexing nature of our practical conflicts requires, according to Jung, a more problematic conception of conscience. First and foremost, he argued that the innate impulse of conscience is not necessarily "moral" as commonly understood but rather may urge a course of action that conflicts with established mores. Jung contended that there is an "inner contradictoriness of conscience"—besides the "right" conscience there is a "'wrong' one, which exaggerates, perverts, and twists evil into good and good into evil just as our own scruples do."[67] This recognition of the ambivalence of conscience radically complexifies the task of discernment and raises basic questions about the meaningfulness—the very intelligibility—of the concept of conscience.

Jung did not attempt to avoid or trivialize this profound problem, but instead brought the issues surrounding the human engagement with right and wrong, good and evil, to the very center of his psychology. An adequate exposition of Jung's views on these ultimate questions can be given only after providing sufficient background to both his thought and theoretical critiques specific to conscience. Yet, anticipating my conclusions, I will argue in the following pages that conscience, properly understood, is the implied heart of Jung's psychology—for it is through conscience that one becomes most poignantly aware of the "divine service" we may perform,[68] that is, engaging in the struggle to become conscious of—and to discern between—the opposites of good and evil, and to endeavor to incarnate the former. Jung's psychology, seen in this light, may offer a theory of conscience both plausible and compelling, serving to narrow the breach between the theory and practice of one's moral life in these troubled times.

PART I

Jung's Moral Framework

Chapter 2

JUNG ON EMBODIMENT
AND PSYCHIC REALITY

In this chapter I will examine Jung's ideas regarding the nature of the human relationship with the physical realm. Specifically, I will explore his understanding of the relationship between the psyche and the body. As stated in chapter 1, the purpose of this exposition is to expound fundamental assumptions of Jung in order to frame the subsequent discussion of conscience. I will endeavor in this chapter to bring forth a positive reading of Jung, yet I will do so only after acknowledging potential problems in both his theory and his presentation. I will provide this preliminary criticism in the form of a foil, a negative stereotype: Jung as an "other-worldly mystic."

JUNG AS "OTHER-WORLDLY MYSTIC"?

Carl Jung is portrayed by some as having elevated the value and significance of the psyche, or "spirit," while denigrating or ignoring the body and the world. Jung, when stereotyped as an "other-worldly mystic," is seen as advocating an introverted retreat from engagement with the world, turning an eye instead toward a self-sufficient form of self-realization, a type of salvation through mystical experience and a privileged brand of consciousness. Although it is my purpose in this chapter to refute such a portrayal and to offer a positive alternative, it must be acknowledged that the basis for such a depiction of Jung may indeed be found, at least in germinal form, within his writings themselves. I have identified four aspects of his work that may support the view of Jung as an "other-worldly mystic": subject matter, forms of experience cited, theoretical positions, and style of writing.

The subjects that Jung chose to discuss were often esoteric and arcane, such as gnosticism, the *I-Ching*, alchemy, and his own self-styled "synchronicity." Sometimes his inquiries into these subjects are suggestive of the eccentric, if not the bizarre, and are admittedly unintelligible outside an appreciation of the inner logic of his metapsychology. For example, what is the reader to make of the following statement, extracted from the introduction to the essay "Flying Saucers: A Modern Myth of Things Seen in the Skies"?

> It is not presumption that drives me, but my conscience as a psychiatrist that bids me fulfill my duty and prepare those few who will hear me for coming events which are in accord with an end of an era. As we know from ancient Egyptian history, they are manifestations of psychic changes which always appear at the end of one Platonic month and at the beginning of another.[1]

Besides the nature of these subjects, which intrigued him and informed his published works, Jung's reputation as a theosophical guru is further promoted by the emphasis he placed on a realm of experience—there on the borderline of psychopathology—that to the sane and centered mind can sound unreal and fabricated, or at least misinterpreted, and at worst, simply delusional. Whereas other theorists and thinkers may appeal to a sound common sense to buttress their theories—something available to all rational minds[2]—Jung often put at the center of his considerations, according them the greatest importance, types of experience that are unfamiliar and strange, if not disturbing. For example, in a contributing essay to Fanny Moser's book *Ghosts: False Belief or True?*, Jung related how, in the summer of 1920, he was a weekend guest at a "haunted" cottage in the English countryside. The apparitions he experienced on successive nights culminated in the following vision:

> I had the feeling there was something near me, and opened my eyes. There, beside me on the pillow, I saw the head of an old woman, and the right eye, wide open, glared at me. The

28

left half of the face was missing below the eye. The sight of
it was so sudden and unexpected that I leapt out of bed with
one bound, lit the candle, and spent the rest of the night in
an armchair.[3]

Still further, certain of Jung's theoretical commitments—
commitments that he claimed were empirically derived—led him
to make statements that may sound fanciful or speculative in
nature. For example, he believed that to fairly represent psychic
processes one must adopt not only the causal point of view but the
teleological one as well. This fundamental claim of Jung led to
descriptions of psychic processes—specifically, dynamic factors
that assume a pseudo-personal character oriented to the realization of innate potentiality—that may seem reminiscent of an ani-
mistic or spiritualistic mind-set. Other theoretical commitments,
particularly his Kantian-derived epistemology, led Jung to make
statements that may seem exaggerated, or at least incautious, by
suggesting a form of idealism, if not solipsism. For example, "the
psyche creates reality every day."[4]

In addition, Jung made certain stylistic choices that rendered
the content of his work open to easy misconstrual. A classic example of this is "Answer to Job," in which Jung employed a subjective idiom—which he explicitly acknowledged and explained—
that may lead the undiscerning reader to believe that Jung was
engaging in speculative metaphysics or declarative theology.[5] If
read as metaphysics, this essay suggests that Jung was moving in
an altogether different realm from us mortals. For example, he
claimed that "God wants to become man, but not quite."[6] But we
might ask, What type of man, after all, purports to know something of the mind of God?

Finally, in addition to the four reasons outlined above—subjects studied, experiences cited, theories of the psyche, and style of
writing—Jung may be seen as negating and dismissive of the body
and world by way of omission, that is, what was largely excluded
from his writings. As a proportion of his collected works, Jung
wrote relatively little about interpersonal dynamics and relationships, social factors and processes, and developmental challenges
of the first half of life. The net effect of this, viewed critically, is
to create an image of the human world whose norm is that of

introverted adults preoccupied with their own dreams and subjective fantasies in pursuit of a mysterious self that supposedly transcends the constraints of space and time. One may justifiably wonder what this world would be like were it dominated by adherents to this strain of Jungian thought.

JUNG'S POLEMICAL SITUATION

Clearly, many of Jung's statements (such as those quoted above) may sound remote and on the "fringe" of mainstream discourse—in short, disembodied from our workaday sensibilities— if they are detached not only from the texture and narrative of his written work, but also from the general intellectual climate in which he operated. Therefore, before proceeding with a constructive response, I will make a few observations about the intellectual situation in which Jung operated and what his personal motives may have been for holding the ontological position he advocated throughout his professional life.

It is fair to say that Jung was driven by a strong sense of vocation to impress upon the world his particular vision of reality.[7] This vision was derived from what he called powerful, unforgettable, numinous encounters with the "objective psyche"[8] that provided the foundation and impetus of his psychology. "All my works, all my creative activity, has come from those initial fantasies and dreams...."[9] Jung believed that his "creative illness"[10] held implications beyond the merely personal, setting him the "task" of trying to understand "to what extent my own experience coincided with that of mankind in general."[11] Moreover, this "task" had a communal character—"My life belonged to the generality"[12]—and was infused with a painful sense of relational necessity: "I did all in my power to convey to my intimates a new way of seeing things. I knew that if I did not succeed, I would be condemned to absolute isolation." All of his works then, to some measure, were aimed at conveying not simply a rationally deduced scientific hypothesis, but rather his most subjective, his most existentially crucial, "way of seeing things."[13]

Jung's root theoretical commitment, born of his own experience, was to "the reality of the psyche." This *ur*-commitment, in its full ramifications, determined the orientation of Jung's ethics and provides the key to understanding his attitude and beliefs toward the "natural world." It is not an exaggeration to say that this foundational commitment to "psychic reality" informed, and subsequently justified, all that followed in his thought.[14]

Jung's statements about the nature of the psyche and, specifically, its relationship to the physical body of self and world, may best be understood as attempts to mediate between other theoretical frameworks that Jung viewed as one-sided and distorting of our actual nature. On one pole of this spectrum are those Jung termed "rationalists"—which included certain philosophers and theologians, as well as the bulk of the general population—who, in his view, exaggerated the radical autonomy and capacities of the conscious ego, denying its inherent epistemological limits and embeddedness in physical, temporal processes. In short, all those who would claim access to transcendent knowledge. On the other end of the spectrum, Jung contended with "materialist reductionists," or those whom he sometimes pejoratively referred to as "realists," who sought to explain the psyche exclusively in terms of neurology, chemistry, and biology, leaving the psyche itself as a "nothing but" epiphenomenon.[15] Together these two groups comprised what Jung once called "the cult of rationalism and realism."[16]

Jung was aware of the analytical nature of this distinction and that in the real world the concepts are often uncritically conjoined.[17] Yet in spite of these terminological ambiguities, Jung found these designations useful in identifying and articulating his intellectual position and those of his opponents. Thus, the designations "reductive materialist" and "uncritical rationalist" signify important and distinct theoretical options that provide a structure for describing and intellectually locating Jung's thought.

Jung's objections to the materialists and rationalists did not reflect a general irrationalism on his part. Rather, Jung reserved his criticisms for those species of rational thought that claimed to have penetrated the secrets of the human personality and yet, by design or accident, resulted in what Jung considered to be a distorting portrayal. This distortion could occur through either uncritical, exaggerated claims about what may be known about the psyche, or a falsifying, diminished portrait based on a partial exclusion of experiential phenomena. His targets thus included any belief system that resisted the discoveries of the natural sciences (e.g., conservative theologies), or denied the distinct, nonmaterial nature of the psyche (i.e., scientific materialism), or ignored the epistemological limits imposed by critical philosophy and the discovery of the unconscious (i.e., "foundationalist" philosophies).

Nonetheless, one may point to certain traits of Jung as seeming evidence of an irrationalist bias: his approving attitude toward paradox, his oft-repeated assertions of the limits of reason, and, more psychologically, the relativization of the ego itself within the psychic economy.[18] While in fact the embracing of paradox and the subordination of the ego to the self were desired "end wisdom-states" for Jung, it was only through hard-won "understanding" that these experiences were to be considered legitimate. In fact, "understanding," or conscious integration, is at the very heart of individuation—almost coextensive with the term—as Jung portrayed the process. It should therefore be no surprise when Jung included "understanding" in his quaternity of virtues, or "great gifts of grace," supplementing the traditional trinity of faith, hope, and love.[19] It thus seems best to understand Jung as someone who was an irrationalist only in the sense of criticizing those forms of rational thought that overestimated the capacities of reason and the value of rational thought. The intellect was a necessary means, but an insufficient end in itself, within Jung's normative vision of the psychic economy.

JUNG'S RHETORICAL STRATEGIES FOR DEVELOPING A CONSTRUCTIVE ALTERNATIVE

Within this polemical context, Jung employed various rhetorical strategies to develop his constructive positions regarding the nature of the psyche and, specifically, its relationship to the body. I locate these forms of argumentation in several overlapping yet distinct categories: empirical, practical, rational (mostly epistemological), and traditional. By *empirical* I refer to

Jung's attempt to include in his hypotheses and conceptual frameworks the full range of experiential phenomena as provided by the methods and instruments of natural science,[20] as well as introspective processes, both spontaneous and systematic. By *rational* I refer to arguments that Jung used based on critical philosophy, particularly a Kantian-based epistemology that issued into a form of phenomenology. By *practical* I mean the positive, if not the primary, status Jung accorded the "living reality" of the particular, existing individual as both evidence for, and justification of, his ideas and their formulations. In short, it is by the "fruits," the real-world effects, that we both know and nurture our ideas. Lastly, by *traditional* I refer to Jung's not-infrequent appeals to the *consensus gentium* or *omnium*[21] as the "objective" basis of what would otherwise be the appeal of a singular subjectivity. These forms of argumentation were presented by Jung not as sources of dogmatic authority but rather as vehicles and representations of knowledge—as humanly prehended, conceptualized, and asserted.

Jung framed much of his debate with the "reductive materialists" in terms of what constitutes "science" and who may rightfully claim the mantle of "scientific." Jung recognized that science was not only a method of inquiry to which he aspired and which he claimed, but was a language conveying the dominant worldview, which he must speak if he were to avoid being relegated to obscurity and irrelevance. Hence, he repeatedly described himself as an "empiricist," dedicated to "facts" and deserving of the title of "scientist" in the fullest sense of the word. Particularly in his early professional years, during his collaboration with Freud and the developmental period of his own analytical psychology, Jung was anxious to establish his scientific credentials and not to be pigeon-holed as an occultist or a closeted theologian. In a letter to Anglican priest Victor White, dated October 5, 1945, Jung acknowledged his polemical motives during his earlier (i.e., roughly thirty-five years prior) professional career and how it influenced his rhetorical strategy:

> My temperamental empiricism has its reasons. I began my career with repudiating everything that smelt of belief. That explains my critical attitude in my Psychology of the Unconscious [orig. 1911/12]. You should know that this

book was written by a psychiatrist for the purpose of submitting the necessary material to his psychiatric colleagues, material which would demonstrate to them the importance of religious symbolism. My audience then was a thoroughly materialistic crowd, and I would have defeated my own ends if I had set out with a definite creed or with definite metaphysical assertions.[22]

Given his desire to locate himself and his nascent psychology within prevailing scientific discourse, Jung took what may be called an indirect approach in his disputations with the reductive viewpoint. That is, he disputed not the applicability of reductionism but rather its adequacy. He therefore argued about what defines and constitutes proper scientific methodology and, relatedly, what range and type of phenomena should be considered scientific data. Jung understood his adherence to the "scientific method" in the sense that it would have then been understood by some on the European Continent, that is, as "any kind of logical and systematic approach," in distinction from the more narrowly conceived Anglo-Saxon understanding, which limited the "scientific" to "physical, chemical, and mathematical evidence only."[23] Therefore, "historical and comparative methods" were considered by Jung to be scientific, meaning that "history, mythology, anthropology, ethnology are 'sciences' as are geology, zoology, botany, etc."[24]

For Jung, psychology was rightfully included in this list, perhaps somewhere between mythology and the "etc.," "even when it [psychology] is not concerned only with (most inadequate[25]) physical or physiological methods." Procedurally, this scientific method meant for Jung the following modus operandi: "I observe, I classify, I establish relations and sequences between the observed data, and I even show the possibility of prediction."[26] Jung acknowledges the difficulties and limitations in this scientific psychology, namely, the fact that repeatable experimentation is not generally possible (but, he points out, neither is it in geology!), and that "in contradistinction to all others [i.e., sciences] it tries to understand itself by itself...."[27] But it is these very limitations that also point to psychology's possible significance, there "on the frontiers of knowledge."[28]

Within this methodological framework of "science," Jung argued for a phenomenological form of empiricism. Jung's understanding of what constitutes "empirical" led him to criticize other psychologies that claimed to be adequate and comprehensive yet failed to account for the full range of what he considered to be relevant data—that is, the richness of all experiential phenomena, whether they arise from the outer world or the inner sphere. Jung made the following rhetorical observation in this regard, which includes an implicit challenge to not dualistically split the world—thereby deciding prematurely—when determining what is empirically relevant and necessary for inclusion in one's *Weltanschauung*. In this passage are two significant points: both a rejection of supernaturalism and an affirmation of the psychic (and empirical) reality of our innermost experiences.

> I know nothing of a "super-reality." Reality contains everything I can know, for everything that acts upon me is real and actual. If it does not act upon me, then I notice nothing and can, therefore, know nothing about it. Hence I can make statements only about real things, but not about things that are unreal, or surreal, or subreal. Unless, of course, it should occur to someone to limit the concept of reality in such a way that the attribute "real" applied only to a particular segment of the world's reality.[29]

In addition to this methodological argument about what constitutes an empirical fact—and the need to include all such phenomena within a generalized theory—Jung was also critical of reductive materialism on more purely epistemological grounds. He recognized that it is important not only to include the full range of phenomena within a general theory but also to interpret and theoretically frame these phenomena within appropriate epistemological categories and constraints. Jung made generalized arguments regarding the inescapable subjectivity of all knowledge, but also, specific to the nature of science, about the inherent limits to achieving "objective" knowledge of "facts." Jung held that efficient causation, mathematical expression, and general laws—all based on objective concepts—are completely appropriate (in fact, necessary) when applied to a specific, circumscribed field of inquiry, for example, chemistry, biology, genetics. Each of these sciences objectifies the terms and elements of its sphere of inquiry in order to provide a "handle" on which to construct its models and theories. Yet, Jung argued, when reductive scientism (inappropriately) extends the objective claims of its theories to psychology it fails to account adequately for the phenomena of the psyche as directly, subjectively experienced. For instance, he wrote:

> The excessive importance attached to objects gives rise in [reductive] science to a certain kind of theory favoured by specialists, which for instance cropped up in psychiatry in the form of the "brain mythology" previously mentioned. In all such theories an attempt is made to elucidate a very wide range of experience in terms of principles which, though applicable over a small area, are wholly inappropriate for other fields.[30]

When exploring the nature of the psyche and its relationship to the body, Jung observed—and criticized—a particular effect of this tendency toward the tacit objectification of the subject matter under investigation. He argued that if one applies concepts suitable for the elementary facts of biology to the more complex phenomena of the psyche, an increasing vagueness arises and a resulting lack of applicability to lived experience. Jung puts it this way:

> If they [psychological concepts] are traced back to their biological foundations they become so imprecise that they lose their psychological meaning. This is not to say that tracing types of consciousness back to instinctive data is superfluous. To understand their structure a knowledge of the biological foundations is essential. But since it is the nature of psychological concepts to point forwards, in the sense of an entelechy, their specific meaning consists in the apprehension of complicated psychic facts. They lose this meaning, as said, when they are looked at retrospectively, in terms of their origin. They then dissolve into extremely general biological conditions.[31]

For Jung, therefore, the supposed "objectivity" of reductive scientism was in fact a very subjective delineation of a portion of reality for the purposes of discrete measurement, manipulation, and control. Extended beyond the appropriate range, such a theoretical approach serves to distort its subject matter. If a psychology aspires, explicitly or otherwise, to provide a "practical moral philosophy," as Jung's psychology in fact did,[32] this distortion is problematic not only in theory but in practice as well. While strict experimental scientism has historically served to free us from the oppression of superstition and (through applied technology) numerous forms of physical deprivation, its grounding in (and promotion of) an objectifying literalism has had, Jung believed, deleterious psychological effects. "As scientific understanding has grown, so our world has become dehumanized. Man feels himself isolated in the cosmos, because he is no longer involved in nature and has lost his 'unconscious identity' with natural phenomena."[33] His criticisms of reductive scientism were thus driven not only by critical reasoning regarding the nature of empiricism and epistemological constraints—nor on his possible nostalgic predilection for a mythic world[34]—but also by the actual negative impact such a view had upon those who sought his consultation. On the practical grounds of mental health, Jung therefore argued against the sufficiency of reductive materialism.

Jung associated the scientific materialism of his day with the loss of myth and its orienting meaning and held that an uncritical appropriation of this viewpoint may result in the atrophication of the spirit and "bondage to the senses." He observed that many who had become neurotic—that is, "divided against themselves"—would not have been so afflicted in an earlier epoch. He called such persons "optional neurotics."[35] In this context, by the standards of mental health and spiritual vitality, he viewed a narrow scientism as inadequate.

> If they [i.e., "optional neurotics"] had lived in a period and in a milieu in which man was still linked by myth with the world of ancestors, and thus with nature truly experienced and not merely seen from the outside, they would have been spared this division with themselves. I am speaking of those who cannot tolerate the loss of myth and who can neither find a way to a merely exterior world, to the world as seen by science, nor rest satisfied with an intellectual juggling of words,

which has nothing whatsoever to do with wisdom....These victims of the psychic dichotomy of our time are merely optional neurotics; their apparent morbidity drops away the moment the gulf between the ego and the unconscious is closed.[36]

Perhaps most basically, Jung held that a reductive, objectified, biologically based explanation is prone to generate what may be called an "existential gap" between theory and practice. In the prologue to his autobiography, *Memories, Dreams, Reflections,* Jung pointed to this gap between our inward experience and our externalized theory by exclaiming, "I cannot experience myself as a [reductive] scientific problem." This implies that to understand oneself—and others—one must use a mode other than, or in addition to, a reductive scientism. Jung, offering such an alternative, continued: "What we are to our inward vision...can only be expressed by way of myth."[37] This is the case because "science works with concepts of averages that are far too general to do justice to the subjective variety of individual life"; therefore, "myth is more individual and expresses life more precisely than does science." Though portrayed as specific and concrete—the most real of all things—reductive science is actually, according to Jung, an abstraction that views life from the outside—objectified—and when adhered to dogmatically "consists to a great extent of mere talk."[38] In this manner the direct experience of human life slips through the net of numbers and laws constructed by science.

Jung observed how it is not only the "primitive man,"[39] but also "the learned," who struggles against a merely naturalistic view of life, seeking instead the freedom of the spirit" as the most effective weapon against the mere truth of the senses."[40] This "truth of the senses," as Jung saw it, is unable to provide the meaning and means for psychological renewal which is a hallmark of religio-mythical belief and practice. The "primitive," whose daily life is often a struggle against basic physical constraints, depends on a connection with the "spirit" to humanize and raise herself above the level of mere compulsion. Through dreams, fantasies, psychic and somatic symptoms, and a naive attribution of "spirit" to numerous everyday phenomena, the primitive person lives in a world both material and spiritual.

> His utter dependence on circumstances and environment, the manifold distresses and tribulations of his life, surrounded by hostile neighbors, dangerous beasts of prey, and often exposed to the pitiless forces of nature; his keen senses, his cupidity, his uncontrolled emotions—all these things bind him to the physical realities, so that he is in constant danger of adopting a purely materialistic attitude and becoming degenerate. His belief in spirits, or rather, his awareness of a spiritual world, pulls him again and again out of that bondage in which his senses would hold him; it forces on him the certainty of spiritual reality whose laws he must observe as carefully and as guardedly as the laws of his physical environment. Primitive man, therefore, really lives in two worlds. Physical reality is at the same time spiritual reality.[41]

Jung thus argued that it is not only the primitive but the sophisticate as well, who needs liberation from literalism through symbolic renewal. Herein lies the point of unity in Jung's critique of both reductive materialism and uncritical rationalism, and the essence of his remedy—the dependency of the conscious ego on its instinctual, unconscious foundations for its continued human vitality. By "human vitality" I suggest, of course, something different from simple animal vitality, something more than basic physiological health or frictionless functioning of the instincts. Rather, "human vitality" walks that razor's edge of alternating expression and repression and somehow reaches an optimum when the "yeas and nays" of the body are harmonized with the "whys and wherefores" of the mind. Jung held that it is the discursive relationship between the ego and its unconscious, instinctive basis, often achieved through the symbolic, that makes this possible.

Jung adopted the story of Nicodemus's encounter with Jesus for his own polemical purposes contra the reductive materialists (which, in this case, Jung associated with the Freudian theoretical framework). Jung cast Nicodemus in the role of the person stuck in literalism or materialistic reductionism, asking the insoluble question about being born a second time and entering into the mother's womb again. Jung stated that "Jesus tries to purify the sensuous cast of Nicodemus's mind by raising it from its dense materialistic slumbers...." The purpose of the symbolic is not an illusory attempt to create a second reality, a spiritual one, superimposed on the physical world. Such naive projections have rightly been criticized as positing as real what in fact is transcendent and lying outside the realm of knowledge. Rather, what Jung suggested is that the symbolic has "great educative force" for liberating one's libido, or what Jung called more generally "psychic energy."

> The reason why Jesus' words have such great suggestive power is that they express the symbolic truths which are rooted in the very structure of the human psyche. The empirical truth never frees a man from the bondage of the senses; it only shows him that he was always so and cannot be otherwise. The symbolic truth on the other hand, which puts water in place of the mother and spirit in place of the father, frees the libido from the channel of the incest tendency, offers it a new gradient, and canalizes it into a spiritual form.[42]

While Jung employed the story of Nicodemus to illustrate the limits of materialism, I believe he could as well have identified this religious leader as an "uncritical rationalist" owing to his inability to conceive of a psychic, spiritual reality that is communicable through the symbolic. Literalism, as Jung understood it, is a hallmark of both reductive materialists and uncritical rationalists, differentiated only by the locus of what is "really real."

By the term "uncritical rationalism" I mean the practice of dislocating certain elements of psychic experience—whether it be an "idea," an article of "faith," an "image," or ego-consciousness itself—from the psychic medium out of which it arose. In short, uncritical rationalism tends to reify elements of consciousness, failing to consider adequately the psychic substratum and matrix out of which all conscious thought emerges and on which all conscious thought remains dependent. Or, put differently, uncritical rationalism denies the conscious mind's dependence on, and relationship with, its own unconscious foundations. Just as a reductive materialism may portray the mind as epiphenomenal and may attempt to convince it of its own impotence, so an excessive, uncritical rationalism may serve to inflate the ego beyond legitimate bounds. In both cases the practical effect is a dissociation of

the conscious personality from its embeddedness in psychic structures and dynamic matrices, more or less unconscious, that merge
into the physical. The theoretical result of either position is a
dualistic splitting of mind and body: "When carried to extremes,
therefore, both types of thinking [reductive materialism and
uncritical rationalism] create a mythology, the one expressed con-
cretely in terms of cells, atoms, vibrations, etc., the other
abstractly in terms of 'eternal' ideas."[43]

Jung contrasted his analytical psychology, based on a psychological phenomenology—"There is not one thing in my philosophy which is not substantiated by actual experience"[44]—with
the speculative nature of intellectual philosophy. Jung wrote:

> The philosopher should always bear in mind that our *point de
> depart* is different, since I approach the problems from the
> scientific, empirical side: what he calls "ideas" I observe and
> describe as *entia*, just like a botanist his plants, a zoologist his
> animals, and alchemist his substances. I am not out to build a
> conceptual system, but use concepts to describe psychic facts
> and their peculiar mode of behavior.[45]

In addition to this methodological difference—in which
Jung claimed the "scientific" for himself—he offered throughout
his writings a wide-ranging critique of an overly rational approach
to life. First and foremost were practical reasons. Jung believed
that efforts by the ego to assert its psychic hegemony, denying its
dependence on the unconscious, were refuted by the demonstrable experiences of psychopathology. The "facts" themselves,
derived from the "mentally ill or 'seekers after truth,'"[46] demonstrate that the ego is only a relative master in its house. Jung cited
as an example a presumably overintellectualized "professor" who
would like to think that "compulsion neurosis is a magic word
used by the modern medicine man, which means (apotropaically!)
nothing but neurosis (imaginary illness)." Yet once the professor
himself succumbed to a compulsion neurosis he found that a "real
compulsion neurosis is one of the most hellish, devilish tortures,
far worse than organic disease. It would be better if the professor
thought he were possessed by the devil! That would be consider-
ably nearer the truth."[47]

Beyond issues of individual psychopathology, Jung repeatedly chided the theologians of his day for failing to provide the contemporary mind with an adequate means of understanding religious symbolism. What this meant for Jung was that appeals to "faith," or "belief"—understood as a sacrifice of the intellect—were likely to fall on deaf ears. Belief in objectified religious symbols that are contradicted by the findings of science has become increasingly problematic for the educated public. What is needed, according to Jung, is a new interpretive foundation for the old symbols that is accessible and real, that is, able to be experienced. Jung therefore eschewed objective claims to metaphysical truth, believing this was but a pretense of an inflated consciousness, unaware of its own limits.[48] Both critical philosophy and depth psychology have led to an epistemological criticism that "treats all metaphysical claims and assertions as mental phenomena, and regards them as statements about the mind and its structure that derive ultimately from certain unconscious dispositions.... Psychology therefore holds that the mind cannot establish or assert anything beyond itself."[49]

Jung acknowledged that these epistemological restrictions entail a loss, a "sacrifice," for "we bid farewell to that miraculous world" in which "mind-created figures populated a metaphysical heaven and hell."[50] Yet it is precisely because our projections have been withdrawn, leaving us with "only psychology," that the objects of our metaphysics are now "experienceable, understandable, and—thank God—real, a reality we can do something with, a living reality full of possibilities." Further, it should be noted that simply because Jung rejected the objective validity of metaphysical statements, this "does not amount, as any intelligent person can see, to a gesture of scepticism or agnosticism aimed at faith and trust in higher powers...."[51] For Jung, the "metaphysical" was similar conceptually to what Kant meant by a "'merely negative borderline concept.'"[52] The metaphysical "thing-in-itself" may, as far as humanly possible, become known in and through experience, and through experience only.

This epistemological position led Jung to criticize what he felt was an unnecessary conflict between religious and scientific thought. Both ways of thinking, when they engage in concretism, fail to take adequate account of their foundations in the psyche. It is the recognition of the mediatory role of the psyche that was the basis of Jung's proposed resolution. The historical conflict between science and religion finds one expression in the theoretical problem of the relationship between mind and body. I quote at some length, as a way of segueing into Jung's proposed alternative to these problems, his statements regarding the nature of the conflict between the religious and scientific and the particular faults of both parties:

> The West thus developed a new disease: the conflict between science and religion. The critical philosophy of science became as it were negatively metaphysical—in other words, materialistic—on the basis of an error of judgment; matter was assumed to be a tangible and recognizable reality. Yet this is a thoroughly metaphysical concept hypostatized by uncritical minds. Matter is an hypothesis. When you say "matter," you are really creating a symbol for something unknown which just as well may be "spirit" or anything else; it may even be God.[53]

And, in contrast, regarding faith, Jung makes the following observations:

> Religious faith, on the other hand, refuses to give up its pre-critical *Weltanschauung*. In contradiction to the saying of Christ, the faithful try to *remain* children instead of becoming *as* children....It [faith] is unwilling to give up the primitive, childlike relationship to mind-created and hypostatized figures; it wants to go on enjoying the security and confidence of a world still presided over by powerful, responsible, and kindly parents.[54]

JUNG'S "THIRD WAY"

In order to offer a positive alternative to the one-sidedness of both reductive materialism and uncritical rationalism (religious and philosophical), Jung adopted a position that he termed *esse in anima*, or "essence in soul," or, loosely, "the psyche is essential and that which is immediately real." Jung saw in this position a way of successfully mediating a myriad of theoretical and practical problems. *Esse in anima* was Jung's attempt to formulate a satisfactory conceptual response to age-old dualisms.

> I do not contest the relative validity either of the realistic standpoint, *the esse in re*, or of the idealistic standpoint, the *esse in intellect solo;* I would only like to unite these extreme opposites by an *esse in anima*, which is the psychological standpoint. We live immediately only in the world of images.[55]

Or, more boldly, Jung claims:

> But between *intellectus* and *res* there is still *anima*, and this *esse in anima* makes the whole ontological argument superfluous.[56]

The constituents of this position may be understood as twofold: the first, epistemological, and the second, ontological. The epistemological component, as has been indicated, is based on a Kantian recognition of the inescapable subjectivity of our knowledge. Or, stated most simply and positively, it is based on the recognition of the psyche as a structuring, shaping, directing, coloring, flavoring, projecting, and even blinding medium for our knowledge. This is unavoidable as "everything is mediated through the mind...."[57] Jung expressed this viewpoint in numberless ways, with the various formulations more or less palatable to common sense. For example, in a relatively moderate formulation, he wrote:

> Living reality is the product neither of the actual, objective behavior of things nor of the formulated idea exclusively, but rather of the combination of both in the living psychological process, through *esse in anima*.[58]

In a letter written late in his life, Jung attempted to express in simple vernacular the nature of the relationship between image and object, mind and body:

> Whatever I perceive from without or within is a representation or image, a psychic entity caused, as I rightly or wrongly

assume, by a corresponding "real" object. But I have to admit that my subjective image is only *grosso modo* identical with the object. Any portrait painter will agree with this statement and the physicist will add that what we call "colours" are really wave-lengths. The difference between image and real object shows that the psyche, apperceiving an object, alters it by adding or excluding certain details. The image is not entirely caused by the object; it is also influenced by certain pre-existent psychic conditions which we can correct only partially.[59]

Yet epistemological issues, though occupying the foreground of many of his works, were always for Jung primarily a means to ontological ends. Jung employed his epistemological arguments to support his ontological position, summed up in the concept "psychic reality." The central role that this concept of "psychic reality" played in Jung's thought is exemplified in the essay "The Basic Postulates of Analytical Psychology," written in 1934. The title of the essay suggests that the reader will find a general outline of a complex system of thought. Yet what one actually encounters is nothing less, nor more, than a singularly focused, protracted defense of the "reality of the psyche" and a parallel critique of the current "spirit of the age" that is entirely "matter of fact" and whose popular psychologies are merely "studies of consciousness which ignore the existence of unconscious psychic life."[60]

In spite of the passage cited above regarding the trumping of the ontological question, Jung was concerned with ontology in the sense that he equated the problem "What is real?" with "What can I experience?" For Jung, everything he could and did experience he considered to be "real," and, conversely, what could not be experienced was simply unknowable. For Jung, the meaningful questions in this regard are, "Is a conscious content present or not?"[61] and "Does it act upon us?"[62] For example, Jung challenged the materialistic perspective on the grounds that it fails to acknowledge the reality of "thoughts" even though their effect is incontestable:

Is a thought "real"? Probably—to this way of thinking [i.e., materialistic]—only so far as it refers to something that can be perceived by the senses. If it does not, it is considered "unreal,"...and is declared nonexistent. This happens all the time in practice, despite the fact that it is a philosophical monstrosity. The thought *was* and *is*, even though it refers to no tangible reality; it even has an effect, otherwise no one would have noticed it. But because the little word "is"—to our way of thinking—refers to something material, the "unreal" thought must be content to exist in a nebulous super-reality, which in practice means the same thing as unreality.[63]

The effects of this "third way" may at first seem entirely negative in character, that is, as simply deflating the hubris of both the materialists and the rationalists by constricting our range of attainable knowledge. Yet Jung's criticisms were in the service of an alternative, positive perspective. By framing the mind/body problem (an ontological problem) as an epistemological problem—or, more accurately, as a *false* epistemological problem—he provided a way of overcoming a theoretical conundrum.

> It is due to our most lamentable mind that we cannot think of body and mind as one and the same thing; probably they *are* one thing, but we are unable to think it. Modern physics is subject to the same difficulty....[64]

This epistemological "overcoming" of the ontological problem provides the theoretical framework for Jung's portrayal of the psyche as being not only of one "substance" with the body but also as sharing in its qualities and effects. That is, Jung not only insisted on theoretical grounds for the essential unity of mind and body, but he was also intent on demonstrating the manner of their present, vital interrelationships. One of the most immediate and obvious areas where Jung explored the implications of mind/body unity was in our conception of "instinct." Our understanding of what is "instinctual" is directly relevant to such basic moral issues as freedom, responsibility, and the will. If something—generally a behavior, or at least an inclination to such behavior—is considered instinctive, there is generally no moral quality attached to it, positive or negative. The moral quality of an act, or intention, or disposition is contingent on the presence of conscious reflection and at least a modicum of freedom of the will. Thus, the instinctual realm and the moral realm are traditionally segregated, perhaps most plainly demonstrated by a general exemption of animals from moral accountability.

Western moral theory has generally maintained a clear distinction—if not positing an irreconcilable hostility—between the instincts and the cognitive processes involved in moral practice. This mutual exclusivity has generally been the case regardless of how a given theorist has valued the passions. Jung challenged this segregation. He attempted to revise and broaden the conception of "instinct" beyond that of physiological behavior alone, to include also the realm of "psychic behavior." Jung made this significant step in the following manner, drawing upon an analogy from the animal kingdom to illustrate his point:

> There are any number of typical situations, each represented by a certain innate form that forces the individual to function in a specifically human way. These are the same as the forms that force the birds to build their nests in a certain way. Instinct takes a specific form, even in man. That form is the archetype....[65]

Or, more succinctly:

> Our instincts do not express themselves only in our actions and reactions, but also in the way we formulate what we imagine. Instinct is not only biological, it is also, you might say, spiritual.[66]

Or, most simply, archetypes are "images of instincts."[67]

Through this theoretical, conceptual move, Jung sought to locate the psyche and its processes within the biological continuum. This changed perspective—where we no longer view the psyche as radically distinct from, and in opposition to, the body—was portrayed visually by Jung in the following, geometrical manner:

> The deeper you go [into the psyche], the broader the base becomes. It certainly does not become narrower, and it never by any chance ends in a point—in a psychic trauma, for instance....Knowledge of the subjective contents of consciousness means very little, for it tells us next to nothing about the real, subterranean life of the psyche.[68]

This inversion of the psychic structure—presenting the ego not as a reigning crown of the psychic realm, but as the visual, perhaps ephemeral expression of the essential—represents a "revolution" more radical, I believe, than that of Freud. Freud's "Copernican revolution" did indeed unseat the ego from its assumed position of hegemonic authority. But what, I ask, really changed? Yes, per Freud's agenda, the pretenses of Reason and its optimism were punctured and deflated. But was the basic attitude—the inner quality or "heart"—of the ego itself transformed? Or was the Promethean attitude made only more defiant through the rapid-fire sequence of Copernicus, Darwin, and Freud? I would suggest that as long as the body and its passions are conceived as being in an oppositional relationship with the ego and, importantly, without moral quality, the self will continue to search for a "location" it may trust and affirm as its "home" other than our physical reality. Freud's diagnosis of Victorian, rational humanity was one of hubris, denial, and defiance. Jung's assessment of his contemporaries pointed instead toward a pervasive state of forlorn alienation and yearning for reconciliation. Only when the ego perceives not only its foundations, but *itself* as continuous with the physiological can it seek its fulfillment through integration and transformation within the physical realm.

For Jung the problem of harmonizing mind and body was of the greatest necessity, not simply for the philosopher but for all of us who partake, for good or ill, in the ethos of our present age. This spirit is marked by "the rediscovery of the body after its long depreciation in the name of spirit. We are even tempted to speak of the body's revenge upon the spirit...."[69] For too long we have divided mind against body, leading to an "unbearable contradiction." But, Jung observed, even if a disembodied mind could endure the split, the concrete, actual life of a human "cannot remain thus divided, for the split is not a mere matter of some offbeat philosophy, but the daily repeated problem of his relation to himself and to the world...."[70] Yet, significantly, for Jung this recognition of the body was not a simple matter of "surrendering" to one's instincts, nor even "sublimating" them in a socially accepted manner. For both these notions still rest upon a belief in an irremediable conflict that may at best reach a state of détente.

Instead of a relatively static model of inherent conflict, Jung suggested that one's reconciliation with the body is part of a progressive, historical movement for humanity in which his psychology played a part:

> Analytical psychology tries to resolve the resultant conflict not by going "back to Nature" with Rousseau, but by holding on to the level of reason we have successfully reached, and by enriching consciousness with a knowledge of man's psychic foundations.[71]

What was suggested here by Jung is a new manner of understanding the problem that not only qualifies its claims but also infuses the problem with a positive function:

> If we are still caught by the old idea of an antithesis between mind and matter, the present state of affairs means an unbearable contradiction; it may even divide us against ourselves. But if we reconcile ourselves with the mysterious truth that spirit is the living body seen from within, and the body the outer manifestation of the living spirit—the two being one—then we can understand why it is that the attempt to transcend the present level of consciousness must give its due to the body. We shall also see that belief in the body cannot tolerate an outlook that denies the body in the name of the spirit.[72]

This claim of an ultimate unity of mind and body, and an affirmation of both as part of a "living reality," provides one of the foundational elements of Jung's moral psychology being explored in these pages. A second question, one of great poignancy— whether it is conflict or harmony that resides at the heart of life— is addressed in the next chapter.

Chapter 3

JUNG ON CONFLICT AND HARMONY

The purpose of the previous chapter was to counter Jung's alleged negativity toward *physis*, the body of self and world, by developing a positive model of his philosophy of nature. I argued that Jung rejected any and all absolute dualisms and instead portrayed as an "indissoluble unity" the mind/body, psyche/matter relationships. Jung developed this viewpoint through a "third way," what he termed *esse in anima*. Psychology (analytical) is the "mediatory science," one that gives ontology an epistemological twist (and vice versa) through the phenomenology of the unconscious. The practical effect of this theoretical position is a portrayal of the psyche as being grounded in, and expressive of, humanity's instinctual nature. Yet, in contradistinction to Freud and the Freudians, for Jung this meant an expansion of the meaning of the term "instinct" to include not only the more purely physiological drives but also what one might call, loosely, the life of the spirit. Psychic structures, symbolic expressions, conscious articulations, and spiritual yearnings were all given an instinctual cast through the concepts and language of the archetypes. In short, the psyche was naturalized, but at the same time, nature was ensouled. Jung claimed this was not metaphysics, but science.

These synthesizing, unifying perspectives constitute fundamental tenets of Jung's psychology and inform a basic element of my argument. Yet it is possible that the previous chapter, in the effort to clarify one of Jung's basic assumptions, in fact served to distort, perpetuating several misconceptions regarding Jung. The polemical challenge of the prior chapter was to offer an alternative to dualistic thinking concerning spirit and matter, *psyche* and *soma*. An emphasis was placed on the synthetic nature of Jung's thought, of reconciling apparent contradictions. Although a simple unity was not suggested, the impression may have been given that Jung minimized or bypassed the reality of conflict in order to emphasize harmony. In short, the prior chapter may have suggested that Jung was a "Pollyannaish preacher of harmony."

The present chapter seeks to refute this negative stereotype by differentiating Jung's positions from alternative, more simplistic categories of thought that were perhaps implied, or at least left unanswered in chapter 2. To achieve this end, the focus of this third chapter will be the complex problem of "conflict and harmony"—how these phenomena are both perceived in theory and engaged in practice, and how Jung's framing of this problem impacts one's understanding of his psychology. As I will discuss, Jung was not an advocate of a simple unity—denying conflict in the name of a false harmony—but rather he embraced multiple values within his moral universe that were often in conflict with one another yet, at the same time, potentially tending toward a higher and wider complex harmony.

What exactly do I mean by "the problem of conflict and harmony"? To answer this most basic of questions, I make several initial observations. First, the problem of conflict and harmony manifests in many forms and may be approached theoretically from many angles. For instance, the nature of conflict may be approached within the religious, natural, social, and psychological spheres and may be called—respectively, and by way of example—the problem of evil, survival, warfare, and psychopathology. Further, it should be observed that within all of these realms the problem may be approached *descriptively*, that is, through an attitude that strives for a faithful articulation of what is clearly seen.[1]

Yet the problem of conflict and harmony may be, and in fact usually is, also addressed *prescriptively* at the very point where theory moves, usually unacknowledged, from "is" to "ought," thereby entering the moral realm. This is particularly true within the social and psychological spheres of inquiry. Whether this transition from fact to value is logically or theoretically defensible, and whether it is explicit or not, the move from description to prescription does occur in major contemporary psychotherapeutic psychologies, according to Don S. Browning. He describes the "modern psychologies, and especially the clinical psychologies," as "practical moral philosophies" or "mixed disciplines" which are "actually instances of religio-ethical thinking."[2] The modern psychologies, according to Browning, engage not only questions about human "tendencies and needs" but also the manner in which these "natural" dispositions are to be morally ordered by "theories of obligation."[3] I do not criticize this practice, for it appears that it is the moral kernel of theories that provides the motive force of its ideas and the possible appeal to the reader's conscience and ethical judgment. In this study I seek to make explicit basic Jungian prescriptive valuations—valuations that he may present as descriptive fact—in order "to distinguish what is scientific from what is moral and quasi-religious and to make some evaluation" of his claims within each of these categories.[4] I will do so by focusing on the problem of conflict through the *description* of *psychological* dynamics and their relation to physiological processes as portrayed in Jung's analytical psychology.

CONFLICT, HARMONY, AND CONSCIENCE

The issue of conflict is relevant to the problem of conscience in several ways. Perhaps most basically, conscience may itself be understood as a factor that precipitates and reveals one's moral conflicts. A "bad conscience," as an experience or state of mind, is by definition a state of conflict. Even a "good conscience" implies the existence of a conflict overcome, that is, at a minimum, the awareness that "the good" that one has managed to realize was fragile—and it may have been otherwise—had not, for example, a temptation been averted. In this sense, then, whatever the form, conscience is inconceivable without the conflict that precipitates and defines it.

Yet conscience implies more than a static state of conflict. Conflicts of conscience, even in their most paralyzing forms, beckon and impel one toward a resolution, an atonement, or, at the least, a psychic détente. In whatever manner one conceives of the mechanics and means, conflicts of conscience suggest at least the possibility of a future different from the conflicted present. A conflict implies its opposite, that is, harmony, as darkness implies light. In this sense conscience is the psychic form of conflict and harmony par excellence. It is a poignant example of the complexity of one's self asserting its pluralism. To begin to understand conscience one must therefore comprehend the dynamics of psychological conflict.

Beyond these general observations about the conflictual nature of conscience, an examination of conflict and harmony serves more specific functions within this work. In order to develop a positive account of Jung's moral psychology it is necessary to address, at least in basic terms, the problem of human freedom both as the basis of moral responsibility and as a moral value in itself. The connection between psychological conflict and human freedom is this: assume for a moment that one understands human beings to be creatures fully enmeshed, without remainder, in the biological order. If one assumes these "naturalistic brackets,"[5] and if one conceives of the self as *unitary* in structure, then the nature of one's conflicts, and one's liberation from them in freedom, will be conceived necessarily in terms referring to the external world. That is, the constraints upon oneself and their dissolution, one's conflicts and their overcoming, reside "without." Neil Weiner describes this freedom as "a purely formal notion," a freedom *from* but not *for* anything in particular. "Negative freedom gives me the right to do as I choose in these presumably personal matters, but it gives me no guidance about which alternative to pick, and it is with these 'personal' matters that the real substance of ethics, character, and virtue lie."[6]

However, if the self is understood as *complex* in nature— potentially admitting of imbalance, disharmony, and fragmentation—then one's conflicts and their resolution in freedom may reside within as well as without. Freedom may then be understood not solely as liberation from external constraints but also as requiring for its fulfillment a freedom from varied forms of inner bondage—compulsions, depressions, and fears—that disrupt one's inner harmony, diminish self-determination, and compound shades of shame. Such an inner freedom is dependent on a form of self-knowledge that entails what Neil Weiner terms "rough virtue," that is, an awareness of one's genuine moral qualities and capacities and their harmonious integration. Weiner identifies the form of freedom dependent on "knowledge of the true object of desire" as *aretaic* freedom. Conscience is a means by which the complex self may address and resolve its inner moral conflicts in order to realize this *aretaic* freedom.

The issue of conflict is relevant to conscience in another manner as well. One of the principal arguments against the traditional notion of conscience as authoritative moral source is the obvious and demonstrable failings of conscience on both a personal and a social level. Individually, conscience may mislead by wrongly accusing or fail by its apparent absence. In either case its reliability as moral guide is cast in doubt. Socially, the very existence of conflict, with each party claiming to act conscientiously, testifies loudly for the skeptic. Logic would seem to dictate in such cases that either there is not a transpersonal moral order or conscience does not serve as moral source of this order. How, after all, could there be such social strife if the universally available conscience is in fact a voice of a "transpersonal good"? Would not this transpersonal good—a god of some magnitude by whatever name—orchestrate its intended moral order by speaking with a consistent voice of conscience? And does not the apparent absence of such a uniform moral impulse provide *prima facie* evidence of the unreliability—or nonexistence—of conscience?

These questions, and more, strike to the heart of the significance of the problem of conscience, for these questions mirror on the human, psychological plane the most profound and inscrutable of all theological problems—the problem of theodicy, the problem of Job. The person who suffers moral conflict—either within one's own self or through the apparent immorality of others—may understandably ask, if conscience is not in some sense a proponent, a "mouthpiece" for a source of transhuman moral wisdom, then just what is it? And what is it worth?

If in fact both conscience and the self are understood as unitary in nature—wholly accessible and clearly discernible—then these "failings" do indeed render conscience impossibly problematic. Theoretical justifications of conscience would tumble into contradictions and emotive assertions, persuading only those convinced of their own infallibility. Yet if conscience is understood not as an objective, graspable "thing," but as a form of awareness, contingent in part on the state of the knower, then these failings do not represent irrefutable arguments against the claims of conscience as moral guide. Rather, one's conflicts of conscience may be seen as reflective of a complex self, not all of this self known or even knowable. In this light, the fallibilities of conscience may become more of a call for deeper discernment than evidence of its moral insignificance. Thus, the complex structure of one's internal conflicts, arising as they do from the nature of the multifaceted self, provide a basis for understanding the fallibility of conscience such that its claims to moral authority may remain plausible.

There is a final consideration regarding conflict and conscience that warrants mention: the way conflict is understood and portrayed is at the very heart of one's general model of psychodynamics and, specifically, moral processes. By exploring the nature of psychic conflict, one's assumptions about general human inclinations and needs may be made more explicit. For example, by analyzing the nature of psychic conflict, questions are raised about "the will" and other determinative factors that govern one's subjectivity. Are these factors multiple or, finally, singular? What is their relationship to the ego and to the physical body? And whatever their numerical configuration and rootedness in body or mind, the critical question arises as to whether these factors comprising one's subjectivity are at heart selfish or altruistic. Further still, in positing the means of resolving these conflicts—the essence of clinical psychology—one's hierarchy of values and the manner in which they are adjudicated and realized are made explicit. For example, one may believe that moral goods are many or, conversely, that they are ultimately singular in nature, requiring purity and exclusionary focus. And one may assume that the surest means to the attainment of the good(s) will be found in yielding to simple bodily passions, or in exercising the power of Reason, or perhaps through the decisive act of choosing an "either/or." In sum, by exploring the nature of psychic conflicts, one's attention is drawn toward the heart of human nature, because strife and the hope of resolution are powerful animating forces in human life.

JUNG AND CONFLICT

How, then, did Jung incorporate conflict within his world-view and psychological theorizing? Was he in fact pollyannish? Academic appraisals of him vary widely in this regard. Don S. Browning in *Religious Thought and the Modern Psychologies*, locates Jung within the "culture of joy," a culture that "sees the world as basically harmonious" and "human wants and needs as easily reconciled and coordinated in almost frictionless compatibility."[7] Yet Salvatore R. Maddi, in his comprehensive comparative study *Personality Theories*, provides what appears to be a diametrically opposed assessment: "For Jung, life, behavior, and psyche reek with conflict."[8] It may be said without risk that academic consensus regarding Jung awaits the future. Elsewhere, in what may be generally termed the "popular culture," Jung is often loosely associated with an assortment of New Age movements. Proponents of various theosophical beliefs often claim Jung as their own, supportive of a feel-good, idealistic worldview wherein evil and suffering are solipsistically wished away. Which, then, of these characterizations is accurate or fair to the spirit and letter of Jung's own writings?

The answer to this question is not simple. As the above quotations suggest, Jung's ideas may be employed to justify a wide range of attitudinal positions corresponding to the needs of both reader and writer. In what follows I attempt to capture something of the complexity of his thought, relating the varied elements of his psychology to one another in a balanced presentation that gets at the heart of Jung's ideas about the range and role of psychological conflicts and their resolution in harmony.

I will initially approach this task by employing a foil, the negative stereotype of Jung as a promoter of a pollyannish attitude that minimizes the intractable nature of humanity's conflicts and the necessity of confronting elementary facts of embodied human life. This negative stereotype of Jung is not simply a fabrication of his detractors,[9] but in fact has several sources within Jung's writings themselves. First and foremost was the pervasive presence in Jung's informing *Weltanschauung* of far-reaching structural and dynamic concepts such as process, development, synthesis, amplification, integration, and realization, which serve to create an overall sense of harmonized purpose, meaning, and possibility. Whatever conflicts Jung did acknowledge seemed to be considered neither irremediable nor without an ultimate sense.

This does not mean that Jung was naively optimistic or prone to denying actual human suffering. In fact, I will argue that Jung's psychology embodies and expresses a worldview that is profound in both its vision of a transcendent and harmonizing purpose and its disturbing recognition of the depth and grave import of present conflicts. In other words, although Jung may be appropriated selectively to support a simplistically optimistic attitude, I will argue that an adequate reading of his works reveals that the indispensable foundation of his affirming worldview was the recognition and, insofar as it is possible, acceptance of inescapable conflict at the heart of human life. In short, the sense of ultimate purpose resident in Jung's psychology need not equate with a denial of present sufferings; rather, it is through a conscious embracing of conflict that one may come to understand one's significance in the human drama, and in this understanding of one's meaning resides the means and end of living the moral life.

Another reason that Jung is perceived by some as being remote from an appreciation of their real-world conflicts is the manner in which he presented his ideas, particularly the case histories derived from his clinical practice. In contrast to Freud, for example, who brought us vivid tales of visceral tragedy through the case histories of "The Rat Man," "The Psychotic Doctor Schreber," and others, Jung's presentation of cases somehow moves the individual life to the background as the presentation of psychic images and fantasies, dream narratives, and a range of historical and literary associations assume the foreground in his explications and theorizing. This tendency to depersonalize what may be seen, and felt, as unique agonies is part of Jung's more general fabric of thought that follows as a guiding principle the objectification of psychic factors originating outside the ego. This "objectification" of elements of the psyche, however, need not mean a "depersonalization" of these elements.

In this regard I will argue what may seem counterintuitive: that Jung's apparent universalizing idealism (e.g., the concept of the archetypes), rather than diminishing one's individuality, in fact is the basis of perceiving each human life as unique and significant within a transpersonal and dramatic context. Conversely, psychologies that seem at first blush to affirm the worth of the individual may actually serve to depress one's sense of worth by reducing the frameworks of one's narratives to mundane and monotonous biographies. Self-identity, whether affirming or negating, is always contextual, rooted in a web of narratives, comprising one's own myth.

Finally, the manner in which Jung conceived and described his central concept of *individuation* could be suggestive of a privatized way of insulating the self from conflict. This would be so if individuation were understood, erroneously, in terms of a single value, that is, consciousness. This critical viewpoint, combining a simplistic emphasis on the individual with a singular focus on consciousness, would, if accurate, locate Jung within the long and tired tradition of introverted idealists seeking self-sufficiency through rational means.

Yet consciousness for Jung is not to be simply equated with intellect, thinking, or the faculty of reason. Rather, an expansive and matured consciousness is one that is appreciatively aware, through direct, firsthand encounters, of the full range of one's composition, including one's impassioned embodiment; one's rich emotional life, which infuses experience with value and beauty; an intuition that fuels one's hopes, dreams, and sense of wonder; and, finally, the capacity to think and understand, which allows one more fully to know others and to create and do works in this light. Further, a broad and deep consciousness is likewise marked by an awareness of what one is *not*. Only to the extent that one is aware of one's own finitude may one reach out toward the infinite—through the others around us and through the other within us.[10]

Finally, psychological wholeness for Jung was not a private affair, pursued in splendid isolation. Rather, he conceived of it as being comprised not simply by a consciousness shaped by broad experience and deep understanding, but also through the taking upon oneself of the moral obligations contained in these insights and the living of one's life accordingly. "Intellectual and emotional understanding require to be not only rationally integrated with the conscious mind, but morally assimilated."[11] This process of individuation is thus dialectical: between the individual and her environment, as well as within one's own psyche as a "discursive cooperation of conscious and unconscious factors."[12] Individuation may therefore be seen as having "two principal aspects: in the first place it is an internal and subjective process of integration, and in the second it is an equally indispensable process of objective relationship. Neither can exist without the other, although sometimes the one and sometimes the other predominates."[13] This dialectic of psychological development introduces multiple moral values into one's practical life that entail the inevitability of conflict. Seen in this light, individuation is a synthetic term, descriptive of a process of human development in which the wholeness of the person emerges, develops, and manifests in ever greater differentiation and complexity. Jung's typology, model of functions, and understanding of transference as pervasive and typical human phenomena form the basis of this evaluation.

As I discussed in the last chapter, Jung employed a variety of polemical forms to build his arguments for the substantial reality of the psyche. Likewise, when he articulated his particular vision of the dynamics of conflict, he utilized a range of styles, logics, and language. On the one hand, he attempted to use the language of the hard sciences, arguing in his essay "On Psychic Energy" for the existence of psychological principles or laws that in some way parallel those found in physics, namely, the "conservation of energy" and "entropy."[14] Elsewhere he employed naturalistic metaphors, drawn from the fundamentals of human experience, to depict psychic processes, for example, the emergence and gradient flow of springwater, or the daily course of the rising and dying sun.[15] Finally, he articulated his theories of psychodynamics by describing and then amplifying his direct encounters with individuals struggling to bring order and sense out of the psychic chaos that initially drove them across the threshold into the consulting room. Each of these approaches—what I call "scientific," "metaphorical," and "practical"—contributed to Jung's portrayal of the dynamics of psychological conflict and harmony.

THE ENERGIC POINT OF VIEW

Jung's "scientific" explanation of psychodynamics went something like this: when one observes physical phenomena, one can adopt either the *mechanistic viewpoint* based on efficient causation or, conversely, the *energic viewpoint* based on final causation. According to Jung, the mechanistic view conceives of events as effects of causes "in the sense that unchanging substances change their relations to one another according to fixed laws."[16] In contrast, the energic view conceives of events in terms of relations of movement based on an "energy [that] underlies the changes in phenomena" and that tends toward a condition of equilibrium.[17] This "energy" is not to be conceived as a substance, but rather is a concept abstracted from the changing relations of matter. "The concept, therefore, is founded not on the substances themselves but on their relations, whereas the moving substance itself is the basis of the mechanistic view."[18]

Whether one accepts this distinction—and accepts the reality of "final" causation—rests on whether one accepts the meaningfulness of an abstract—that is, nonhypostatized—conception of "energy" derived from observations of relationship. Jung acknowledged this basic philosophical issue and choice:

> Finality and causality are two possible ways of understanding which form an antinomy. They are progressive and regressive "interpretants" (Wundt) and as such are contradictory. Naturally this statement is correct only if it is assumed that the concept of energy is an abstraction that expresses relation. But the statement is not correct if an hypostatized concept of energy is assumed.[19]

Jung described the mechanistic and final approaches to understanding phenomena as "modes of thought"[20] or "viewpoints," that is, "not *constituent* (objective) principles—as it were, qualities of the objects—but purely *regulative* (subjective) principles of thought, and, as such, not mutually inconsistent." He stated, "I consider both these points of view necessary, the causal as well as the final, but would at the same time stress that since Kant's time we have come to realize that the two viewpoints are not antagonistic."[21]

To adjudicate this apparent contradiction epistemologically Jung adopted the "antinomian postulate," which asserts that one's conception of the world is a psychically conditioned phenomenon: "Certainly it is necessary for science to know how things are 'in themselves,' but even science cannot escape the psychological conditions of knowledge, and psychology must be peculiarly alive to these conditions."[22] Utilizing a viewpoint developed in his *Psychological Types*, Jung claimed that it is not so much the objective behavior of things that determines one's view of causation as it is the attitude of the investigator: "Empathy leads to the mechanistic view, abstraction to the energic view."[23] Jung then claimed that this "intolerable contradiction" is really a result of projecting one's subjective concepts into the object itself, falsely believing that the asserted principle is "identical with the behavior of the thing itself."[24] Therefore, when dealing with the physical world, Jung advocated an epistemologically nuanced perspective, in a Kantian vein, that recognizes the relative truth claims of both efficient and final causation.

Jung also adopted what may be termed a phenomenological position to argue for the validity of the energic point of view:

> In my opinion the nature of the human mind compels us to take a finalistic view. It cannot be disputed that, psychologically speaking, we are living and working day by day according to principles of directed aim or purpose as well as that of causality. A psychological theory must necessarily adapt itself to this fact.[25]

One may argue that Jung's statements display a circular logic that makes his point fallacious, that is, that the mere existence of the experience of purposefulness does not attest to its validity. This is certainly true in regard to claims of objectivity and correspondence between inner and outer states. But that is not the point Jung was making. As discussed in chapter 2, Jung argued for the "reality of the psyche" as a phenomenon that must be included, in its own right, in any adequate worldview. This would include the phenomena of purposefulness. Therefore, by claiming the need to include final causation in one's psychological theories, Jung was making a metatheoretical claim that is not intended to be strictly empirical in nature (i.e., objectively referential) but rather is meant to serve as a basis for understanding the full range of psychic phenomena. Erazim Kohák addresses this issue of circularity and metatheory in the following manner:

> The circularity [of one's argument], however, need not be vicious. Metatheoretical arguments must be circular, self-confirming, since they seek to provide a global matrix of intelligibility—unlike theoretical arguments, which presuppose such a matrix. The condition is that the circle be wide enough to embrace all there is. Circles, much like dogs and other small animals, become vicious only when they sense that they are too small to cope with the task with which they are confronted.[26]

Jung believed that as long as one insisted on the singular validity of historical explanations then the "essence" of psychological life was missed. If one views psychological processes in terms of substance, efficient causation, and objective fact, the tendency is to deny the ubiquitous experience of purpose, goal, and directed activity. According to Jung, the "final point" of view is inseparable from the observation and experience of psychological differentiation and development wherein "causes are understood as means to an end."[27] Jung uses the process of "regression" to illustrate his point.

> Regarded causally, regression is determined, say, by a "mother fixation." But from the final standpoint the libido regresses to the *imago* of the mother in order to find there the memory associations by means of which further development can take place, for instance from a sexual system into an intellectual or spiritual system.[28]

According to Jung, psychic phenomena are themselves facts with causal efficacy, a truth made evident by their effective and necessary role in processes of psychic transformation. Finally,

Jung argued that the causal point of view actually impedes psychological development—because a *reductio ad causum* "binds the libido to the elementary facts."[29] And what is *fact* to the causal point of view is *symbol* to the final point of view. Briefly put, Jung understood a *symbol* as a visual or conceptual representation that is the best possible expression currently available for what is not yet fully known or understood. In contrast, a *sign* refers to a consciously known, or at least knowable, factor. A symbol may be collectively or individually held and may have its origin in individual intrapsychic experience or in the accumulated wisdom of generations. It is the attractive power of the symbol that allows for the transformation of libido from an exclusive focus on the historical cause to an imagined positing of "the way that lies ahead."[30]

QUANTITATIVE AND QUALITATIVE

In addition to differentiating efficient and final causes, Jung further developed his "scientific" ideas regarding psychic energy by making a distinction between *quantitative* and *qualitative* concepts. This terminology was used by Jung in his book *Symbols of Transformation* (1911–12), in which he equated "libido" with "psychic energy," in contrast to what he conceived as the Freudian equation of libido with "sexuality."[31] Jung later explained what the motivation and rationale were behind this theoretical move. "What I wished to do for psychology was to arrive at some logical and thorough view such as is provided in the physical sciences by the theory of energetics....In physics we speak of energy and its manifestations, such as electricity, light, heat, etc. The situation in psychology is precisely the same." The result was a theory of the libido that conceived of psychic energy in "quantitative," abstract terms.[32]

> I conceived the libido as a psychic analogue of physical energy, hence as a more or less quantitative concept, which therefore should not be defined in qualitative terms. My idea was to escape from the then prevailing concretism of the libido theory—in other words, I wished no longer to speak of the instincts of hunger, aggression, and sex, but to regard all these phenomena as expressions of psychic energy.[33]

His polemical motivation was thus to resist conceptual hypostatization that, seemingly, draws the mind irresistibly into reductive, mechanistic modes of thought deleterious to symbolic, amplified, and teleological thinking. Jung described a quantitative concept as one that refers to relations of intensities, while a qualitative concept is a description of a substance.[34] These definitions, at least as I understand them, are contrary to normal associations for these two terms. *Quantity* I associate with measurement, which I then associate with objects and extended substance. Conversely, it is relationships and their intensities that I associate with *qualitative* factors. But Jung asked us to reverse these connotations, and in this inversion lies an important aspect of his thought.

Jung used this distinction between quantitative and qualitative to sharpen his definition of *energy*, and, importantly, to distinguish it from *forces* and *drives*. *Energy*, for Jung, was a quantitative concept, "based on the one hand on an immediate, *a priori*, intuitive idea, and on the other a concrete, applied, or empirical concept abstracted from experience."[35] Energy, when defined in this manner, is a complex concept. This complex nature of the concept of "energy"—based on both *a priori* and *a posteriori* elements—is often occluded by the fact that in practice one's direct experiences of energy are in the form of definite, concrete forces. In the psychological realm these forces appear "in the form of sexual, vital, mental, moral 'energy,' and so on," that is, as specific "drives." Jung observed that, because of the visceral, repeated impact of immediate experience, there is a tendency to merge or conflate the intuitive idea of energy with its applied concept, thereby leading us to equate "energy" with "force." In this manner one's conceptualization and understanding of the complex nature of energy are reduced and restricted to its simple, manifest form. Jung recognized that this conceptual confusion—this urge to think tangibly—is nearly inevitable since "we are incapable of imagining a quantum unless it be a quantum of something."[36]

Jung acknowledged that exact quantitative measurement of psychic energy, beyond the simplest of psychological phenomena, is not possible as it is with physical events. Yet this empirical imprecision need not negate the possibility of applying the energic point of view to psychological phenomena. Jung believed that a quantitative *estimate* of energy is possible, for in fact "our psyche actually possesses an extraordinarily well-developed evaluating system, namely the *system of psychological values*."[37] In an unusual juxtaposition, Jung attempted to bridge the usually impassable gap between fact and value through the simple observation that "values are quantitative estimates of energy."[38] Subjectively experienced, "estimates" of energy are determined through the intensity of feelings.[39] Humanity's moral and aesthetic values have accrued collectively in a variety of laws, mores, traditions, canons, and prejudices. These form an "objective system" of value and measurement, but they have only indirect relevance for individual psychological conditions.

The individual person experiences this energic process of valuation through a "subjective value system." Jung acknowledged the difficulties, and in some ways the incommensurabilities, of relating subjective values to the generally established values. A similar difficulty arises within the individual's psychic economy when comparing "value intensities of different qualities, say the value of a scientific idea compared with a feeling impression." One's subjective valuations are, however, more easily, or at least possibly, evaluated in relation to one another than are those between persons. The relative strength of one's different values can be recognized through different levels of intensity of psychic processes and/or states of equilibrium.[40] The "psychological value" of a psychic process is "implicit in its determining power," for example, through affects and feelings.[41]

This subjective adjudication of values depends on conscious awareness of not only rational ideas and deduced judgments but also the discernment of influences originating from the unconscious. Though not directly experienceable, by definition, the unconscious manifests itself through a range of feelings, thoughts, and intuitions—experiences that form the basis of conscience.

Jung's motives for his theoretical constructions regarding psychic energy may therefore be stated as follows: he distinguished between quantity and quality, and energy and force, in order to avoid what he considered any form of concretism that would support a reductive psychology. Jung identified "qualitative" concepts with the "specific," "concrete," and "applied." A qualitative concept of energy is therefore applicable only in the description of a force. This understanding of energy—as applied force—is entirely appropriate, in Jung's view, when employed within a specialized science, as long as it is recognized as a "regional ontology" and does not make excessively wide, generalized claims beyond its rightful domain.[42] Conversely, a quantitative concept of energy may make claims to broader applicability and adequacy by including the various forces in a "higher concept of relations" that seeks to acknowledge the particular, distinctive reality of each of these different drives.[43] Jung attempted to use this theoretical framing to affirm the specific (i.e., limited) applicability of psychoanalytic theory while simultaneously relativizing it.

> Since Freud confines himself almost exclusively to sexuality and its manifold ramifications in the psyche, the sexual definition of energy as a specific driving force is quite sufficient for his purpose. In a general psychological theory, however, it is impossible to use purely sexual energy, that is, one specific drive, as an explanatory concept, since psychic energy transformation is not merely a matter of sexual dynamics. Sexual dynamics is only one particular instance in the total field of the psyche. This is not to deny its existence, but merely to put it in its proper place.[44]

THE CONSERVATION OF ENERGY AND ENTROPY

The application of the energic point of view to psychological theory has several basic effects that are directly relevant to Jung's modeling of the psychodynamics of conflict and harmony. As Jung developed the idea, the central principle of the energic viewpoint—also the first principle of thermodynamics—is that of the "conservation of energy" (or "principle of equivalence"). Simply stated, this means that "for a given quantity of energy expended or consumed in bringing about a certain condition, an equal quantity of the same or another form of energy will appear elsewhere."[45] This "principle of equivalence" is, of course, central as well to psychoanalytic theory, employed through the concepts of "repression," "substitute formations," and symptomatology in general. Yet, according to Jung, Freud's theories suffered from a habitual reduction of complex phenomena (i.e., the full range of psychic experience) to an oversimplified, mechanical-causal explanation based on a single manifestation of force, that is, sexuality. Because "it cannot be asserted that sexuality is the only fundamental psychic instinct...every explanation on a sexual basis can be only a partial explanation, never an all-sufficing psychological theory."[46] Reductive causalism, combined with the "principle of equivalence," translated into Freud's adoption of the "Nirvana Principle" and its conservative anthropological corollaries.

In contrast to this pessimistic, quiescent attitude, Jung understood the principle of equivalence through the framework of his energic point of view. The result stands in marked contrast to psychoanalytic theory. Jung saw in the "conservation of energy" not a force allied with stasis or death but rather a way of conceptualizing certain processes of psychological development—or, more accurately, processes of transformation—marked by structural and dynamic self-regulation. But just how is the "conservation of energy" a vehicle of change? This requires an explanation.

The principle of equivalence (i.e., the conservation of energy) finds its theoretical complement in the concept of "entropy." The combined application of these two principles provided the theoretical basis for Jung's model of psychic transformation. Many of the phrases and expressions commonly used by Jung and subsequent Jungians[47]—such as "one-sided," "polar," and "self-regulating"—are based on these two principles derived from, or at least analogous to, those found in the physical sciences. Without an appreciation of these theoretical foundations, these root commitments of Jung's, any discussion that utilizes these and other common terms is prone to sound speculative, fuzzy, and ungrounded.

Simply stated, entropy is the idea that within a closed energic system variances in intensity seek a state of equilibrium, proceeding from "improbable" to "probable" states. It is through the relations of different intensities, and the resulting processes of movement toward states of reduced tension, that transformations of energy may occur. Jung illustrated this idea of a self-regulating system tending toward equilibrium with examples from the physical realm:

> Heat can be converted into work only by passing from a warmer to a colder body. But mechanical work is continually being converted into heat, which on account of its reduced intensity cannot be converted back into work. In this way a closed energic system gradually reduces its differences in intensity to an even temperature, whereby any further change is prohibited.[48]

Jung viewed the psyche in an analogous manner, as a system that is "relatively closed" and therefore subject to the operations of the principle of entropy. Jung claimed that the entropic viewpoint was applicable to the psyche—"at least [as] a provisional view"—because of the "immediate experience of quantitative psychic relations on the one hand, and the unfathomable nature of a psychophysical connection on the other."[49] By adopting this position, Jung was attempting to articulate the view that as a *"relatively closed system"*[50] the psyche could not be reduced to physiological terms, but rather maintained its own integral form of energy and causal nexus.[51] That is, while clearly dependent on the body for basic sustenance, the psyche is within its own sphere autonomous and *relatively* insular.

This entropic tendency helps to explain both the caustic and reconstructive dynamics of transformative processes. As psychic tension builds—for example, between certain conscious and unconscious states—the capacity of old forms of personality to accommodate the demands of a wider world is threatened. An unstable personality may be understood as oscillating between opposite poles. Yet heightened tension, experienced as mental suffering in one form or another, brings with it an accumulation of energy that may serve a positive, reconstructive role. Jung writes that the "greater the tension between the pairs of opposites, the greater will be the energy that comes from them; and the greater the energy, the stronger will be its constellating, attracting power."[52] This "constellating, attracting power" refers to affects and symbolic, archetypal contents that facilitate, and in some sense represent, an emergence of a transformed personality.

Entropic processes yield, ideally, a more grounded, wider personality that has, as it were, a "lower center of gravity" that is difficult to unseat and disturb. As a commonplace example of this process, Jung cited the development of a mature, balanced attitude following the "storms of youth," in which opposites oscillate violently and "the final stability of which is the greater in proportion to the magnitude of the initial differences."[53]

This energic viewpoint informed Jung's depiction of *libido*, a term immediately derived from psychoanalysis but possessing a lineage tracing back to the ancient world.[54] Jung sought to deliteralize the use of the term, or, in the language of this chapter, to provide it with an energic, quantitative sense, in contrast to its concrete connotations of biologically expressed sexual energy. While on one hand Jung sometimes equated libido with psychic energy,[55] he elsewhere distinguished the two concepts. The equation, and distinction, rest on the same line of thinking that informed his understanding of the relation between force and energy. One experiences libido directly in the form of various appetites. Looked at causally, or genetically, it is basic "bodily needs like hunger, thirst, sleep, and sex and emotional states or affects, which constitute the essence of libido."[56] Jung did not deny humanity's current rootedness and indivisible unity with its physiological nature, nor did he neglect the evolutionary processes that may seem to give effective primacy to the more elementary factors of human nature: "even the highest differentiations were developed from simpler forms. Thus, many complex functions, which today must be denied all trace of sexuality, were originally derived from the reproductive instinct."[57] Yet Jung refused to exhaustively reduce the more complex into what is simpler, or what exists now by what has preceded. Rather, Jung suggested that in the "highly complicated human psyche" the more basic instincts have become ramified and finely differentiated, achieving varying degrees and forms of "functional independence." For example, "Although there can be no doubt that music originally belonged to the reproductive sphere, it would be an unjustified and fantastic generalization to put music in the same category as sex."[58]

Jung thus arrived at a conception of *libido* as a general term for "striving" and "desire," of "intentionality in general," or, most generally, "the energy of the life process"⁵⁹—all being phenomena of energy. Libido is thus an "energy-value which is able to communicate itself to any field of activity whatsoever, be it power, hunger, hatred, sexuality, or religion, without ever being itself a specific instinct."⁶⁰ Libido is thus an "inclusive term for psychic intensities," that is, "the intensity with which psychic contents are charged."⁶¹

PSYCHOLOGICAL ADAPTATION: EVOLUTION AND ALIENATION

The emergence of self-reflective consciousness makes possible a humanly distinctive form of conflict—the alienation of the conscious mind from its unconscious instinctual foundations. Jung spoke of these "unconscious instinctual foundations" as the human species' "natural history." This view of the unconscious informed his framing of this conflict, unique to *homo sapiens*, in terms of "adaptation" as it applies both to the emergence of the human species and in the challenges of the life of the individual.

The process of human psychological adaptation was understood by Jung as occurring, most basically, within the psyche's bipolar structure, what Edward F. Edinger called the "ego-self" axis.⁶² This bipolar model provided the conceptual superstructure within which the energic processes were conceived as dynamically operating. Within this basic structure it is the unconscious that was given phylogenetic and ontogenetic primacy by Jung. By *primacy* I do *not* mean that the unconscious was more highly valued, by any standard, than consciousness. Nor do I mean to suggest that Jung believed ego consciousness, and its attendant sense of autonomy and responsibility, to be illusory and ineffectual. Rather, by *primacy* I mean that Jung viewed the unconscious as temporally or developmentally prior to consciousness for both the individual and the evolution of the species. This "developmental prioritization" refers not only to a certain sequencing of psychosexual and psychospiritual patterns, but also to a causal significance in the emergence of the whole range of individual mental phenomena. This view prompted Jung to characterize the unconscious as the creative matrix out of which novel cultural products have, and still do, emerge.

Phylogenetically, Jung depicted a process of evolution in which the human species has gradually evolved from a state of primitive consciousness in which individuals and peoples are governed more by instinct and affect than by conscious will and rational judgment. This form of consciousness is marked by a conservative aversion to what is new, strange, or different—a misoneism—because a changing environment threatens maladaptation for the relatively fixed forms of instinctive response. When circumstances remain relatively constant, a "primitive state of psychic health" may prevail, but when progressive adaptation is demanded by a dynamic, novel environment, a "higher and wider consciousness" is necessary for "the assimilation of the unfamiliar."[63]

As consciousness expands and differentiates through encounters with novel objects and events, the threat of dissociation from its unconscious foundations likewise grows. This propensity to dissociate is related to the fact that consciousness experiences itself as radically autonomous—able to recognize only those "contents that are individually acquired" and to overvalue conscious contents to the "detriment of the unconscious."[64] For the individual, this tendency frequently results in the fallacious belief that simply because one has consciously decided something, or even decisively acted externally, one is truly independent and free from a whole host of complex unconscious factors.[65]

Yet according to Jung, radical autonomy and complete independence are not possible. This is because "all conscious ideation and action have developed on the basis of...unconscious archetypal patterns and always remain dependent upon them."[66] Yet, in spite of this dependence, a partial or relative autonomy is possible, as the very existence of dissociation demonstrates. Thus it is that with the development of consciousness and "free will" there is a commensurate possibility, if not propensity, to "deviate" from the instinctive, archetypal patterns and gradients.[67] This situation creates an "uprooted consciousness" that risks "instinctual atrophy." This "instinctual atrophy" manifests itself not only in dramatic instances of psychopathology but also in mundane maladies such as a vague sense of disorientation, emotional sterility, nervousness, an inflated and godless hubris, and "entanglement in impossible situations and problems."[68] If, or when, a breakdown actually ensues, one discovers that the unconscious is "in full revolt against the conscious values."[69]

It should be stated clearly that Jung did not suggest that it is either possible or desirable to avoid this process of evolving consciousness, for the "emancipation" of consciousness and the freedom of the will "may well continue to be considered the highest cultural achievements of humanity."[70] Consciousness and freedom of the will are necessary for moral agency,[71] and human culture itself is inconceivable not only without consciousness but, more specifically, in the absence of the dramatic tension manifested in the struggle between consciousness and its instinctive foundations.

Thus, the problem of psychic disequilibrium does not reside in the fact of consciousness itself nor in the unconscious *qua* unconscious, nor in the external environment. Rather, Jung identified the root problem of psychopathology—and all of the centrifugal suffering that this causes—as a conscious attitude that has failed to adapt adequately to the demands of either, or both, the "outer" and "inner" conditions.[72] The problem is thus one of relational adaptation on the part of consciousness. This claim that "attitude"—a conscious phenomenon—is the root of psychological conflict may initially seem to be contradicted by the usual portrayal of analytical psychology as giving primacy of value and dynamic significance to the deep interior world of the unconscious. But it is Jung's claim that it is the conscious attitude that fundamentally determines the nature of one's psychic life, including the degree of health and harmony present and the goodness manifested.

PSYCHOLOGICAL ADAPTATION: ATTITUDE AND EQUILIBRIUM

In order for these claims to be intelligible and plausible, the role of attitude and the varied challenges of adaptation will now be considered. "Attitude" was described by Jung as "a particular arrangement of psychic contents oriented towards a goal or directed by some kind of ruling principle."[73] One's attitude has a "point of reference" and reflects a predisposition to act, and react, in definite directions and ways. Attitude expects, selects, and directs. It reflects a "readiness of the psyche to act or react in a certain way."[74] It is not simple or easily malleable, but a complete "resultant" of one's "individual education," "innate disposition," "environmental influences," "general experiences of life," and personal "insights and conviction" gained through collective views and their differentiation.[75] Attitude, as Jung understood it, is thus not a mere veneer of the persona but represents the locus of the manifest personality itself. Moreover, the individual's "habitual attitude brings about such great displacements of energy, and so modifies the relations between the individual functions, that effects are produced which often cast doubt on the validity of general psychological laws."[76] Attitude, thus defined, dramatically affects both the manner and relative success of one's adaptation in life.

Jung conceived of the process of psychological adaptation as requiring a balanced relationship to both inner and outer conditions. In a short monograph titled *Adaptation, Individuation, Collectivity*,[77] Jung described neurosis as a disturbance or diminished process of adaptation to either outer or inner conditions. By "outer conditions" Jung meant not only the "surrounding world" but also "conscious judgments...formed of objective things." By "inner conditions" he meant "those facts or data which force themselves upon my inner perception from the unconscious, independently of my conscious judgment and sometimes even in opposition to it."[78] Exclusive adaptation to either inner or outer conditions leads to an imbalance, or a disruptive fusing of the two spheres. In this essay, Jung described the "energetics of adaptation" as follows:

> When the libido invested in a particular function cannot be equilibrated by the exercise of the function, it accumulates until it attains a value which exceeds that of the neighboring functional system. Then a process of equilibration begins, because a potential is present. The energy flows over, as it were, into another system. When, therefore, adaptation to the inside is not achieved, the libido intended for that purpose accumulates until it begins to flow out of the system of inner adaptation into the system of outer adaptation, with

the result that characteristics belonging to inner adaptation are carried over into outer—that is to say, fantasies intervene in the relation to the real world. Conversely, when the system of outer adaptation overflows into the system of inner adaptation, characteristics belonging to the former are carried over into the latter, namely, qualities belonging to the reality-function.[79]

This passage captures, in simple terms, the character and heuristic usefulness of Jung's energic viewpoint. This theoretical perspective allows for an understanding of psychic processes within the framework of transformative and defensive adaptation and, by implication, evolutionary thought. The central dynamic of this energic perspective of adaptation is the conscious mind's capacity to arbitrate between the demands of both inner and outer domains, and to maintain an equilibrium of these spheres through the exercise of "functions" that express libidinal energies. When libidinal energies are not given normal expression, they may accumulate increasing energy differentials and the potential, or the eventual necessity, of symptoms that indirectly express the heightened tension.[80]

This particular essay—really more of an outline he sketched to clarify his own thinking—was written in 1916, three years after his formal break with Freud and toward the end of his own "creative illness." It remained unpublished during Jung's lifetime. While some of the basic dynamics of this model sound like simple replications of Freud's own theorizing, basic differences exist, as I have discussed, in the characterization of libido and the origin and aim of the dynamic processes themselves. Chapter 5 will explore at some length the similarities and differences between the psychoanalytic perspective and that of analytical psychology through an examination of Freud's concept of the super-ego in comparison to Jung's understanding of conscience. For now, though, a consideration of the different ways in which libido "cannot be equilibrated" through the exercise of functions will tell us much about how Jung understood conflict and the various ways it may reach resolution, or termination, in the human psyche.

To understand Jung's modeling of conflict, it is important to recognize that, while he did describe certain structural and dynamic elements of human psychology as essentially universal and constant—for example, the energic process itself and the existence of archetypes—the manner in which these factors operate varies significantly among individuals. Further, even within the course of a single lifetime, the relative predominance of the various functions—even one's general type—may alter and invert.[81] This recognition of the particular, the concrete, the individual, is often overlooked in Jung's psychology—in spite of the fact that "individuation" was the "central concept" of his psychology.[82] The affirmation of the unique individuality of each person permeated his work and practice, expressed in statements such as "the cardinal rule for the psychotherapist should be to consider each case new and unique. That, probably, is the nearest we can get to the truth."[83] This emphasis on the individual, and "individuation," is generally overshadowed because Jung *did* generally focus on a particular class of problems that have their origin and means of resolution in the relationship of the individual to collective phenomena and processes. It is the element of the "collective," particularly the "collective unconscious," that makes Jung's psychology different, if not unique, among major contemporary psychotherapeutic psychologies.

PSYCHOLOGICAL ADAPTATION: INDIVIDUAL VARIABILITY

This recognition of the variability of the individual psyche translates into equally variable ways of understanding psychological conflict and the manner of its resolution. For example, although Jung demonstrated a predilection for the energic (final) viewpoint, he recognized that the causal perspective was necessary for a complete judgment, and, in certain cases, was the appropriate and preferred perspective. It was this recognition of relative applicability that allowed Jung to express qualified appreciation of Freudian theory. The causal and energic viewpoints were the basis of two methods of interpretation, which Jung called the reductive and constructive methods, respectively. These methods translated into two ways of approaching the cause and cure of psychic conflict. The reductive method is applied in all cases where it is a question of illusions, fictions, and exaggerated attitudes. On the other hand, a constructive point of view must be considered for all cases where the conscious attitude is more or less normal, but capable of greater development and refinement, or where unconscious tendencies, also capable of development, are being misunderstood and kept under by the conscious mind.[84]

Generally, Jung held that the reductive method of interpretation was applicable to "the neuroses of the young" which "generally come from a collision between the forces of reality and an inadequate, infantile attitude, which from the causal point of view is characterized by an abnormal dependence on the real or imaginary parents, and from the teleological point of view may be unrealizable fictions, plans, and aspirations. Here the reductive methods of Freud and Adler are entirely in place."[85] For the young, a conscious recognition of infantile entanglements and a purging of one's personal history may be enough to release in a forward movement the instinctual forces that had previously been bound up and expressed through the neuroses. For the young, for whom a "beckoning future lies ahead, rich in possibilities," it may be sufficient to "break a few bonds; the life urge will do the rest." Typically this means the transference of the parental imagos to "more suitable figures," that is, lovers, spouse, respected authority figures, institutions, and organizations. This does not, however, in Jung's view, represent a "fundamental solution," but rather is a pragmatic one that typically proceeds somewhat unconsciously and "therefore with no notable inhibitions and resistances."[86]

Yet, for the adult, the typical task is quite different, and it is toward this form of psychological conflict that Jung devoted most of his energies and produced his greatest contribution. To the person in the second half of life, the path of psychic development that is demanded "no longer proceeds via the dissolution of infantile ties, the destruction of infantile illusions and the transference of old imagos to new figures: it proceeds via the problem of opposites."[87]

What exactly does this mean, "the second half of life" and "the problem of opposites"? Jung often identified the age of thirty-five as a typical, representative point in the life course when the psychological tides would shift. But the actual chronology is incidental. What defines the second half of life is the presence of a psychological maturity in which the biological, collective demands have been dutifully fulfilled such that the "cultural task" of the conscious development of one's individual personality can properly, morally, now be the orienting principle of one's life.[88] This "conscious development of one's individual personality" entails an encounter with oneself in a new manner and to a new degree of depth. That is, this entry into the the second half of life is marked by the "problem of opposites." Jung described in the following passage this transition into the demands of adulthood.

> He has put this part of the road [i.e., biological, collective demands] behind him with or without difficulty. He has cut loose from his parents, long since dead perhaps, and has sought and found the mother in the wife, or, in the case of a woman, the father in her husband. He has duly honoured his fathers and their institutions, has himself become a father, and, with all that in the past, has possibly come to realize that what originally meant advancement and satisfaction has now become a boring mistake, part of the illusion of youth, upon which he looks back with mingled regret and envy, because nothing now awaits him but old age and the end of all illusions. Here there are no more fathers and mothers; all the illusions he projected upon the world and upon things gradually come home to him, jaded and way-worn. The energy streaming back from these manifold relationships falls into the unconscious and activates all the things he had neglected to develop.[89]

By the *problem of opposites*—a term that can sound so metaphysical, so Heraclitean—Jung thus referred most basically, on a psychodevelopmental level, to the insistent demand of the psyche as a whole to impel the conscious mind toward a recognition and integration of previously unrecognized, undeveloped, and even denigrated parts of one's own personality. Jung described this heretofore unknown part of one's personality as the "counterpart" of the conscious attitude, a "mysterious part" of the personality, the "other" personality, or, most simply, "oneself."[90] The problem of opposites entails the problem of recognizing the fullness of one's interior nature, of not only integrating the meaning and value of one's complex makeup into one's conscious attitude and identity but also confronting the "moral demands" contained in these recognitions.[91]

Jung provided an example of this problem of opposites through a description of one of his patients, a "typical American self-made man who had worked his way up from the bottom," "founded an immense business," and "become very successful." Jung employed this example to describe how psychological conflicts may emerge and manifest "naturally," in accord with his energic model of the psyche. The businessman had taken an early retirement—planning a "well deserved" life of leisure—but he had quickly fallen into a state of deepening anxiety and "hypochondriacal mopings." He returned to his business, hoping for a renewal of his former robustness, but this could not be resurrected through either overt activity or by sheer force of will. His condition worsened. His former mode of adaptation now failed him. "All that had formerly been living, creative energy in him now turned against him with terrifying force." The energy that previously had been directed toward building the business, unable to find a natural gradient through which it could now be expressed, became "damned up" and regressed destructively to "former situations." The patient began to recall earlier traumas in life and came to see that "it was the original relationship with his mother that mapped the course of his symptoms." For some this engagement with personal memories—a reductive, historical explanation—may have been sufficient to resolve their conflict.

Yet for the businessman, this stage of reconnoitering with the historical layers of oneself was not to be the last. Indeed, Jung believed that "his depression and hypochondriacal illusion," and "the fantasies which proceed from such a condition" indicated that "the ultimate goal was to drive him back, as it were, into his own body, after he had lived since his youth only in his head. He had differentiated one side of his being; the other side remained in an inert physical state." The "hypochondriacal 'depression'" sought to push him "down into the body he had always overlooked"—and it was precisely this "other side" that was now needed in order "to live."[92]

PSYCHOLOGICAL ADAPTATION
AND NEUROSES

Jung reported that this particular patient was, in the end, unable to consciously grasp and follow the promptings implicit in his symptoms, and thus the psychic energy followed its own destructive gradient, finding expression in his psychopathology. Jung viewed this conflict, in its most basic terms, as a disjunction between the conscious personality and the deeper stratum of the self—the latter seeking actual realization with the former resisting disruption of the psychic status quo. Yet, as this case illustrates, the "energic demands" for equilibrium achieve their ends in one form or another, and it is the conscious attitude that significantly determines the form and character of this realization. Jung thus urged his patients to see in their conflicts and neuroses not an invasive body to be exorcised, but a "strange, unrecognized" part of their personality seeking to compel their recognition through painful symptoms.

> We should not try to "get rid" of a neurosis, but rather to experience what it means, what it has to teach, what its purpose is. We should even learn to be thankful for it, otherwise we pass it by and miss the opportunity of getting to know ourselves as we really are. A neurosis is truly removed only when it has removed the false attitude of the ego. We do not cure it—it cures us.[93]

Energically understood, the neurosis reflects a heightened potential of energy, a buildup of tension that is full of vitality. If the "accent" of the neurosis is toward the future, toward the "will to adapt," then a reductive interpretation may, in Jung's view, do positive harm by concealing the demands of one's "other" personality. Contained in this "inner antithesis" is the energy necessary for the forward movement of life, "the conflict that must be fought out again and again if life is to go on."[94] The "task" of one's personality in these cases is to "discover [in the neurosis] the opposite to the attitude of the conscious mind."[95] A lack of conscious recognition does not, of course, mean that the energy has disappeared, but rather that the energic buildup simply flows on "unconsciously in ever-renewed and ever-changing forms of neurosis." Only by accepting and understanding the neurosis can one avoid "stagnation," "rigidity," and "neurotic subterfuge."[96]

Such acceptance is no simple feat, for in a neurosis one finds both one's "worst enemy and best friend." A neurosis may be felt to be "one's worst enemy" because of painful psychosomatic symptoms that are felt to be a most private affair but which also obsess and compel us, making life "complicated" and setting "apparently impossible tasks." Yet a neurosis may also be one's "best friend" because in, or through, the neurosis one finds the "other half" of oneself, that which "belongs" to oneself, that which "creates organic balance," and "in the deepest sense" serves to "complete oneself."[97] Whether one's psychic conflicts are seen and felt to be friends or enemies depends in large part on the conscious attitude one takes toward the attendant suffering. It is the conscious attitude that may enable a transformation of the enemy into a friend.

In his essay "A Review of the Complex Theory," Jung discusses what is perhaps the most basic of conflicts.[98] He examines how the ego attempts through a variety of apotropaic means to avoid acknowledging the fact that it is not the autocratic ruler of its own psychic house but is instead dependent on unconscious foundations that exhibit varying degrees of autonomy. It is not uncommon for one to attempt to explain away the autonomous complexes as "nothings," as "trivial things," and to conceal them from others and oneself. One attempts to make them "unreal" as long as one can—thus maintaining one's respectability and one's illusion of absolute self-control. There is a shameful quality that surrounds a secretly held neurosis. But, for those still healthy enough (paradoxically), it is the very pain caused by dissociated complexes that serves to assert the reality of these dynamic psychic factors. Unseen, they are not unfelt. Through symptomatic pain, variously registered in the psychosomatic system, the neurotic complex forces the psyche to realize something about itself. The "outbreak of neurosis signifies the moment" when "the complex establishes itself on the conscious surface," seeking to assimilate the ego "step by step," just as the ego had sought to assimilate the complex. In this manner, a "neurotic dissociation" ensues.[99]

The neurotic attitude that lay behind the dissociation in the first place perceives the emergence of neurotic symptoms as an unwanted, even hated enemy that threatens the adaptation of the organism, that is, the ego as it understands itself. This is because "we should prefer to be always 'I' and nothing else."[100] This statement points to a central element of Jung's psychology, namely, the progressive relativization of the ego as the defining feature of the second half of life. Or, stated positively, the progressive expansion of the ego's awareness of the range and nature of its relations.

For Jung, the common thread that runs through many of the psychological conflicts arising in the second half of life is the ego's false, maladapted, disproportional attitude characterized by an overvaluation of its capacities, claims, and values. It is the ego's defensive attempt to rigidly control the construction of one's life that often leads to a narrowness of the conscious personality, which, in turn, engenders conflict. Frequently, "a narrowness of the personality" is causally related to an acceptance of "inadequate or wrong answers to the questions of life." When living within the narrow confines of the ego, that is, when the ego sees itself as *sui generis*, there is a tendency to seek significance or meaning for one's life through an accumulation of possessions—broadly understood—and the pursuit of goals that support this self-inflated attitude. The result of these hollow pursuits is that "we demand that the world grant us recognition for qualities which we regard as personal possessions: our talent and our beauty."[101]

Yet these false possessions do not constitute what is essential and enduring but rather are limited—and thus limiting. These endeavors may translate into a life in which position, marriage, reputation, outward success, and money "are sought and attained, and yet leave the individual unhappy" and, eventually, "neurotic."[102] Such persons were described by Jung as "optional neurotics," for in an earlier epoch "in which man was still linked by myth with nature" as "truly experienced and not merely seen from outside, they would have been spared this division with themselves."[103]

> I am speaking of those who cannot tolerate the loss of myth and who can neither find a way to a merely exterior world, to the world as seen by science, nor rest satisfied with an intel-

lectual juggling with words, which has nothing whatsoever to do with wisdom.[104]

THE RATIONAL AND THE IRRATIONAL

In this passage is the essence of Jung's criticism of the dominant *Weltanschauung* and its significant role in contributing to many contemporary psychological problems. Jung objected to what may be called the externalization of life as promoted by the *Weltanschauung* of the "hard" sciences, specifically their objectification and depersonalization of both subject and object. A result, or at least a corollary of this objectifying tendency, is the intellectualization of the psyche, both descriptively and as directly experienced. That is, the tendency is to overvalue the rational—specifically, "thinking"—at the expense of the nonrational wholeness of life. Jung's prescription for this condition was to close or narrow the gap between the ego and the unconscious through what he termed the "transcendent function."[105]

Several clarifications may be helpful at this point. By *nonrational*, or *irrational*, Jung did not mean *contrary* to reason, but *beyond* reason, that is, something not reducible to purely rational terms, something "not grounded on reason." This includes elementary facts (e.g., "the earth has a moon"), and occurrences of "chance" (or, relatedly, "synchronicity"). More broadly, the irrational is an "existential factor" that always exists when one encounters, and attempts to comprehend, actual objects and experiences. "A completely rational explanation of an object that actually exists (not one that is merely posited) is a Utopian ideal."[106] By this Jung meant that, while the ego may direct the attention of certain psychic functions—thinking and feeling—to specific objects and their qualities in a manner consistent with rational principles, there are always "accidentals" and "contingent" factors excluded in the exercise of these rational functions. Yet once perception is directed toward, or allowed to be sensitive to, the "flux of events," to "react to every possible occurrence," and to "be attuned to the absolutely contingent," then it becomes irrational. Intuition and sensation are functions that "find their fulfillment" in the perception of such a "flux of events,"[107] and here may be considered irrational functions.

It is upon this distinction and description of the functions that Jung was able to describe "feeling" as a rational function. It is important that this description of the feeling function as rational not be understood to mean a gross attempt by Jung to usurp through conceptual sleight of hand the distinct reality and value of feelings, passions, and affects of all sorts by what is normally thought of as rational, that is, conscious thinking. This understanding would amount to the very opposite of what I believe Jung was trying to convey. That is, Jung was not urging the subordination of emotional life to the powers of reason. If this were the case, Jung would have been advocating a dualistic morality, conceived in terms of reason versus passion and marked by constraint and law. However, Jung argued that passions are not to be conceived as necessarily in conflict with reason, nor as essentially unruly and devoid of significance for a life that seeks in experience not only affect but understanding. In short, Jung understood "feeling" as the element of experience, the dynamic within one's psyche, that confers value and motive force to what would otherwise be merely intellectual and conceptual judgments. Feeling is "a kind of *judgment*, differing from intellectual judgment in that its aim is not to establish conceptual relations but to set up a subjective criterion of acceptance or rejection."[108]

It should be noted that Jung distinguished between feeling and affect. Affect (which, in Jung's lexicon, was synonymous with "emotion") is a "state of feeling characterized by marked physical innervation" and "a peculiar disturbance of the ideational process."[109] Conversely, feeling, in its pure or primary state, "produces no perceptible physical innervations, i.e., neither more nor less than an ordinary thinking process."[110] Further, feeling is a "voluntarily disposable function," that is, subject to the rationally reflected will.[111] In contrast, affects were defined by Jung as outside the control of the will. The "dividing line" between the two—affect and feeling—is, however, admittedly "fluid." Affects, depending on their magnitude and duration, may compel emergent feelings, and, conversely, every feeling, when reaching a certain strength, "releases physical innervations" and thus becomes an affect. The basic point here is that Jung wished to emphasize that there is a significant component of the emotional-feeling continuum that is rational in nature and is an essential element of our most complex and valued psychological systems and their resulting behaviors.[112] Jung held that these feeling "values" are rational in the sense that they "are assigned according to the laws of reason." Feelings "arrange" the contents of consciousness "according to value" in a manner analogous to the way our thinking organizes the contents of consciousness according to concepts.[113]

This juxtaposition of the terms *values* and *rational* requires an explanation. Jung defined the rational as "that which accords with reason." Reason was not an abstract "thing" or even a function for Jung, but was an "attitude" of consciousness. Reason is an attitude "whose principle is to conform thought, feeling, and action to objective values." What are these "objective values?" In a compact paragraph in the section entitled "Definitions" of *Psychological Types*, Jung made far-reaching statements that he unfortunately failed to develop explicitly. Jung stated that "most objective values" and "reason itself" (i.e., reason as an attitude of conforming experience to objective values) are "not the work of an individual subject, but the product of human history."[114] In psychological terms, "objective values" may be understood as "firmly established complexes of ideas handed down through the ages." This statement can admittedly take on many meanings. Jung proceeded to explore the status of these ideas by considering their origin. In a single sentence he asked whether these ideas might not in some sense derive from a "pre-existent, metaphysical, universal Reason," but then asserted—in claimed agreement with Schopenhauer—that such Reason is dependent on the "adapted reaction" of humans for its existence. The emergence of human reason and society's "objective values" is then, in conclusion, given an ostensibly naturalistic explanation instead.

> Human reason, accordingly, is nothing other than the expression of man's adaptability to average occurrences, which have gradually become deposited in firmly established

complexes of ideas that constitute our objective values. Thus the laws of reason are laws that designate and govern the average, "correct," adapted attitude. Everything is "rational" that accords with these laws, everything that contravenes them is "irrational."[115]

SUMMATION

In summary, Jung understood feeling—and the other three basic functions—within the broad context of human adaptation to both inner and outer conditions. Experience is divided into two broad functional categories, the rational and the irrational. The rational functions—thinking and feeling—are based on a degree of *reflection* and represent some form of judgment. The irrational functions—sensation and intuition—instead aim toward *perception* of the general flux of events. These four functions, according to Jung, are "irreducible to one another"[116] and *"sui generis."*[117] The values (and principles) held by reason, and reason itself (as attitude), are understood to be psychological complexes accrued through the course of history. This implies a malleability to rational norms and values, yet also a degree of constancy and gravity, yielding a manner of authority consistent with that accorded the experience of the generations within the obvious— and because obvious, often forgotten—context of the embodied life here on Earth.

This discussion of the rational and irrational is not intended to provide a philosophically airtight theory of forms of knowledge. Rather, Jung seemed to make this critical distinction to support his observations that it is precisely the demand for absolutely rational explanations for life's problems that lies behind many psychological conflicts. Jung was attempting to provide a rational explanation of why the rational itself is contingent, relative, and limited. "The expectation or exclusive conviction that there must be a rational way of settling every conflict can be an insurmountable obstacle to finding a solution of an irrational nature."[118] While this encounter with the irrational is experienced in manifold ways in relation to others and the world at large, it is most poignantly felt at the base of one's own personality. And it is toward this process that Jung directed his attention.

It is perhaps not an exaggeration to say that it is the development of a transformed conscious attitude, marked by the acceptance of the irrational elements of oneself, and life itself, that is the defining characteristic of both Jung's therapeutic approach and his philosophical temper. Again, by "irrational" he did not mean contrary to, or denigrating of, reason or rational operations, but rather as denoting those elements of experience that simply cannot be grasped conceptually, nor articulated linguistically, because of inherent epistemological and cognitive limitations. For Jung this acknowledgment of the limits of consciousness was not cause for despair, but rather was the basis for widening one's view of the possibilities inherent in reality. "Rational truths are not the last word, there are also irrational ones. In human affairs, what appears impossible by way of intellect has often become true by way of the irrational."[119]

While Jung acknowledged the significance of humankind's evolutionary origins, his theoretical and practical orientation was generally toward complex phenomena evolving forward. Thus, he understood conflict in terms of adaptation—to both inner and outer conditions. At times he portrayed consciousness itself in terms of its adaptive function. "The reason why consciousness exists, and why there is an urge to widen and deepen it, is very simple: without consciousness things go less well," and it is "the conscious man that has conquered the earth and not the unconscious one."[120] Yet Jung's admiration of consciousness was qualified—"a higher consciousness is exposed to dangers undreamt of by the primitive"—due to the conflicts that surround its transformative existence. Individuation was thus considered "at once a charisma and a curse."[121] Therefore, he concluded, "whether in the last analysis, and from a superhuman point of view, this [the emergence of consciousness] is an advantage or a calamity we are not in a position to decide."[122]

Generally, the ego—the center of consciousness—was portrayed by Jung as relatively conservative, seeking to develop and rely on its strengths or, in Jungian terminology, "superior function." While this one-sided adaptation may lend practical competency and force to the personality through applied focus, it also could prepare the conditions for psychological problems. For example, conflicts may, and do, arise when developmental demands inherent in the personality itself are not allowed realization in the person's life through direct expression or more subtle integration into the whole of the personality. The problem of expressing the whole of one's personality brings me to the question of the relations between the individual and the collective, to be discussed in the following chapter, "Jung on Individuation and Individualism."

Chapter 4

———◦———

JUNG ON INDIVIDUATION
AND INDIVIDUALISM

In this chapter I will explore Jung's understanding of the relationship between the individual and society and, specifically, whether he conceived of the relationship as primarily one of conflicted discontent or harmonious symbiosis. And, given that conflicts do in fact arise, how did he conceive of their origin, forms of manifestation, and the possibility and means of their resolution or, at least, mitigation? Further, where did Jung locate his primary moral value, with the individual or the community? I will engage these topics by comparing "individuation"—the central concept of Jung's psychology[1]—with egoistic "individualism." It is important to note that Jung was not a sociologist in either disposition or avocation. He did not engage in complex organizational or political theorizing through which he might debate the relative merits of different social structures and the claims of vested partisans. Rather, he wrote as a medical psychologist whose insights and contributions to the field of sociology reside in the sphere of the psychodynamics of group behavior and were driven by his existentialist moral agenda defending the individual in the face of collective pressures.

Indeed, Jung's psychology, *if* evaluated through the frameworks of secular sociology or the natural sciences (including most psychologies), may appear to favor a form of egoistic individualism at the expense of the social welfare. Basic to such a criticism, however, is a stated or inferred distinction between the individual and society that does not accurately describe Jung's thinking. Besides the individual and society, there was for Jung a third factor, the objective and extra-individual "interior world." For Jung, this interior world was as "real" as the sentient world of everyday life and was, moreover, not identical in either scope or identity with the individual, conscious personality. Acknowledging the full reality and claims of both the internal and external realms is, according to Jung, difficult.

> In my picture of the world there is a vast outer realm and an equally vast inner realm; between the two stands man, facing now one and now the other, and, according to temperament and disposition, taking the one for the absolute truth by denying or sacrificing the other.[2]

If one accepts the heuristic validity of this spatial portrayal of human experience, then the ethical situation is, in its essentials, triadic in structure. That is, moral value may be located "outside," "inside," or with "one's individual person." This depiction of the moral realm is contingent on two premises: (1) that the "interior realm" exhibits a sufficiently certain degree of autonomy and objectivity such that it may be considered separable from the individual ego, and (2) that moral categories and concerns pertain to this "interior realm" no less than to the social or individual realms.

In addition to this framing of moral space, Jung's social ethic was built upon a distinction between types of human relations: those relationships that are face-to-face and personal, and those that the individual engages in the context of large "collective" groups. Jung maintained very different attitudes toward these two types of relationship, generally affirming the potential of the former while highlighting the hazards of the latter. If the rationale and implications of this distinction are to be understandable, however, certain concepts need to be defined and explained.

First, one must distinguish between psychological description and moral assertion. By "psychological description" I mean, simply, the articulation of psychic qualities, states, and processes that are, in themselves, ethically neutral. For instance, Jung wrote, "the mechanism of convention keeps people unconscious...."[3] Whether or not one agrees factually with the statement, this is a "psychological description" that in itself is value-neutral. There may be, and in fact is, within Jung's moral psychology as a whole, a moral implication, but this statement itself was intended by Jung to be an objective account. This type of phenomenological description was the methodological basis of Jung's claims of adherence to a form of empiricism.

Alternatively, by "moral assertion" I mean a claim about the existence, or location, or relative worth of a moral value, understood as an end in itself. Moral goods may be diffuse and many, or perhaps few in number coalescing around a singular referent—God, Humanity, Life, etc. In either case, when affirmed, they are experienced as "really real," of inherent worth, and of significant if not ultimate concern. As stated above, Jung was rarely explicit about his moral values, choosing to write in a nondisputational style using a language that aspired to appeal to the scientifically minded. Yet on occasion, depending on audience, genre, his stage of life, and perhaps his current state of mind, Jung was relatively open and confessional about his commitments. For example, he began the essay "The Development of Personality" with the assertion, echoing Goethe, "that the ultimate aim and strongest desire of all mankind is to develop that fulness of life which is called personality."[4] Jung stopped short of saying, "And I think this is good...and to this I devote myself." But there was no need. For the entire essay is informed and infused with an opening moral assertion—*not* description—that the purpose, and hence the good, of human life lies in the development of personality. This moral value, this ultimate concern, served as first principle, confirmed (but not established) by the subsequent deductive arguments of his essay.

Typically, however, Jung's moral values were more densely veiled and furtive, forming a subtext that is both backdrop and end point for his polemics. This is why, after reading one of his essays, one may sense a subtle alchemy working upon oneself, challenging if not changing one's outlook, and yet one may feel hard-put to articulate exactly why and how this is so. Hence, one of the objectives of this chapter is to make explicit Jung's moral values and to explore their implications for how he described the psychological relationship between the individual and various collective groups.

This distinction between psychological observation and moral evaluation is central to the development of my ideas in this chapter. My claims are (1) that, although Jung's psychological descriptions were predominantly negative toward the impact of the collective on the psychological well-being of the individual *and* the general welfare of society; (2) this does not necessarily mean that Jung placed exclusive ethical value on the welfare of the individual; but rather (3) that his social ethic conceived of the welfare of the individual and that of society to be, in the end—and along the way—mutually dependent. Many of Jung's explicit critiques of the collective were based on pragmatic, psychological grounds, that is, the purported deleterious effect of collective relationships on the psychological condition of *both* the individual and the group. His practical criticisms did not necessarily equate with moral valuation. This point serves as an important qualifier to the charge that Jung was a simple ethical egoist, indifferent to concerns broader than those indigenous to the analytic hour.

Before proceeding directly into the argument of this chapter, a final, yet indispensable, clarification needs to be made. The task of distinguishing psychological observation from ethical evaluation is complicated by the fact that for Jung the realm of ethical values was in a complex—in fact inseparable—relationship with the psychic sphere. This point refers me again to Jung's triadic structure of moral space. For Jung, the psyche, as the locus of conscious agency, was the necessary and essential factor for actualizing ethical goods. The entirety of the moral life—dependent as it is on a sense of freedom and responsibility, capacities for creative and critical reflection, and sustained commitment of the self—is simply inconceivable apart from the human psyche. Yet the psyche is itself the locus for the realization of the individual personality—an ethical good, for Jung, second to none. Psyche is thus both *means* and, often, the *end* for the realization of moral goods. Consequently, psychological description and ethical claim interpenetrated in Jung's thought—the two spheres merged. Therefore, many (or most) of his psychological analyses and narratives were not value-neutral. They implied moral claims.

OBJECTIFICATION AND SCIENTIFIC REDUCTIONISM

Contemporary American culture idealizes and idolizes the value of interpersonal relationship, particularly that of romantic love. American movies, magazines, even scandals—its collective public fantasies—reveal this fascination. This idealization of romance, of the search for a soul-mate who satisfies all, may be regarded as mythic, imaginal, and archetypal in American society. Relationship thus lies at the heart of the American psyche's storied blueprint of fulfillment.

Yet this insatiable longing for another, for deep personal rapport, may be seen as the psyche's compensatory assertion against a countervailing trend in our culture that objectifies reality—including the human subject—and which serves to dislocate us from the surrounding world of personal relationships. This tendency to objectify the individual is at the root of several theoretical problems: the framing of moral life in terms of either/or choices and the portrayal of the relationship between the individual and others as oppositional in nature. Through this objectifying lens, human fulfillment is not sought in expressive unity with the romantically conceived "great current of life" in which the individual, and all that is, participates and belongs.[5] Objectifying viewpoints pit the individual against the collective in hostile terms in which a gain for one is a loss for the other. For example, classical Darwinism equates "self-interest" with individual biological survival and propagation. Objectification of the human subject may also lead to opposite conclusions—that the welfare of the individual pales before the good of the group—whether the group be family, cult, church, party, or the state.

Jung used "objectification" in multiple senses with different implications. Sometimes it referred to a psychodynamic process in which the infant "self," previously merged in undifferentiated identity with its surroundings, coalesces its subjective identity through a differentiation with the "objects" in its environment (including, most significantly, human persons in close rapport). This process of "objectification" was deemed absolutely essential for the development of a healthy personality structure marked by a realistic appraisal of the boundaries of self and external world. Hopefully, this process continues, in some secondary sense, throughout life through the withdrawal of psychological projections that serve to distort one's engagement with reality. In this sense, the term *objectification* had for Jung a basically positive connotation.

Objectification, however, has a more complex meaning that was problematic for Jung. Objectification resides at the heart of the Enlightenment view of reality that portrays humans "as both subject and object of an objectifying scientific analysis,"[6] and, insofar as Enlightenment views continue to influence our culture, objectification in this sense permeates contemporary attitudes, tempers, and dispositions. This objectifying outlook may be considered the opposite of "expressivism"[7] or "personalism."[8] As it permeated Enlightenment culture it entailed a view of humans as the "subject of egoistic desires, for which nature and society provided merely the means of fulfillment."[9] Humans, as creatures continuous with an objectified natural realm, were portrayed as causally determined by environmental and physiological factors and thus lacking moral freedom. For the individual, a decision to objectify one's approach to reality may be considered of primary moral importance because it informs one's basic attitude and moral framework. Objectification supported a worldview that is "utilitarian in its ethical outlook, atomistic in its social philosophy...and which looked to a scientific social engineering to reorganize man and society and bring men happiness through perfect mutual adjustment."[10]

Contemporary American culture promotes this objectification of the world by habituating consciousness toward numbers—calories, pounds, years, dollars, square feet, Dow Jones, GPA, and GDP. The effect is a compulsive measuring of our lives—our status, our worth, our prospects—in these numeric terms. When operating within this mathematical mind-set, the justification of the individual seems to depend on belonging and contributing to a numerically superior collective group. The solitary individual has substance, meaning, and enduring value only vis-à-vis an aggregate of others. Seemingly, if one's individual life is to have significance, it must be through identification with a larger "body of others" that is of superior power and that outlives the individual.[11]

Beyond such existential reflections, the status of the individual may be diminished by scientific theories. Scientific disciplines typically seek to portray and account for the individual as a minor factor in a large equation in which the person is claimed to be constructed, shaped, and propelled by impersonal forces. Through these paradigms the conscious, choosing, dreaming, wondering, willing, suffering, and loving experiences of the existing individual are contextualized and dispersed into fragments of centrifugal explanation. Or, if not dispersed, then the individual is reduced to subhuman, impersonal terms. In either case, the unique, experiencing individual is lost. Through our rigorous, disciplined ways of knowing, the significance of the existing individual is, subtly or explicitly, diminished to the point of disappearance.

Such objectifying naturalism places the burden of proof upon anyone who would assert the moral value of an individual life, not only as a means to a seemingly more enduring collective end but as a moral end in itself. Any assertion about the moral value of the individual would seem to rest on ignorance or arrogance, denial or despair. An altruistic ethic of reciprocity— whether utilitarian or rational—positing a social, aggregate good as the demonstrable end of the moral life, would seem to be the only positive alternative available to those living in an objectified, numeric world.[12]

Jung responded to the objectification of the human person— and the attendant diminishment of the status and worth of the individual—by critiquing the assumptions and implications of such a viewpoint. His imagination seemed to readily and happily supply metaphors that depreciated claims of the primacy of the collective at the expense of the individual. "A million zeros joined together do not, unfortunately, add up to one."[13] And elsewhere, in a letter intended to discourage the formation of a learned committee designed to engineer social progress, he wrote, "The heaping together of paintings by Old Masters in museums is a catastrophe; likewise, a collection of a hundred Great Brains makes one big fathead."[14] In a slightly more generous tone, Jung elsewhere acknowledged that society is indeed a "necessary condition" for life—but then again, he adds, so too are "oxygen, water, albumen, fat, and so forth." Just as it would be absurd to claim that we live to breathe, it would be "equally ludicrous to say that the individual exists for society."[15] For Jung, the individual was "the essential thing,"[16] "the sole carrier of life,"[17] and that "infinitesimal unit on whom a world depends" and "in whom even God seeks his goal."[18] How then can he be taken seriously as a psychologist who has something serious to contribute to the psychology of social responsibility?

If these quotations are taken at face value and in isolation, one may prematurely conclude that Jung's ethics is simply egoistic, asserting the supreme moral value of the individual against the impinging, if not oppressive, forces of the collective. Yet, while Jung is critical of, if not hostile toward collective mores and large groupings of all sorts, he elsewhere made statements about the hazards of alienation from others and the determinative role of relationships in shaping personal life. Often, these assertions were not explicit and must be inferred. For example, in a late-life lecture Jung described schizophrenia as "a fundamental disturbance of relationship, that is, of the patient's rapport with his surroundings" that "menaces" the individual with "isolation."[19] Relationships with others, oneself, and the world at large are not mere accouterments, but are necessary and constitutive of mental health. Elsewhere, in a letter discussing the possible merits of communal religion, he asserted that "individualistic isolation" is the "sickness of our time."[20]

Beyond these general statements about the necessity of relationship for psychic health, Jung's writings contain both singular statements and systematic reflections on the pivotal role of personal, intimate relationships on the life course of an individual. For example, responding to a correspondent who had lost an intimate loved one, Jung explored the ensuing effect of this severed relationship in the following manner: "It frequently happens that when a person with whom one was intimate dies, either one is oneself drawn into the death, so to speak, or else this burden has the opposite effect of a task that has to be fulfilled in real life. One could say figuratively that a bit of life has passed over from the dead to the living and compels him towards its realization."[21] It seems apparent that this statement was not written by a man who saw the individual as self-sufficient and insular, but rather by one who understood and appreciated social relatedness. Finally, we read that individuation "is not 'individualization' but a conscious realization of everything the existence of an individual implies: his needs, his tasks, his duties, his responsibilities, etc. Individuation does not isolate, it connects."[22] These remarks are nonsystematic and make no claim of "proof." However, they suggest a more complex picture of the nature and role of relationship within Jung's analytical psychology.

JUNG AND HISTORICAL, EVOLUTIONARY PROCESSES

In the introductory chapter, I stated that the method of this study would be largely ahistorical and noncontextual. At this juncture, however, several points of a historical nature need to be considered. Jung's adult life[23] straddled the World Wars, a time of collective upheaval and organized violence that convulsed the foundations of European civilization and threatened Switzerland, the island refuge where Jung made his home. From the outbreak of the Great War—to the Bolsheviks, to the ensuing economic tumult, to Stalinism, to fascism and its dictators, to the conflagration of the Second World War, to the descent of the Iron Curtain and the splitting of the world—impinging historical forces threatened, for Jung and his contemporaries, the livelihoods and the very lives of individuals and communities in ways that are not easy for the cyber-age mind to grasp.[24]

Although Jung was inclined generally to discount the significance of these "outward events" in the unfolding of his own life story—deferring instead to "the imperishable world," to "the 'other' reality," to his "bouts with the unconscious"[25]—his historical context did in fact profoundly shape his attitudes toward collective social organizations of all forms (religious, professional, political, etc.), as well as the specific formulations through which he expressed his beliefs. It was not the case, however, that Jung was unaware of the manifold ways that context conditioned his thought. For example, Jung on numerous occasions sought to locate his ideas within the philosophical and spiritual traditions to which they were indebted and of which they were kindred spirits.[26] On a more intimate autobiographical level, Jung related the emergence of his early intrapsychic experiences to the influence of the surrounding ethos. He wrote that "the peculiar 'religious' ideas that came to me even in my earliest childhood were spontaneous products which can be understood only as reactions to my parental environment and to the spirit of the age."[27] This passage is significant in that even the most supposedly "spontaneous" of psychological phenomena are given an animating cultural context. The relationship between the individual and society is dialectical in nature, one in which "reactions" occur between the two, each factor only relatively independent. What Jung resisted and sought to refute throughout his writings was not the basic recognition of our embeddedness in manifold relations but rather any attempt to exhaustively reduce psychic experience to cultural conditioning.

In addition to considering the impact of direct social and historical forces on the shaping of the contemporary mentality, Jung's perception of his present day was infused with a belief in the ongoing phylogenetic evolution of consciousness and its role in human adaptation.

> The species repeats itself in the embryonic development of the individual. Thus, to a certain degree, man in his embryonic life passes through the anatomical forms of primeval times. If the same law holds for the mental development of mankind, it follows that the child develops out of an originally unconscious, animal condition into consciousness, primitive at first, and then slowly becoming more civilized.[28]

He also framed his basic structural model of the psyche and the core dynamic of psychopathology (the conscious mind's alienation from the unconscious) in the context of evolutionary, historical process:

> The resistance of the conscious mind to the unconscious and the depreciation of the latter were historical necessities in the development of the human psyche, for otherwise the conscious mind would never have been able to differentiate itself

at all. But modern man's consciousness has strayed rather too far from the fact of the unconscious. We have forgotten that the psyche is by no means of our design, but is for the most part autonomous and unconscious.[29]

Further, although Jung embraced Darwinian theory,[30] he did not believe that the meaning of consciousness could be exhausted by exploring its practical, adaptive functioning. For Jung, a purely functional viewpoint when claiming full adequacy in the realm of the human spirit represents a theoretical suppression of the living psyche, which we experience as purposeful and directed toward aims that transcend those of mere efficient causation.[31] For Jung, the development of consciousness was not merely functional, reducible to biology, genetics, or the will-to-power, but was the culmination, or fulfillment, of evolutionary processes and the very raison d'être of human existence.[32]

Finally, for Jung, "history," understood not as a chronicling of past events but as consciousness of our participation in the "stream" of time, not only "looks back" but points forward as well. Therefore, Jung's portrayal of relations between individuals and collectives always assumed the presence of an emerging consciousness that presses outward toward realization into the future but which brings with it an awareness of the past. For example, "Everything living dreams of individuation, for everything strives towards its own wholeness."[33] Moreover, "[e]verything in the unconscious seeks outward manifestation, and the personality too desires to evolve out of its unconscious conditions and to experience itself as a whole."[34] This purposeful, imaginal impulse of the psyche makes human beings historical creatures who traverse back and forth along a time line, pivoting in the present but always living imaginatively forward or backward from the current point of time.

Jung's historical view of both the individual and culture should not be confused with an attitude of triumphalism or devotion to a myth of progress. Jung regularly sought to deflate human fantasies of an achievable earthly paradise by pointing out the ever-present reality of evil and life's precarious balance between joy and suffering.

> The sad truth is that man's real life consists of a complex of inexorable opposites—day and night, birth and death, happiness and misery, good and evil. We are not even sure that one will prevail against the other, that good will overcome evil, or joy defeat pain. Life is a battleground. It always has been, and always will be; and if it were not so, existence would come to an end.[35]

This description of the world as morally static was held in tension with his affirming attitude regarding the possibility of individual growth and metamorphosis.

THE COLLECTIVE AND THE INDIVIDUAL

For Jung, the most significant conflict between the individual and the collective was *not* that of the necessary repression of physiological instincts but rather the thwarting of the development of personality—including, not insignificantly, moral responsibility—through pressures to conform and the seductions of both power and powerlessness. Jung argued that the mitigation of this pervasive conflict was not, however, realized through a self-sufficient individualism or unconstrained freedom. Instead, the fulfillment of the individual was to be achieved *only* in and through real relationship, and only insofar as persons truly relate to others may they contribute ethically to the welfare of the group. In order to defend these propositions an examination of the terms *collective* and *individual* now follows.

Jung used several terms with almost synonymous intent to describe large organizations and gatherings of people that are able to command strong allegiance from their members and with which the identity of the individual is merged. These terms, variously pejorative, include *mass movements*, the *organized State*, the *herd*, or, simply and most often, the *collective*. These terms at times referred to a political party, a nationalist movement, a collective religious fervor, a secret society—in short, any grouping of people in which the individual level of consciousness of its members is diminished through participation in the group. This reduction in the level of critical awareness, Jung argued, is a result of the group's ability to represent and constellate archetypal contents that originate within its members' psyches, leading to an externalization, that is, projection, of these dynamic contents upon the group's leaders, symbols, and abstract principles. The general result of this process is a diminished sense of individual responsibility, precisely because the locus of significance and capacity for agency, that is, the numinosity of the archetypal energies, is now believed to be outside oneself. Thus, as the size of a group grows, individual moral responsibility diminishes, so much so that Jung asserted that "the morality of society as a whole is in inverse ratio to its size."[36]

Jung's conceptual counterpole to "the collective" is "the individual." The individual, as Jung portrays him or her, is not a static, immutable being, but rather is one whose very being is a process of becoming. As discussed in chapter 3, the objective world of efficient causation is, in Jung's view, properly complemented by the subjective experience of purposeful, final causes. In this sense, then, one's "individual becoming" may justifiably assume the character of a narrative—a drama, a myth—with a plot centered on the fulfillment of potentialities inherent in the protagonist. Jung gave voice to this conviction in the opening words of his autobiography—the very first sentence—where he stated, "My life is a story of the self-realization of the unconscious."[37] It is no exaggeration to see in this statement a summation of Jung's vision of the human being—its essence, its primary process and purpose, and the nature of the good toward which this purpose seeks fulfillment. This "self-realization of the unconscious" manifests in the individual life through transformations of personality and in collective life through numerous cultural expressions— "principally in the various religious systems and their changing symbols."[38]

INDIVIDUATION AND INDIVIDUALISM

This process of psychic self-realization informed Jung's concept of "individuation," and it is through the rubric of individuation that he subsequently expressed his social ethic. In oversimplified summation, that which hinders individuation is faulted, and that which enables it is praised. Jung often described individuation in simple terms, such as a "'coming to selfhood' or 'self-realization,'"[39] or "the process of becoming an 'in-dividual,' that is, a separate, indivisible unity or 'whole.'"[40] Yet to his detractors Jung's descriptions and advocacy of individuation were not so simple but were in fact problematic in both theory and practice. Walter Kaufmann contended that Jung's account of his own individuation process did not reflect the valorous journey of a man who "faced up to his own shadow and attained a degree of self-knowledge not possible until he discovered the collective unconscious and the archetypes," but was rather a "shrouded and falsified account" that provided "an escape" not only for Jung but "for others" as well.[41] In a more temperate tone, Anthony Stevens summarizes the criticisms of Jung's concept of individuation and its practical corollaries as follows:

> It has been alleged that his theory of individuation cannot possess general validity, since it is too closely linked with his own experiences and with his own psychological type; that his therapeutic approach is too inner-directed for life in the modern world, since it places too much emphasis on archetypes and mythology and too little on the problems of relationship and social adjustment; that he is élitist in his assumptions; and that, as a method of treatment, analytical psychology is suitable only for the leisured, cultivated, and rich.[42]

I distill the above criticisms into several questions relevant to the current argument: Is individuation elitist in the sense of being accessible and possible for only the few? Is individuation elitist in its effects; that is, does it translate into an ethic of individual egoism or elitism? Is devotion to individuation, even if this means in others as well as oneself, inimical to broader moral commitments in society?[43]

Jung acknowledged that individuation *is* elitist in the sense that it is experienced in its full ramifications by only the few and often serves in these individuals to segregate them psychologically and socially from others.

> The words "many are called, but few are chosen" are singularly appropriate here, for the development of personality

from the germ-state to full consciousness is at once a charisma and a curse, because its first fruit is the conscious and unavoidable segregation of the single individual from the undifferentiated and unconscious herd. This means isolation, and there is no more comforting word for it.[44]

Further, by the very nature of the experience of individuation and the resulting forms of knowledge, claims arise with moral relevance that are neither open to demonstrable proofs in the public realm nor readily communicable through ordinary language. "The experience of the unconscious is a personal secret communicable only to very few, and that with difficulty."[45] Yet the claims that individuation is an empirically uncommon phenomenon and that it yields knowledge not accessible to all do not necessarily entail an unacceptable or pernicious form of elitism. Neal O. Weiner makes several useful distinctions about elitism.

It is inherent in the logic of virtue and the unconscious that, in general, only the virtuous can know the specifics of virtue and that they will be unable to explain themselves to others in terms that are rationally convincing. This is an elitism of character, but it is not an elitism of intellect, education, or wealth. It is an elitism that is open to anyone who for whatever reason happens to be relatively free of anxiety and self-deception. Thus it does not correspond to any social class, race, gender, economic condition, degree of education, or religious persuasion.[46]

If one substitutes in the above passage the word *individuation* for *virtue* (and *individuating* for *virtuous*) we have a fair account of how Jung conceived of the form of elitism that individuation entailed. Weiner describes this form of elitism as an "elitism of character" or a "democratic anti-elitism."[47] Unlike other forms of oppressive and exclusionary elitism, based on money, education, ethnicity, or narrowly defined intelligence, an "elitism of character" is potentially open to all, hence essentially democratic and antielitist. It is in this sense that I understand the elitism of individuation, and it is on this basis that Jung conceived of individuation as a *possibility* for all, yet *actualized* in varying degrees by relatively few.

Only those individuals can attain to a higher degree of consciousness who are destined to it and called to it from the beginning, i.e., who have a capacity and an urge for higher differentiation. In this matter people differ extremely, as also do the animal species, among whom there are conservatives and progressives. Nature is aristocratic, but not in the sense of having reserved the possibility of differentiation exclusively for species high in the scale. So too with the possibility of psychic development: it is not reserved for specially gifted individuals. In other words, in order to undergo a far-reaching psychological development, neither outstanding intelligence nor any other talent is necessary, since in this development moral qualities can make up for intellectual shortcomings.[48]

In many cases, particularly in his early writings, Jung described individuation in heroic terms that admittedly convey an air of heroic superiority and exclusivity.[49] Yet, as Jung matured, he increasingly described individuation in more modest terms, embedding the process in the general fabric of our workaday world. For example, individuation is "by no means a rare thing or a luxury of the few."[50] Rather, individuation is "a natural necessity"[51] that simply develops "a unique combination, or a gradual differentiation, of functions and faculties which...are universal."[52] And elsewhere, "Individuation is just ordinary life and what you are made conscious of."[53] From this perspective, individuation is a process in which we all participate, the question being not "whether," but "to what degree" and "in what manner."

And the individuated person—what would she or he be like? "He will have no need to be exaggerated, hypocritical, neurotic, or any other nuisance. He will be 'in modest harmony with Nature.'"[54] To the outside world such a person would likely hold no special interest, for their greatness is not measurable or quantifiable through scientific means, nor is it necessarily productive of a loud cultural splash. "Society does not value these feats of the psyche [i.e., attaining to a wider consciousness] very highly; its prizes are always given for achievement and not for personality, the latter being for the most part rewarded posthumously."[55] Such a person is simply their own unique being, fulfilling the individual qualities given them, becoming "the definite, unique human being" that he/she "in fact is."[56]

In this manner Jung used the term "individuation" loosely, referring to both the general process of psychological development, shared by many if not all, and a more specific process engaged in by few. He acknowledged that individuation, in its more pronounced, consciously engaged sense, is an "unpopular undertaking" and a "strange adventure" that "few embark upon."[57] Why is individuation, in this more uncommon form, so unpopular and rare? In one formulation Jung stated that both "causal necessity" and "moral decision" are needed for the development of personality. "If the first is lacking, then the alleged development is mere acrobatics of the will; if the second, it will get stuck in unconscious automatism."[58] Yet elsewhere he observed that even necessities and moral decisions are not sufficient:

> What is it, in the end, that induces a person to go their own way and to rise out of unconscious identity with the mass as out of a swathing mist? Not necessity, for necessity comes to many, and they all take refuge in convention. Not moral decision, for nine times out of ten we decide for convention likewise. What is it, then, that inexorably tips the scales in favour of the extra-ordinary?[59]

Jung answered his question in the following manner:

> It is what is commonly called *vocation:* an irrational factor that destines a man to emancipate himself from the herd and from its well-worn paths. True personality is always a vocation and puts its trust in it as in God, despite its being, as the ordinary person would say, only a personal feeling. But vocation acts like a law of God from which there is no escape.[60]

The process of consciously engaged individuation is thus marked by a sense of vocation, of being "addressed by a voice,"[61] that provides the requisite differentiation from surrounding personalities.[62] Yet, as with individuation itself, Jung at times described a "sense of vocation" not as an "either you have it or you don't" phenomenon, but rather as an experience common to all, varying in degree, not kind.

Vocation, or the feeling of it, is not, however, the prerogative of great personalities; it is also appropriate to the small ones all the way down to the "midget" personalities, but as the size decreases the voice becomes more and more muffled and unconscious....The smaller the personality, the dimmer and more unconscious it becomes, until finally it merges indistinguishably with the surrounding society, thus surrendering its own wholeness and dissolving into the wholeness of the group. In the place of the inner voice there is the voice of the group with its conventions, and vocation is replaced by collective necessities.[63]

In this passage Jung seemed to suggest a polarizing conflict between listening to either one's own voice or that of the collective. Yet this conflict is not necessary. To explain why, Jung distinguished sharply between *individuation*, which, he argued, ultimately serves the interests of the collective, and *individualism*, which does in fact produce real and destructive conflicts between individuals and society. Individualism is an ego-driven effort to lay claim to a supposed "specialness" that elevates oneself in the eyes of others, while ignoring "collective considerations and obligations."[64] While identifying with the *persona* generally leads to conformity, a crude individualism seeks social approval precisely though the opposite device, that of a supposedly distinguished uniqueness. The common element between the two—conformity and uniqueness—is the focus on external approbation for a positive sense of self.

In contrast to individualism, Jung described individuation in terms more conducive to personal-public mutuality, if not harmony:

Individuation means precisely the better and more complete fulfillment of the collective qualities of the human being, since adequate consideration of the peculiarity of the individual is more conducive to a better social performance than when the peculiarity is neglected or suppressed.[65]

The above passage, admittedly vague and requiring clarification, contains an important point. I understand "collective qualities" to mean socially directed virtues such as duty and empathy, while the "peculiarities of the individual" are precisely those aspects of the personality that are attributable to one's innate psychological processes and not reducible to social conditioning. The point Jung was making is that the inwardly directed individual is more likely to be creative and energetic in his contribution to society, ultimately benefiting it more, than the person governed solely by external factors. Social conformity was considered by Jung to be all too often driven by heteronomous coercions or one's own neurotic resistances to individuation.

Yet Jung believed that individuation was conducive to the betterment of society not simply for practical reasons regarding social performance, but rather because individuation leads to a strengthened sense of identification with others, which in turn benefits the collective. This identification with others would, presumably, make one less inclined to dehumanize them, to project upon them one's own shadow, and to place them outside one's moral community. A self-identity grounded on the conviction of a shared nature with others is, according to Jung, the basis of harmonious relations with oneself and others. He held that in its deepest, most completed form, individuation is productive of a socially aware and concerned consciousness, achieved in parallel with a transformed self-identity:

> The natural process of individuation brings to birth a consciousness of human community precisely because it makes us aware of the unconscious, which unites and is common to all mankind. Individuation is an at-one-ment with oneself and at the same time with humanity, since oneself is a part of humanity.[66]

Jung acknowledged the difficulty in distinguishing between crude individualism and the supposedly laudatory individuation. He used the language of vocation to articulate his viewpoint:

> [The one who heeds the voice of vocation] has been called by that all-powerful, all-tyrannizing psychic necessity that is his own and his people's affliction. If he hearkens to the voice, he is at once set apart and isolated, as he has resolved to obey the law that commands from within. "His *own* law!" everybody will cry. But he knows better: it is *the* law, *the* vocation for which he is destined, no more "his own" than the lion that fells him, although it is undoubtedly this particular lion that

kills him and not any other lion. Only in this sense is he entitled to speak of "his" vocation, "his" law.[67]

The critical question here is whether one is heeding what
Jung described as an "all-tyrannizing psychic necessity" that
addresses oneself as "*the* law" and to which one may not claim
personal possession or credit, or one is pursuing an egocentric
course of action with which one identifies and claims as one's
own. This inner voice of vocation, Jung said, confronts one
objectively and is not a simple creation or whim of one's ego.
Vocation may thus be seen as an element of individuation—as a
merging of identity with one's general life purpose—as well as
that which heralds and supports the process of self-realization
itself. In heeding one's vocation, the process of differentiation, of
individuation, of "coming to selfhood,"[68] is consciously begun. In
following one's vocation one "does not become 'selfish' in the
ordinary sense of the word, but is merely fulfilling the peculiarity of his nature, and this, as we have said, is vastly different from
egotism or individualism."[69]

In contrast to this vocational nature of individuation is the
ego-driven quality of individualism. As Jung portrayed it, individualism is often, or usually, a futile and vain effort, leading to a
sense of frustration and bitterness the more one identifies with
social perception while ignoring the genuine impulse toward individuation. This individualism amounts to a "fixing of our interest
upon...goals which are not of real importance," resulting in a
"demand that the world grant us recognition for qualities which
we regard as personal possessions: our talents or our beauty." Yet
these "false possessions" distract from "what is essential," leading
to dissatisfaction with life and oneself. The individualist feels
"limited" because, in truth, he or she has "limited aims," and the
"result is envy and jealousy."[70]

Although Jung obviously placed great value upon supporting
individuation, he was *not* advocating a publicly sanctioned program of individuation that sought to compel all individuals to
embark on a routinized set of psychological exercises toward a
common standard of success. This would be neither possible nor
desirable because individuation is not properly inspired from

without, but must be impelled from within. External imposition ignores the variety among individuals and would thus become oppressive: "What sets one man free is another man's prison."[71] The goal of individuation—the image of wholeness for that particular individual—therefore varies in accord with the "manifold needs and necessities" of humankind.[72] This recognition of the uniqueness of each individual also expressed itself in Jung's therapeutic practice, where he sought to minimize the occluding effect of generalized theory and instead endeavored to engage every client in a particularized manner.[73]

Further, although recognition of individual difference is at the center of Jung's psychology, his views should not be confused with theories that depict humans as capable of limitless self-construction without structuring, constraining, and guiding forces in their lives. While Jung's understanding of individuation was precisely the emergence of the individual in his or her specific expression, it is a process he conceived of as occurring within both a social context and the universal structures and dynamics of the psyche. In this manner—locating the concrete actuality within generalized forms—Jung attempted to do justice to both the multiplicity and the unity that constitute our lived experience as individual social beings "who have a world to which we belong."[74] Jung's social ethics was determined by the question of whether one listens to the voice of genuine vocation (i.e., individuation) or seeks collective recognition through conformity (i.e., a well-managed life of the *persona*) or for outstanding, ostensibly superior, qualities with which one identifies (i.e., individualism).

THE INDIVIDUAL AND THE COLLECTIVE: LEVELS OF CONSCIOUSNESS

Jung identified a number of not-so-laudable motives for the individual to join mass movements and identify with the collective. The following passage, rhetorical in nature, provides a useful introduction to this topic:

> Where the many are, there is security; what the many believe must of course be true; what the many want must be worth

striving for, and necessary, and therefore good. In the clamour
of the many resides the power to snatch wish-fulfillments by
force; sweetest of all, however, is that gentle and painless slip-
ping back into the kingdom of childhood, into the paradise of
parental care, into happy-go-luckiness and irresponsibility.[75]

In this passage Jung was making several distinct points. The
most basic motive he identified for those seeking a collective
identification is security. This presumably includes first and foremost the securing of bodily safety and survival. Increased safety
in numbers is an undeniable reality on one level, rooted in our
species' historical experiences of competitive adaptation and survival—an experience shared with other social creatures. Yet the
lure of the collective is not limited to physical survival. The collective also serves to define, through various institutional and
cultural means, what is true and good for its individual members,
and thus constitutes prevailing psychological and ethical values.
Groups engage in "world construction" and "world mainte-
nance," establishing plausibility structures and justifying individual and collective pursuits through publicly sanctioned ends.[76] As
Jung saw it, this social construction of reality is, to a degree,
inevitable and not wholly undesirable. Social structures, traditions, and all manner of cultural content (e.g., language, religion,
philosophy, and technology) make available the accrued experience of countless generations in which our individual lives may
take root and grow. This cultural context is the necessary foundation for all of human life.

Jung became critical of the process of social construction,
however, when he perceived that the individual personality was
being stunted by collective forces. Jung held that collectively
sanctioned ideas and values may suppress, through a wide array of
physical, institutional, and psychological instruments, the creative, particular, and often marginalized impulses and expressions
of the individual. As a clinical psychiatrist, Jung naturally focused
on psychological forms of the social suppression and control of
the individual, as opposed to economic, legal, or physically coer-
cive means.

What could induce an individual to, in effect, relinquish his
or her own selfhood and autonomy for these heteronomous ideas,

these collective promises? Jung indicated a polarity of motives, most likely varying in relative predominance between individuals and circumstances—the lure of both power and the yielding of power. The collective may promise a greater capacity for the exercise of violence in order to snatch the objects of one's desire, or it may promise the replication of parental protection so that one may remain in, or return to, a state of mental and moral infantilism.

Such, in summary, are the temptations of identifying with the collective at the expense of one's individuality. Jung believed the costs of sacrificing one's unique personality to the collective are numerous, to both the individual and society. An excessive identification with the collective results in a certain restless, unfulfilled dissatisfaction for the individual. Insofar as individuation is a necessity, the "leveling down to collective standards is injurious to the vital activity of the individual."[77] Conforming to social expectations entails the construction of a suitable *persona*, and to the degree that the ego identifies with this *persona* a certain "soullessness" emerges.[78] This sense of soullessness reflects a growing alienation from one's own unconscious as the personality's center of gravity shifts outward.[79] This process of "imitation"—no matter how extravagant it may appear outwardly—results in psychic "sterility"[80] and, if the psychic center becomes too imbalanced, in a compensatory activation of the unconscious.[81]

As suggested earlier, Jung held that identifying with groups is not simply negative, in the sense of seeking security and/or the renunciation of responsibility. It is also possible that one may realize—however imperfectly—genuine moral and psychological values through participation in a group. When an individual is identified with a group, collective experiences of transformation may indeed occur. However, there are several problems inherent in these collective experiences. Most important among them was Jung's contention that such group experiences occur "on a lower level of consciousness than the experience of an individual."[82]

The idea of "levels of consciousness" plays an important role in Jung's psychology and requires some clarification before continuing. The basic meaning of the term "level of consciousness" refers to the extent and range of one's awareness in terms of perceiving what actually exists and understanding what animates and motivates the factors of one's experience. A greater level of consciousness is not to be equated simply with a heightened predominance of reason or the accumulation of facts. As Jung used the term, a higher level of consciousness included not only a broadened awareness of one's environment but also a complexified and clarified sense of one's personality. The process of individuation may be understood as comprised, in part, by a growing consciousness of the manifold elements of one's own self.[83] Hence, the Jungian "higher consciousness" is suggestive of a practical form of awareness that includes both the world and one's own personality.

Implicit in the term *levels* is the idea that movement between levels is possible. As the above passage indicates, Jung held that the human psyche was capable of moving not only "upward" but also "downward" through levels of consciousness. In a basic sense, the movement between levels refers to the common experience of gaining a higher level of consciousness through understanding something of which one was previously ignorant or confused. Moving to a "lower" level of consciousness is also a common experience, as when one is tired, sick, or psychologically fragmented.

Critical to the present argument is Jung's view that one's level of consciousness is determinative of how problems are encountered, framed, and resolved. Jung held that with greater consciousness the individual personality is more autonomous, that is, less governed by unconscious forces and thus capable of genuine moral deliberation and choice: "A higher and wider consciousness resulting from the assimilation of the unfamiliar tends towards autonomy,"[84] and "our freedom extends only as far as our consciousness reaches."[85] Conversely, at lower levels of consciousness individuals are more prone to act from mere convention: "An individual who is guided more by the unconscious than by conscious choice therefore tends towards marked psychic conservatism. This is the reason why the primitive does not change in the course of thousands of years, and also why he fears anything strange and unusual."[86] Or, more dangerously, lower levels of consciousness exhibit what Jung described as a "possession" by unbridled and destructive instinctuality.[87] More commonly, lower levels of consciousness allow the projection of one's own shadow upon one's environment and others.[88]

Jung made distinctions between different levels of consciousness based on the criteria of mental health as evidenced within his clinical practice and through inference by observing individual and group behavior. Regarding the former, Jung held that a higher level of consciousness enabled individuals to better "solve" life's problems:

> I had always worked with the temperamental conviction that at bottom there are no insoluble problems, and experience justified me in so far as I have often seen patients simply outgrow problems that had destroyed others. This "outgrowing," as I formerly called it, proved on further investigation to be a new level of consciousness. Some higher or wider interest appeared on the patient's horizon, and through this broadening of his outlook the insoluble problem lost its urgency. It was not solved logically on its own terms, but faded out when confronted with a new and stronger life urge. It was not repressed and made unconscious, but merely appeared in a different light, and so really did become different. What, on a lower level, had led to the wildest conflicts and to panicky outbursts of emotion, from the higher level of personality now looked like a storm in the valley seen from the mountain top.[89]

Perhaps the use by Jung of the term "*levels* of consciousness," here and elsewhere, was unfortunate in that it may imply a Neoplatonic ascension away from the material realm toward a noncorporeal reality. This is *not*, however, what Jung meant by the term. For Jung, attaining a "higher level of consciousness" requires, metaphorically, a descent into what is dark, hidden, and shadowed, including the depths of one's unconscious. "One does not become enlightened by imagining figures of light, but by making the darkness conscious."[90] Thus, terms such as *broadened* and *wider* are used by Jung to complement the term *higher* when denoting a positive progression in states of consciousness.[91] Jung recognized that gaining these higher levels of consciousness— "outgrowing" one's problems—entails a clear recognition of one's embodied reality and acknowledgment of the travails this entails.

This does not mean that the storm is robbed of its reality, but instead of being in it one is above it. But since, in a psychic sense, we are both valley and mountain, it might seem a vain illusion to deem oneself beyond what is human. One certainly does feel the affect and is shaken and tormented by it, yet at the same time one is aware of a higher consciousness looking on which prevents one from becoming identical with the affect, a consciousness which regards the affect as an object, and can say, "I *know* that I suffer."[92]

In addition to clinical experience, Jung distinguished levels of consciousness based on observations of the apparent moral quality of an individual's or group's behavior. Jung held that the level of a group's consciousness tends to decline in proportion to its size. "The psychology of a large crowd inevitably sinks to the level of mob psychology."[93] Jung considered the impact of large numbers upon the individual's psychology in his essay "Concerning Rebirth," where he discussed forms of psychological transformation. He made a distinction between transformation "in a group" and transformation "in oneself"—"two totally different things."

> This [distinction] is due to the fact that, when many people gather together to share one common emotion, the total psyche emerging from the group is below the level of the individual psyche. If it is a very large group, the collective psyche will be more like the psyche of an animal, which is the reason why the ethical attitude of large organizations is always doubtful.[94]

Because this collective experience takes place on a lower level of consciousness and, because of the presence of the group, amid a charged atmosphere of suggestibility, the experience is more easily achieved than that of individual transformation, which entails a heightened level of consciousness.[95] This collective experience is alluring because, "The regressive identification with lower and more primitive states of consciousness is invariably accompanied by a heightened sense of life...."[96] However, this collectively induced transformation is typically ephemeral since:

The group experience goes no deeper than the level of one's own mind in that state. It does work a change in you, but the change does not last. On the contrary, you must have continual recourse to mass intoxication in order to consolidate the experience and your belief in it. But as soon as you are removed from the crowd, you are a different person again and unable to reproduce the previous state of mind.[97]

These statements do not mean, however, that Jung did not recognize the possible value of group experiences, particularly if they occur within the context of ritualization focused on a sacred center other than one's own ego or the group itself. The mob or mass mentality is to be distinguished from the "transformation rite, which, though performed before an audience, does not in any way depend upon group identity or necessarily give rise to it."[98] Ritualization that serves to heighten consciousness, to make one's conflicts more acute, to relate oneself to a transpersonal center outside the group is a positive function of the group.

> The inevitable psychological regression within the group is partially counteracted by ritual, that is to say through a cult ceremony which makes the solemn performance of sacred events the centre of group activity and prevents the crowd from relapsing into unconscious instinctuality. By engaging the individual's interest and attention, the ritual makes it possible for him to have a comparatively individual experience even within the group and so to remain more or less conscious. But if there is no relation to a centre which expresses the unconscious through its symbolism, the mass psyche inevitably becomes the hypnotic focus of fascination, drawing everyone under its spell.[99]

If the group can serve as a transmitter of traditions that remain symbolically alive—and thus psychologically effective—and *not* as the preserver of outmoded forms no longer plausible, then individual participation in community may be positive in terms of its individuating effect. Jung's primary concern appears to have been the tendency of groups to reinforce the human propensity toward slothfulness, specifically the urge to "expect everything from outside—even that metamorphosis which external reality cannot provide."[100] At bottom, individual transformation simply cannot be derived from collective experience, rather "the inner man remains unchanged however much community he has. His environment cannot give him as a gift something which he can win for himself only with effort and suffering."[101]

The dangers of identification with the group, however, extend well beyond purely personal psychological consequences. Jung believed that the externalization of one's sense of self inclines the individual toward projecting "this same collective psyche [upon] others." This results in an ignorance or suppression of the particular qualities of persons, leading to "the suffocation of the single individual."[102] Jung claimed that the general level of morality in society, which "rests entirely on the moral sense of the individual and the freedom necessary for it," necessarily declines as individual factors are "blotted out."[103]

The moral level of the group declines, according to Jung, precisely because the sense of individual responsibility decreases in proportion to a heightened sense of suggestibility. As the identity of the individual is increasingly externalized through group identification, "environmental influences, be they good or bad," become determinative and lead to a state of "individual bondage." The "discriminative capacity"—that is, the ability to determine the cause of things, and the moral qualities that are attached to them, or that one attaches to them—is weakened.[104] As the discriminative capacity declines, so do one's freedom and sense of responsibility. Moreover, by identifying with a group's solution to life's problems one may "avoid any personal conflict but fuel the general one instead." For example, by obstinately clinging to a psychologically dead *credo* one may actually contribute to the eventual decline of both the creed and its institutional basis. "Every hardening of the denominational standpoint enlarges the crack [between Catholics and Protestants] and diminishes the moral and spiritual authority of Christians."[105] Jung contended that by identifying with the collective psyche one will "infallibly try to force the demands of his unconscious upon others, for identifying with the collective psyche always brings with it a feeling of universal validity—"godlikeness"—which completely ignores all differences in the personal psyche of his fellows."[106]

For Jung, the individual was the source of creative cultural change, for it is the individual that provides the complexity, novelty, and "differentiation" necessary for social progress.[107] Thus, an individual who merely conforms to societal norms and expectations, perhaps identifying with the persona, contributes only indirectly and incompletely to society's needs to evolve and adapt to changing circumstances. Jung based his assertion about the necessity of the individual to effect cultural change *not* on the grounds that the nature of the individual is unambiguously good. "All the highest achievements of virtue, as well as the blackest villainies, are individual."[108] Nor did Jung believe that harmony between individuals and society is the natural and normal course of things, disrupted only by quirks of character or history. The European experience in the first half of the twentieth century had the effect of coloring Jung's thought with a pervasive sense of trepidation about the threat of "mass mindedness" to the individual. "Masses are always breeding grounds of psychic epidemics."[109] These "epidemics" do not necessarily depend on large numbers to incite them. "Everywhere in the West there are subversive minorities who, sheltered by our humanitarianism and our sense of justice, hold the incendiary torches ready, with nothing to stop the spread of their ideas except the critical reason of a single, fairly intelligent, mentally stable stratum of the population." Jung added, ominously, "One should not overestimate the thickness of this stratum.[110]

So it is not a naive optimism that supported Jung's bias toward the individual as the source of cultural developments. It was rather the perception that the larger a group becomes the more it will rely on conventions and "conservative prejudices detrimental to individuality."[111] These "conservative prejudices" reinforce existing social structures and promote a leveling down of individuality and a diminished state of consciousness. "The mechanism of convention keeps people unconscious, for in that state they can follow their accustomed tracks like blind brutes, without the need for conscious decision."[112] Further:

> [In a collective atmosphere everything individual] is doomed to repression. The individual elements lapse into the unconscious, where, by the law of necessity, they are transformed

into something essentially baleful, destructive, and anarchical. Socially, this evil principle shows itself in the spectacular crimes—regicide and the like—perpetrated by certain prophetically-minded individuals; but in the great mass of the community it remains in the background, and manifests itself indirectly in the inexorable moral degeneration of society.[113]

This condition of repressed individuality presents dangers for society both from within and from without. Jung made the argument that when external conditions change—conditions "not provided for under the old conventions," and thus requiring a new cultural adaptation—it is the relatively conscious individual who is able to facilitate this adaptation. However, "just as with animals, panic is liable to break out among human beings kept unconscious by routine, and with equally predictable results." Yet it is the "personality," the individual who has encountered his/her own private terrors of personal adaptation, that is "able to cope with the changing times" and "does not allow itself to be seized by the panic terror of those who are just waking to consciousness."[104]

In addition to the ability to adapt to changing external circumstances, Jung claimed that the suppression of individuality, the predominance of "the mere routine of life...in the form of convention and tradition," carries with it the danger of "a destructive outbreak of creative energy" from within the social body.[115] Jung argued that this "creative energy," that is, unconscious libido seeking manifestation, presents a danger only when it is "a mass phenomenon, but never in the individual who consciously submits to these higher powers and serves them with all his strength."[116] It is precisely when the unconscious manifests itself through collective contagions, "not assimilated by any consciousness," that it may "precipitate a catastrophe."[117] Thus, although the objective psyche is universally shared,

> [The] objective psyche must nonetheless individuate itself if it is to become actualized, for there is no other way in which it could express itself except through the individual human being. The only exception to this is when it seizes hold of a group....[118]

The manifestation of the objective psyche "outside" individual consciousness is socially and individually dangerous because its impulses cannot be subjected to conscious scrutiny and deliberation, but rather "runs on in it [the group] like an uncontrolled law of nature."[119] Jung placed his hope in the individual for the creative, conscious realization of the unconscious forces of life, for it is only the individual who can bring consciousness to bear on basic instinctual impulses.

> Only the [person] who can consciously assent to the power of the inner voice becomes a personality; but if he succumbs to it he will be swept away by the blind flux of psychic events and destroyed. That is the great and liberating thing about any genuine personality: he voluntarily sacrifices himself to his vocation, and consciously translates into his own individual reality what would only lead to ruin if it were lived unconsciously by the group.[120]

Jung's understanding of the psyche as a dynamic source of energy that requires individual consciousness for its constructive realization was the basis of his understanding of how human evil may become manifest in history. When individuals become "caught in mass movements" the archetypes function and govern events and "all human control comes to an end."[121] When social conditions degenerate and hopes collapse, identification with the archetypes increasingly takes the place of external reality, resulting in dangerous inflations and corresponding justifications for psychologically blind, "godlike" acts with inevitably destructive consequences.[122] This state of dissociation from reality, a psychosis, may threaten both the individual and society.[123]

In summary, Jung located his primary value in the development of the individual personality. He did so for both pragmatic and ethical reasons relating to the well-being of both the individual and society. The foundation of his ethical arguments, essentially "religious" in nature, will be discussed in the concluding chapter. Whatever conflicts exist between the individual and society are not inherently intractable nor irremediable but are open to the possibility of individual transformation, which in turn changes the nature of the problems themselves. Jung is no "progressivist," placing his hope for a better world in the ongoing development of technology and culture. However, he did perceive a purposeful process at work in the evolution of human life, and specifically in the development of human consciousness. This relatively optimistic perspective was grounded not on faith in either the individual's conscious intentions or further collective organizing, but on a transpersonal source outside of consciousness. Conscience is one medium for the manifestation of this source.

PART II

Jung and the Problems of Conscience

Chapter 5

JUNG AND THE NATURALIZATION OF CONSCIENCE

In part 1, "Jung's Moral Framework," I took an expository approach to explicating Jung's thought regarding meta-ethical issues, namely: his philosophy of nature (vis-à-vis the psyche); his modeling of the psychodynamics of conflict and harmony; and his understanding of the nature of relations between individuals and the collective. These issues were identified as being central to the problem of conscience because they constitute the underlying assumptions that determine the way conscience is conceived, interpreted, and evaluated within generalized theories of human nature.

The second part of this study, "Jung and the Problems of Conscience," becomes critical and comparative in method as I engage in a dialogue with pivotal arguments against the significance and plausibility of conscience; namely, the naturalization of the person and the loss of moral agency (chapter 5); the perspectival nature of knowledge and, relatedly, the genealogy of morals (chapter 6).

In the current chapter, "Jung and the Naturalization of Conscience," I will focus on what may be termed "ontological" aspects of conscience, that is, the "what is it?" of this moral locus. I will do so by asking questions regarding the origin, formational process, and operative role and status of conscience within the psychic economy. In the next chapter I will focus on epistemological questions and related problems of discernment. There I will ask the "how does one know?" and "how does one know what one knows?" questions regarding conscience.

These two chapters, comprising part 2 of this work, address what I consider to be the two nodal points of contemporary thought that serve to make unintelligible and implausible, for many, the traditional sense of conscience. These nodal points, as the etymology suggests, are theoretical "knots" that serve to tie together a complex range of phenomena—hence their utility and popularity—yet with a corresponding cost of constraining and occluding any phenomenon that seeks independence from their interpretive nets. The first nodal point to which I refer is the *objectification* of reality, including human beings, in a manner that depersonalizes and, through a process of homogenization, devalues the elements of experience that comprise our life. Objectification, as habitual attitude and mode of perception, alienates one from a sense of genuine contact with deeper, meaningful realities that are predicated on—there are many names for it—community, relationship, personalism, *participation mystique*, the web of life, and so on. These deeper meanings to which I allude include those that arise through one's conscience and resulting acts of conscious moral incarnation. Objectivism, as it were, locks one out of vital reality.

The other nodal point of contemporary thought, in some ways the opposite of the first, is *subjectivism* (and, relatedly, *perspectivalism*), an epistemological viewpoint through which genuine access to intersubjective realities is denied. Moral experience, including that of conscience, is not refuted *per se* by the subjectivist position, but is instead redefined in a manner that denies its moral significance for anyone other than the experiencing subject. Subjectivism, as it were, locks one into a private reality.

In the next two chapters I will address these challenges to contemporary ways of understanding and experiencing the moral dimension of life by positing a renewed basis of moral awareness and sensitivity through Jung's psychology of conscience. Further, I will argue that the true character and full significance of Jung's theories may be best understood in light of his theory of conscience. I will characterize this perspective of his thought as an "ontic moral psychology," a phrase I will discuss more fully in chapter 7 after discussing Jung's ontological and epistemological viewpoints regarding conscience in chapters 5 and 6, respectively. Tentatively, though, an "ontic moral psychology" is based on the claim that morally related psychological processes—particularly those of conscience—are to be seen as potentially expressive of psychic substratum of such rootedness and depth that substantive, ontological ramifications, and resulting epistemological claims of a moral nature, are at least implicit.[1]

This framing of Jung's psychology is predicated on a relational, personal sense of life that interprets the purely objectivist and subjectivist worldviews not as denoting permanent, mutually exclusive states—whether considered constraining or liberating—but rather as modes of knowing that reflect the varying interpretations and abstractions of a conscious being in engagement with reality, sometimes valid and desirable, sometimes fallacious and symptomatic of estrangement. In short, these two "nodal points" of the contemporary mind-set are each but contingently, provisionally true, and incapable of claiming to have exhaustively captured the nature of reality in their interpretive framework. Further, Jung's depiction of conscience as a relational phenomenon, when understood as such and engaged accordingly, may have the salutary effect of helping one overcome the varied entrapments within the isolated ego that objectivism and subjectivism induce. This breakthrough into a wider relational world is precipitated by, and issues into, a repersonalized sense of communion with others, the world, and the depths of self. Conscience may be determinative in awakening this awareness of relationality, for in a most immediate and compelling way it can persuade—through what we call empathy, compassion, ardor, devotion, guilt, remorse, longing—that one participates, is bound to, is of the very fiber and fabric of being itself, now felt to be morally infused and pregnant with meaning. The Jungian conscience is a midwife of this realization.

In order to give analytical force and rational substance to these claims, the sequence of exposition will be as follows: I will first describe the emergence of reductive naturalism, which is both a method that informs and an attitude that supports our current ethos of objectivism; then I will consider some of the costs of this objectification of reality for both the individual and society; a model of critique will then be offered, centered on the criterion of the adequacy of a theory's informing ontology; then a modern exponent of reductive naturalism—evolutionary psychology—will be outlined in order to bring into contemporary relevance the extended discussion of the psychoanalytic super-ego that follows; in conclusion, an alternative framework to reductive naturalism, and the portrayal of conscience that logically ensues, will be introduced using Jung's psychology.

OBJECTIFICATION—ORIGINS AND COSTS

The objectification of the world, that is, that particular perception of the world that sees its essential nature to be that of impersonal particles of substance, shaped and moved by necessary laws, has an ancient lineage. In the West, Democritus is considered the seminal exponent of this worldview. A thorough recounting of this tradition, widely available,[2] is not needed here. Rather, I will stay closer to the theme of this work by considering how this viewpoint, in alignment with the scientific culture of the nineteenth and twentieth centuries, found expression in the psychoanalytic theory of conscience.

The origins of the modern form of this reductive naturalism are a result of a complex of philosophical and scientific factors. At the heart of this process was "a more or less self-conscious devaluation of nature."[3] Alexandre Koyré, in his *From the Closed World to the Infinite Universe*, captures something of the impact of this development on our worldview:

> This scientific and philosophical revolution...can be described roughly as bringing forth the destruction of the Cosmos, that is, the disappearance, from philosophically and scientifically valid concepts, of the conception of the world as a finite, closed, and hierarchically ordered whole (a whole in which the hierarchy of value determined the hierarchy and structure of being, rising from the dark, heavy and imperfect earth to the higher and higher perfection of the stars and heavenly spheres), and its replacement by an indefinite and even infinite universe which is bound together by the identity of its funda-

mental components and laws, and in which all these components are placed on the same level of being. This, in turn,
implies the discarding by scientific thought of all considerations based upon value-concepts, such as perfection, harmony,
meaning and aim, and finally the utter devalorization of being,
the divorce of the world of value and the world of fact.[4]

In chapter 1, I described how this severing of fact and value
migrated through the sciences until human nature itself was
increasingly understood in naturalistic terms. The deleterious
effects of this naturalized view of humanity are as profound as
they are numerous, and I will briefly outline here what I consider
to be some of the relevant issues and what is at stake in their outcome.

Perhaps the most significant effect of a naturalized anthropology is not simply theoretical, but rather most immediate and
practical. When the theory of reductive naturalism is applied to
oneself—when the abstract becomes immediately concrete—an
alienation from oneself may be engendered with a corresponding
attitude of enervated uncertainty. Neal Weiner, in *The Harmony of
the Soul*, makes a relevant observation:

> It is seldom recognized that in ethics the major consequence
> of the devaluation of nature concerns a change in the per-
> ceived relationship of human beings to their own desires.
> Nature is represented most poignantly in the human being
> by the body, and the body is a moral presence as desire—as
> the collection of what are called the "bodily desires," which
> is really the collection of *all* desires insofar as they stem from
> the natural forces that have made us.[5]

Weiner's statement suggests that the severing of fact from
value dramatically affects the way one relates to one's own desires
as expressed through feelings, thoughts, fantasies, and vague
impulses toward action. Within the context of reductive naturalism, one's impulses to act are no longer conceived within the
framework of possible moral goods, but rather are understood to
be expressions—or, more mechanically, impulses and drives—of a
depersonalized nature. Psychologically, one's impulses to act are
then understood not as originating from or pointing toward per-

sons, acts, and objects of moral value, but rather are to be explained reductively in elementary terms devoid of moral significance.

This changed conception of one's own motivations—from moral soul to amoral *id*—may precipitate a sense of estrangement with oneself. This alienation results from a conflict between the theoretical abstraction of humans as constituted wholly by bio-chemical process and the immediacy of one's practical life, which, unlike abstract theory, is not primarily analytical and rational in nature, but is imaginal and dramatic in character and mythic in its metastructures. The experience of oneself as a responsible, free moral agent—modern ethical language for alluding to what was once sensed as soul—is so immediate, so irrepressible, that to attempt to conceptually override this seemingly inherent psychic pattern of behavior is to invite a caustic split within oneself. Erazim Kohák describes this conflict in terms of "constructs" and "experi-ential givens."[6] The depersonalization of one's relationship with oneself naturally leads to a changed relationship with others, as they too are seen as being, at their core, motivated by impersonal forces.

This devaluation of one's desires—devalued because theoret-ically conceived as uncaring quanta of one form or another—has the effect of calling into question not only the meaning of specific plans and purposes in life but the import of one's life as a whole. When one's desires are demythologized through quantification and reductive explanation, then teleology is no longer accorded significance within rational discourse. This, in spite of the fact that every day one awakens from sleep and arises with some sense of purpose, however consciously inane or noble this purpose may be, that governs or at least orients one's behavior. When objectivism prevails in one's assessment of human nature, constructed theories supplant practical concepts that emerged organically within moral traditions. Theories about adaptation and necessary laws that drive us forward replace textured descriptions of virtues, the cultivation of which was previously both means and end of living life well.

In an effort to redress the most basic of problems associated with an objectivist anthropology, theoretical hybrids, while still seeking scientific credibility, have arisen that attempt to stay near to lived experience, arguing for the pseudo-teles of "health" and "flourishing," in both a bodily and a mental sense. Yet, when "rigorously" pursued to their logical end, even the notions of health and flourishing as "rational goods" and "natural ends" are considered merely functional processes serving the "interests" of genetic self-perpetuation.

One of the more far-reaching effects of this naturalized portrayal of human moral capacities is that conscience itself becomes objectified and depersonalized; that is, it is not accorded the status of effecting the conveyance of genuine, suprapersonal moral insight or obligation. Rather, the naturalized conscience is treated, at best, as the socially useful internalization of mores or, more critically, as a capricious agent of amoral forces from which we are best liberated. Conscience becomes a result, not a generative source; becomes symptomatic, not seminal. In sum, the naturalization of the person results in a negation of the moral significance of conscience.

OBJECTIFICATION—BASIS OF CRITIQUE

The manner in which one conceives of conscience is directly related to, if not derived from, one's very first ontological principles. Psychological theories are often presented otherwise, as if, for instance, the "super-ego" were "discovered" and its particular formulation were independent of the metatheoretical claims upon which it rests. Yet, as has been convincingly documented and demonstrated, these metanarratives, by whatever name—mythic structures, cosmologies, religions, ultimate concerns, first principles, metatheories, *Weltanschauungen*—are omnipresent and inescapable in their seminal effect upon all conscious, reflective activity.[7] Likewise, these principles are operative, consciously or otherwise, in one's practical life. Moral psychologists are certainly no exception to these facts of cognitive constraint and the finitude of philosophizing. My intention in this chapter, therefore, is to unearth and examine key elements of the informing metatheories and resulting claims of the psychoanalytical and Jungian theories of conscience. By making explicit the core assumptions of these theories the applicability and adequacy of the amplified ethical superstructures may be better determined.

According to Alfred North Whitehead, the four criteria for assessing a cosmology are whether it is logical, applicable, coherent, and adequate.[8] It is the fourth criterion—the adequacy of one's theories—that I will focus on as the basis of my critique of theories of conscience. By "adequacy" of a generalized theory, I mean (1) that no item of experience is incapable of interpretation through the theory's system of ideas,[9] and (2) that all items of experience are in fact capable of such interpretation. That is, the way that one judges the adequacy of the metatheoretical ideas informing one's more specific theories, for instance, that of conscience, is by determining whether the metatheories sufficiently account for the full range of phenomena that fall under one's observations. Erazim Kohák makes this point in the following manner:

> Metatheoretical arguments must be circular, self-confirming, since they seek to provide a global matrix of intelligibility— unlike theoretical arguments, which presuppose such a matrix. *The condition [determining their adequacy] is that the circle be wide enough to embrace all there is.*[10]

In chapter 2, I argued that Jung advocated neither an otherworldly idealism nor a reductive materialism, but rather sought to articulate a way of prehending and understanding reality that recognized the essential character and relative autonomy of the psyche—*esse en anima*. As discussed, Jung conceived of the psyche as the only reality that one may experience directly and immediately, and that its phenomena were, in and of themselves, "facts" deserving of recognition as such. In so doing, he was not suggesting a solipsistic philosophy, but was rather advocating, as he saw it, an intellectually honest practice of recognizing both the inherent limits and generative capacities of the psyche.

Seen through this heuristic framework, the psyche assumed for Jung the pivotal role as mediator, and proximate foundation, of contending ontological and epistemological viewpoints—such as reductive materialism and uncritical idealism—that in his view were guilty of asserting universal applicability at the expense of their adequacy. Jung argued that "one-sided" ontological or epistemological positions fail the test of adequacy because, at the most fundamental level, they omit the very basis of experience—the sentient psyche—and of which any given metatheory is itself an expression. Idealistic epistemologies may be judged inadequate because they fail to acknowledge and account for the inherent constraints upon human cognitive capacities imposed by the ontological embeddedness—the embodiment—of the human psyche. Conversely, a narrowly naturalistic ontology may be judged inadequate for failing, through lack of self-reflexivity, to account for the conscious agent that is the animating basis of the theory itself. In short, the full range of embodied psychological phenomena—life as actually experienced, not as rationally constructed and subsequently applied in a "regional" context—is the basis on which the adequacy of metatheories is to be tested.

Another way of speaking about theoretical adequacy is through the language of ontology. Kohák makes a distinction between a "general" and a "regional" ontology, which in certain ways parallels his distinction between a metatheory and a specific theory. He explains his ideas regarding different forms of ontology in the following manner:

> Ontology here refers to an inventory and an ordering of what is taken to be. A general ontology would have to include all that presents itself and functions as real in lived experience, including intentional objects. For the purpose of a special inquiry, however, whether it is chemistry, physics, or psychology, the researcher necessarily restricts the totality of the phenomenal field to the region of whatever is relevant to the inquiry. Such a restriction is essential, but it means that the ontology of that inquiry is *regional*, a correlate of particular science.[11]

My task in this chapter is to explore the effect of a naturalized view of the person on one's understanding of conscience by way of examining the adequacy of such a naturalistic view. The language of "regional" and "general" ontologies is useful here, enabling the question of a theory's plausibility and truth claims to be asked not in absolute "either/or" terms but rather through the criteria of range, degrees, and scope of application.

EVOLUTIONARY PSYCHOLOGY AS CONTEMPORARY EXPONENT OF PSYCHOANALYTIC MORAL THEORY

My examination of how the objectification of reality has informed contemporary views of conscience turns now to the seminal theories of Freud and, specifically, his conception of the superego. My discussion of Freud is not intended to provide a comprehensive review of his theories, but rather is employed as a critical foil to clarify the significance of Jung's thought. I will focus on salient features of Freud's theories that have contributed to the development of the current moral climate, specifically those that pertain to conscience. While Freud (and, in chapter 6, Nietzsche) is certainly a phenomenon in himself, my purpose in this study is to consider very specific aspects of his thought and the resulting impact of his theories on the development of contemporary culture.

But, the reader may ask, has not Freud been superseded, is he not in certain ways passé, and should not our attention be given to more relevant contemporaries? While in fact many theorists— for example, A. Freud, Erik Erikson, D. W. Winnicott, Heinz Kohut, Lawrence Kohlberg, and others—have extended Freud's ideas in fruitful directions that mitigate some of his own limitations, both the root assumptions that informed Freud's thought and the basic formulations of psychoanalytic theory continue to exercise a pervasive and profound influence over contemporary thought. By returning to the source of the psychosexual construction of conscience, the contours of its repercussions will be made more visible and the contrast with Jung made more evident.

One such example of a theoretical repercussion is the field of "evolutionary psychology." Robert Wright, author of *The Moral Animal*,[12] has emerged as one of evolutionary psychology's more prominent theorists and spokespersons. A brief review of Wright's ideas will serve to illustrate how Freud's moral psychology may be amplified when its basic assumptions, combined with more recent developments within the biological and genetic sciences, are carried to their logical conclusions.

As suggested above, theoretical positions may be valid within a "regional" context and yet may fail tests of adequacy when their claimed range of application is broadened to that of an all-encompassing metatheory. The primary basis of my evaluation of Wright will be whether he has overstated his theory's range of proper application. That is, does he claim more than is rigorously defensible? Does he assert a "general applicability" when in fact his theory merits only a "regional' claim to relevance?

Wright himself is not bashful when making assertions about the significance—and adequacy—of evolutionary psychology. He believes that this field of inquiry holds the "promise of creating a whole new science of mind."[13] This "science," as Wright sees it, will yield such revolutionary insights and discoveries that nothing less than "a new worldview is emerging."[14] Wright is confident about the future prospects of this "science"—though he acknowledges that its current theories are incomplete and will require future confirmation—because evolutionary psychology is "firmly grounded in logic and fact."[15]

Wright's "new worldview" is conceptually rooted in a Darwinian form of biological materialism. The causal chain of assumptions that inform this particular species of anthropology are outlined in succinct form by Neal O. Weiner, when he writes, "Roughly speaking, anthropology within the naturalistic brackets will simply assume that human behavior is governed by thought, thought by emotion, emotion by psychodynamics, psychodynamics by protoplasm, protoplasm by DNA, and DNA by natural selection."[16]

Within this assumptive framework, morality and, specifically, conscience are explained "genetically," that is, in terms of motivations or, more precisely, the animating impulses behind the motivations. Through this manner of reductive analysis, evolutionary psychology does not trace or seek human "motivations" in the conscious subject, nor in any other locus of responsible agency, but rather in the "interests" of the DNA. This interpretive framework may be termed "genetic essentialism." Wright articulates the logic and character of this theory throughout his writings in various forms, yet one citation should suffice to convey the essence of this perspective:

Our generosity and affection have a narrow underlying purpose. They're aimed either at kin, who share our genes, at
nonkin of the opposite sex who can help package our genes
for shipment to the next generation, or at nonkin of either
sex who seem likely to return the favor.[17]

This passage expresses the heart of evolutionary psychology's moral theory: that human behavior is governed, in the final
analysis, by impersonal forces that somehow, and for some "reason," seek to survive and multiply, struggling to do so within the
operative dynamics of natural selection. Wright expresses—one
may assume to the advantage of his DNA—a tolerant attitude
toward this potentially discouraging, if not sobering, fact of the
selfish gene: "Though there's nothing inherently good about
genetic self-interest, there's nothing inherently wrong with it
either. When it does conduce to happiness (which it won't
always), and doesn't gravely hurt anyone else, why fight it?"[18]

Although Wright believes he has satisfactorily explained the
actual causal nature of our seemingly moral behavior, he is still
confronted with the fact that people *experience* and *believe* that they
possess freedom of choice, that they are able to prehend, however
imperfectly, spheres of self-transcending moral truth, and that
their conscience does transmit moral claims that may wield superior authority to that of the conscious will. Wright begins to
address this practical problem within the framework of his theory
by asking the question, "Why did natural selection give us that vast
guilt repository known as the conscience?"[19] And he answers, logically consistent with the rest of his theory, by ascribing to our
moral sense a merely *functional* significance in the service of natural selection: "It is amazing that a process as amoral and crassly
pragmatic as natural selection could design a mental organ that
makes us feel as if we're in touch with higher truths. Truly a
shameless ploy."[20]

In Wright's view, our cultural and moral history are explained
through, if not subsumed by, the narrative of organic history:
"Sympathy, empathy, compassion, conscience, guilt, remorse, even
the very sense of justice, the sense that doers of good deserve
reward and doers of bad deserve punishment—all these can now be
viewed as vestiges of organic history on a particular planet."[21]

Conscience, in Wright's view, is thus seen as a psychological operation in the service of elementary physiological drives and genetic forces. Conscience is presented as a faculty that misrepresents itself—presenting itself as altruistic and expressive of "moral truth"—while actually serving only the narrow self-interests of genetic self-perpetuation. Wright summarizes his psychological structural theory along explicitly Freudian lines in the following manner:

> Freud's "id"—the beast in the basement—presumably grows out of the reptilian brain, a product of presocial evolutionary history. The "superego"—loosely speaking, the conscience—is a more recent invention. It is the source of the various kinds of inhibition and guilt designed to restrain the id in a genetically profitable manner; the superego prevents us, say, from harming siblings, or from neglecting our friends. The "ego" is the part in the middle. Its ultimate, if unconscious, goals are those of the id, yet it pursues them with long-term calculation, mindful of the superego's cautions and reprimands.[22]

In my judgment, Wright's ideas have the degree of immediate appeal that they do, not because they are theoretically incontestable but rather because they receive powerful, immediate experiential confirmation through both our "will to live" and our sex drive, which is then "transferred" imaginatively and conceptually to the genes. My intention here is not to argue against the significance of humanity's embodied, biological nature, nor to diminish the determinative role that the instincts for survival and reproduction have in shaping a wide range of our psychological phenomena and behavioral expressions. Rather, my criticism focuses on whether evolutionary psychology's portrayal of human beings adequately accounts for the full range of human experience, and, in this accounting, whether the defining qualities of humanity are in fact distorted. Wright's theories *can be* argued against directly and may be shown to be not so "logical" and "factual" as the author claims. But I believe the more productive approach to engaging evolutionary psychology is to acknowledge the insights of this young hermeneutical science while at the same time constructing a more comprehensive framework for understanding conscience that is in accord with the full breadth of our experience as actually lived and felt by the concrete, particular subject. In short, I will attempt to appreciate evolutionary psychology as a specialized theory based on a regional ontology.

This outline of evolutionary psychology's views of conscience was intended to bring into contemporary relevance the following discussion regarding the psychoanalytic super-ego. By way of entry into Freud's theoretical framework, the following quotation is offered, which contains an implicit question. Freud wrote, late in his life, that "even if conscience is something 'within us,' yet it is not so from the first. In this it is a real contrast to sexual life, which is in fact there from the beginning of life and not only a later addition."[23] How then, as Freud saw it, did this "conscience" come to be and with what "voice" did it speak?

THE PSYCHOANALYTIC SUPER-EGO: BASIC STRUCTURAL MODEL

To address these questions, I will approach Freud's theory of conscience by first exploring its origins in the context of his structural model of the psyche. Following this structural analysis, I will discuss the basic assumptions Freud held regarding the character and dynamics of the instincts, and how this affected Freud's views of the different components of the psyche. Finally, I will consider how Freud viewed the various manifestations of conscience.

As is well known, the term Freud used that most closely approximates *conscience* is *super-ego*.[24] The Freudian super-ego was more inclusive than what is normally considered to be the phenomenon of conscience. For example, the super-ego, in addition to generating a sense of guilt, melancholia, and of prompting us to strive for high ideals, is also conceived as the agency of repression and certain repetition compulsions driven by aggressions.[25] A function of such range and significance would seem to require an esteemed lineage within Freud's system, and indeed that is the case. In order to understand Freud's concept of conscience it is necessary to review his theory regarding the emergence of the ego itself, and, specifically, the central drama that it must confront and overcome, that is, the Oedipus Complex, for it is out of this conflict that the super-ego emerges. The following quotation from *The Ego and the Id* (1923), the text in which Freud amplified the structural model introduced in *Beyond the Pleasure Principle* (1920),[26] provides a suitable introduction to the topic.

> *The broad general outcome of the sexual phase dominated by the Oedipus complex may, therefore, be taken to be the forming of a precipitate in the ego, consisting of these two identifications* [father and mother] *in some way united with each other. This modification of the ego retains its special position; it confronts the other contents of the ego as an ego ideal or super-ego.*[27]

The logic behind this statement rests on the basic postulate of psychoanalytic theory—and depth psychology in general—that the unconscious is older than, and prior to, the conscious mind. Within Freud's topographical model this translated into the terminology that the *id* is prior to the *ego*. This "prior to" not only refers to the sequential order in causal processes for both the evolution of the species and the development of the individual, but also connotes the relative significance accorded to the various psychological structures for shaping and determining our psychological expressions. Though in the later structural model the term *unconscious* was transformed from noun to adjective, and was broadened to include (or, rather, to apply to) elements of the ego, the basic description of the *ego* as derivative of the *id* remained unchanged throughout Freud's writings. Because of this "prior to" status, the *id* served, in effect, as Freud's "first principle" from which, and upon which, his psychological models were built. Given this significance, the *id* is central to understanding the nature of the Freudian conscience.

Freud recognized that the *id* could not be directly perceived, for it is, by definition, unconscious in nature. It is therefore to be approached, experientially and in theory, by way of its manifestations—that is, its effects or, pathogenically, one's symptoms—and is to be discussed deductively and by way of "analogies." Most basically, Freud held that the *id* is grounded in the physiological processes and is "filled with energy reaching it from the instincts."[28] The *id* was variously and colorfully described by

Freud as "instinctual cathexes seeking discharge,"[29] "a cauldron full of seething excitations," or, simply, "a chaos."[30] This conception of the *id* as being fully interpenetrated with the instinctual, physiological substrate enabled Freud to claim for his nascent science the credentials of empiricism associated with the fields of biology and medicine. This supposed grounding in tangible empiricism was for Freud the basis of his methodology and the bedrock upon which his theoretical amplifications stood and asserted their claims to scientific truth. In an early letter (April 19, 1908), Freud shared with Jung his dispositional inclination toward approaching the psyche as a phenomenon derivative of the organic, and how sexuality manifests this psychosomatic relationship: "I am rather annoyed with Bleuler for his willingness to accept a psychology without sexuality, which leaves everything hanging in mid-air. In the sexual processes we have the indispensable 'organic foundation' without which a medical man can only feel ill at ease in the life of the psyche."[31]

If indeed the *id* is grounded in, and expressive of, the physiological instincts, then one would expect the character of these instincts to be determinative of the nature of the psyche as a whole. Although Freud's precise delineation of the instincts varied during the course of his life,[32] a common attitude and character pervaded his representations of the instincts regardless of their specific configuration within different dynamic models. At their core, the primary instincts were portrayed as impersonal, elemental forces of a netherworld far removed from the concerns of the waking, walking world of humanity. For Freud, the instincts represent, or *are themselves*, primal forces governed by the *pleasure principle*[33]—with all pleasures being erotic in their essence—moderated by constraining forces collectively known as the *reality principle*.[34] Dynamically, the interplay between the lure of "pleasure" and the repulsion (through the reality principle) of "unpleasure" was conceived by Freud as somehow favoring the latter. In a statement that seems more confessional than empirical, Freud wrote that "sensations of a pleasurable nature have not anything inherently impelling about them, whereas unpleasurable ones have it in the highest degree."[35] This attitude, or assessment, translated into psychoanalytic formulations that claimed that the psyche, in spite of its dynamic nature, ultimately seeks a state of relative quiescence.

> The facts which have caused us to believe in the dominance of the pleasure principle in mental life also find expression in the hypothesis that the mental apparatus endeavors to keep the quantity of excitation present in it as low as possible or at least to keep it constant.[36]

Thus, in spite of the fact that love and hate[37]—the two essential forces at work in Freud's final formulation—may seem to be the epitome of volatility and the essence of exuberant living, Freud suggested that there is something akin to a regressive, gravitational pull to the whole of the instinctual realm that resists emergence and outward expression, seeking instead an insular stasis.

This conservative characterization of the psyche is admittedly hard to reconcile with other aspects of psychoanalytic theory. After all, Freud's theories of sexuality were based on a dynamic, expressive model—seemingly the very opposite of what I assert above. To a degree this dynamic characterization is accurate—and it is this aspect of his thought that has apparently appealed to so many individuals seeking to affirm human embodiment and sexuality. Yet, when Freud's ideas are extended to their logical implications, or traced back to their underlying assumptions, a picture emerges in which the expression of instinctual impulses is not affirmed as a positive value in itself, nor as a means of progressive exploration and insight. Rather, instinctual expression is portrayed simply as a necessary function of relief. This conservative view of the instincts (as dualistic, and bound in a struggle tending toward a state of quiescence) and the *id* (as an aggregate of formless instinctual impulses) informed Freud's speculative[38] theories regarding the emergence and formation of the ego.

THE ORIGIN AND NATURE OF THE FREUDIAN EGO

Freud portrayed the ego as "a frontier creature," mediating between "three masters": the "external world," the "libido of the *id*," and the "severity of the super-ego."[39] In a certain sense this complex struggle takes a distilled and concentrated form in the singular struggle between the ego and the super-ego, since the latter is the exponent of both the *id* and the cultural repression of the *id*'s impulses. Therefore this relationship between the ego and the super-ego is of great significance in determining how one conceives of the human being—her freedom and dignity—as a moral agent in the face of these impersonal forces.

Freud explored the phylogenetic emergence of consciousness through what I would describe as a microbiological evolutionary standpoint. The heart of his theory is the notion that adaptive reactions to stimulations impinging on a primordial organism from outside its cortex gave rise to the emergence of differentiated psychological capacities, beginning with a rudimentary form of consciousness. He wrote:

> Let us picture a living organism in its most simplified possible form as an undifferentiated vesicle of a substance that is susceptible to stimulation....It would be easy to suppose, then, that as a result of the ceaseless impact of external stimuli on the surface of the vesicle, its substance to a certain depth may have become permanently modified.[40]

This modified surface, a "crust...thoroughly 'baked through' by stimulation"[41] is nothing other than a rudimentary form of the ego. "The ego is that part of the *id* which has been modified by the direct influence of the external world through the medium of the *Pcpt.-Cs.*; in a sense it is an extension of the surface-differentiation."[42] The purpose of this cortical modification is framed in evolutionary terms, and, as Freud portrayed it, is primarily defensive in nature. I quote at length here because Freudian metatheoretical assumptions relevant to our arguments are contained in this passage:

> This little fragment of living substance [the primal "vesicle" cited above] is suspended in the middle of an external world charged with the most powerful energies; and it would be killed by the stimulation emanating from these if it were not provided with a protective shield against the stimuli. It acquires the shield in this way: its outermost surface ceases to have the structure proper to living matter, becomes to some

degree inorganic and thenceforward functions as a special envelope or membrane resistant to stimuli. In consequence, the energies of the external world are able to pass into the next underlying layers, which have remained living, with only a fragment of their original intensity; and these layers can devote themselves, behind the protective shield, to the reception of the amounts of stimulus which have been allowed through it....*Protection against* stimuli is an almost more important function for the living organism than *reception of* stimuli. The protective shield is supplied with its own store of energy and must above all endeavor to preserve the special mode of transformation of energy operating in it against the effects threatened by the enormous energies at work in the external world—effects which tend toward a leveling out of them and hence toward destruction.[43]

This modified cortex, which will later evolve into the ego, serves to shield against external energies, yet it has no such protective capabilities toward "excitations from *within*...[which] in the deeper layers extend into the system directly and in undiminished amount, in so far as certain of their characteristics give rise to feelings in the pleasure-unpleasure series."[44] This description of the emergence of consciousness results in a portrayal of the human subject that I would describe as a distinctly psychoanalytic version of the Lockean *tabula rasa*. On the surface this comparison may seem erroneous and reflective of a misunderstanding of Freud's location in intellectual history, for psychoanalysis and its dynamic view of the psyche may justifiably be considered the polar opposite of British empiricism.[45] Yet the critical point I am trying to make through this description—the psychoanalytic *ego* as *tabula rasa*—is that within the Freudian framework the ego itself is described as a precipitate and its contents as derivative of atomistic excitations.

These excitations, coming both from the inside and from the outside, were characterized by Freud in impersonal, reflexive terms. For example, Freud wrote, "What consciousness yields consists essentially of perceptions of excitations coming from the external world and of feelings of pleasure and unpleasure which can only arise from within the mental apparatus."[46] The terminology describing the two impinging spheres is of course different— "perceptions of excitations" and "feelings of pleasure and unpleasure"—yet the moral quality of the two realms, both described in naturalistic terms, is similar. Both spheres are devoid of apparent moral character. The resulting disposition of the ego toward the two realms—inner and outer—from which it was derived, was portrayed by Freud as similarly defensive and wholly pragmatic in nature. In this sense, the Freudian ego, serving the adaptive demands of the organism in the face of a hostile environment, may be more precisely termed a *moral tabula rasa*.

FORMATION OF THE PSYCHOANALYTIC SUPER-EGO

The above portrayal of the *ego* as a precipitate of the amoral *id*, interfacing with the impinging external world, provided the basic structural elements for Freud's theory of the formation of conscience. From the very beginning of the ego's development, according to Freud, there is a basic conflict between its own wishes and the imposition of external, heteronomous rules regarding what is considered good and bad.

> We may reject the existence of an original, as it were natural, capacity to distinguish good from bad. What is bad is often not at all what is injurious or dangerous to the ego; on the contrary, it may be something which is desirable and enjoyable to the ego. Here, therefore, there is an extraneous influence at work, and it is this that decides what is to be called good or bad.[47]

This "extraneous influence" is at first, for the young child, localized *objectively* in primary caregivers who come to represent authority, power, and the sustenance of life itself. This "extraneous influence" is *subjectively* experienced as a pervading sense of helplessness before the dangers of the world and a corresponding awareness of dependency on others. This dependency translates into a fear of losing the "love" of those protectors necessary for one's survival. "At the beginning, therefore, what is bad is whatever causes one to be threatened with loss of love."[48] Yet "above all," more significant than even the dread of losing love, is the related fear of punishment from these stronger individuals—punishment for either misdeeds actually done, or such deeds merely considered. Thus love and fear toward the world of external objects motivate the emerging ego to adopt external norms of good and bad.

This first stage of moral development, though certainly accompanied by strong affects, was considered by Freud to exhibit merely a "social anxiety," and not an expression of what he later termed the "super-ego." The emergence of the super-ego, a momentous event for both the individual and culture, constitutes what Freud called the "second stage of development of conscience"[49] and rests on the internalization of moral norms previously experienced as outside, if not alien, to oneself.

The complex psychodynamics that result in the formation of the super-ego may be summarized in the following manner: the most significant object-cathexes for the developing child are, of course, those of the parents (or primary caregivers). The child, from the very emergence of its individual identity,[50] idealizes the parents and imputes to them godlike qualities of power and perfection. The *ego ideal*, that internalized image to which child and adult alike aspire, is the precipitate of these early experiences of the parents' omnipotence and omniscience.[51] As the child develops, it is compelled to relinquish its leading role in the Oedipal drama, because of a growing awareness of the impossibility of fulfilling its imagined program. Concurrent and integral to this process, but pertaining to a wider context, the child is likewise experiencing failures in measuring up to its *ego ideal*. These failures create for the child a conflict, experienced as frustration and lack of conformity with the *reality principle*. This process—the necessary abandonment of the Oedipal drama in conjunction with an increasingly realistic appraisal of one's own disjunction from the *ego ideal*—provides the psychic impetus for a transformation of the relationship with the *parental imagos* from that of *objectification* to that of *identification*. Freud makes the following distinction between the mechanisms of *identification* and *objectification*:

> "identification" [is] the assimilation of one ego to another one, as a result of which the first ego behaves like the second in certain respects, imitates it and in a sense takes it up into

itself....If a boy identifies himself with his father, he wants to *be like* his father; if he [through "objectification"] makes him the object of his choice, he wants to *have* him, to possess him.[52]

According to Freud, the very strength of these earliest of object relations makes their loss most difficult, if not impossible, to accept without some form of compensating relationship. Thus, because the child cannot *have* the parents, it opts to *identify* with them.[53]

> With his abandonment of the Oedipus complex a child must, as we can see, renounce the intense object-cathexes which he has deposited with his parents, and it is as a compensation for this loss of objects that there is such a strong intensification of the identifications with his parents which have probably long been present in his ego.[54]

It is the dynamic of compensation—perhaps an instance of nature abhorring a vacuum—that informs the intense identification with the parental *imagos* and facilitates the formation of the super-ego agency. The heightened identification and corresponding introjection of the Oedipal object relations results in an emergent precipitate attached to, yet structurally distinct from, the ego, that is, the *super-ego*.[55] Although the dynamic of introjecting abandoned object relations is not limited to the Oedipal objects,[56] the super-ego has a special status within the psychic economy because the Oedipal objects are themselves "the most momentous objects" in one's life, and the identification with them occurs when "the ego was still feeble" (and thus presumably more impressionable).[57]

THE SUPER-EGO: OUR HIGHER NATURE AND GUILT

The mechanisms of the formation of the super-ego within the individual were sometimes placed by Freud within a wider context of what he terms "biology and the vicissitudes of the human species."[58] By this he meant the evolutionary processes, constituted by the full range of "natural" forces experienced within an emerging "cultural" context, that shape the development of the human species. When the formation of the super-ego is placed in this broader context, it is seen to signify more than simply a "compulsion to obey" one's parents or a fear of societal recriminations. Rather, the super-ego is, in a roundabout manner, a representative of the instinctual realm. Whereas the ego is "essentially the representative of the external world, of reality," the super-ego is "the representative of the internal world, of the id."[59] The super-ego "is close to the id," "reaches down into the id," and therefore may serve as "its [the id's] representative vis-à-vis the ego."[60] Moreover, because the super-ego is derived from the "first object-cathexes of the id," it is in close proximity to the "phylogenetic acquisitions" of the *id*, and thus may serve as "a reincarnation of former ego-structures which have left their precipitates behind in the id."[61] Through this mechanism the super-ego is expressive of our ancestral experiences that have accrued in the structures of the psyche.

It is this "partnership" with the *id* that informs the "character" of the super-ego, that is, the nature of its functions and the measures it employs to realize its "aims." As Freud portrayed it, our conscience is generally punitive in nature, known to us most often through a sense of guilt: "The super-ego applies the strictest moral standards to the helpless ego which is at its mercy; in general it represents the claims of morality, and we realize all at once that our moral sense of guilt is the expression of the tension between the ego and the super-ego."[62] Yet the super-ego is not limited to generating a bad conscience but is also the basis of what Freud called our "higher natures."[63] By linking the emergence of the super-ego with our "phylogenetic acquisition," psychoanalytic theory attempted to provide an explanatory model through which the "higher nature of man" was accounted for within the framework of a naturalistic ontology. To those critical of psychoanalysis and its apparent negative assessment of human nature—those with "agitated apprehensions as to the whereabouts of the higher side of human life"—Freud rhetorically responded:

> Very true [there is a higher nature], and here we have that higher nature, in this ego ideal or super-ego, the representative of our relation to our parents. When we were little chil-

dren we knew these higher natures, we admired them and feared them; and later we took them into ourselves.[64]

According to Freud, through the formation of the super-ego "the lowest part of the mental life of each of us is changed," or at least transformed, within our conscious awareness and our overt expression, "into what is highest in the human mind by our scale of values." In this manner, what is generally held to be virtuous, even saintly, is in fact an expression of our "archaic heritage."[65] It is the deceptive "foreground" of virtuousness that Freud sought to unmask and expose.

> It is easy to show that the ego ideal answers to everything that is expected of the higher nature of man. As a substitute for a longing for the father, it contains the germ from which all religions have evolved. The self-judgment which declares that the ego falls short of its ideal produces the religious sense of humility to which the believer appeals in his longing. As a child grows up, the role of father is carried on by teachers and others in authority; their injunctions and prohibitions remain powerful in the ego ideal and continue, in the form of conscience, to exercise the moral censorship. The tension between the demands of and the actual performances of the ego is experienced as a sense of guilt. Social feelings rest on identifications with other people, on the basis of having the same ego ideal.[66]

Within this framework the super-ego—as "heir of the Oedipus complex" and "the expression of the most powerful impulses and most important libidinal vicissitudes of the id"[67]— was seen as the animating agency behind a wide range of phenomena. For example, a "normal, conscious sense of guilt (conscience)...is based on the tension between the ego and the ego ideal and is the expression of a condemnation of the ego by its critical agency."[68] Various neurotic conditions were also interpreted as arising through the mechanism of the super-ego exerting control over the conscious personality, for example, a "negative therapeutic reaction," an inferiority complex, an obsessional neurosis, and melancholia.[69] And as described above, psychoanalytic theory discerned in our "higher natures" and "strivings for perfection" the workings of our super-ego.

The punitive, harsh, exacting nature of our super-ego was explained by Freud through the instinct of aggression, or, in its final form, the instinct of death.

> His aggressiveness is introjected, internalized; it is, in point of fact, sent back to where it came from—that is, it is directed towards his own ego. There it is taken over by a portion of the ego, which sets itself up over against the rest of the ego as super-ego, and which now, in the form of "conscience," is ready to put into action against the ego the same harsh aggressiveness that the ego would have liked to satisfy upon other, extraneous individuals.[70]

Freud made the basic observation that the more a person controls their aggressiveness, the "more intense becomes his ideal's inclination to aggressiveness against his ego. It is like a displacement, a turning round upon his own ego."[71]

Freud recognized the need to explain how a process dependent on the identification with the earliest and most significant object relations—that is, the formation of the super-ego—could become so determined by aggression, as opposed to Eros, libido, sexuality. Freud addressed this problem within the context of the dualistic struggle between the erotic and destructive instincts. He claimed that every identification involves a certain "desexualization" or "sublimation." When this "transformation" (i.e., identification) occurs a simultaneous "instinctual defusion" occurs within the erotic component such that it "no longer has the power to bind the whole of the destructiveness that was combined with it, and this is released in the form of an inclination to aggression and destruction."[72] The resulting tension between the aggressive super-ego—the "dictatorial 'Thou shalt'"—and the defensive ego is experienced as guilt and "expresses itself as a need for punishment."[73]

According to Freud, this sense of guilt has two causes and may be stated chronologically to conform with the developmental sequence: at first, the fear of punishment by an external authority for an actual deed; and later, fear of the super-ego for deeds both done and those merely considered. The first of these cases calls for a simple "renunciation of instinctual satisfactions." Yet once the super-ego has been instituted, the individual not only is called to renounce the actual satisfaction, but also is pressed for ongoing punishment "since the continuance of the forbidden wishes cannot be concealed from the super-ego." That is, the super-ego equates "bad intention" with "bad actions."[74]

Freud then made the observation—or, rather, a claim based on the presumption that our "intentions" are apparently constant both in their moral quality and in their opposition to our conscience—that the installation of the super-ego results in a state of chronic self-recrimination. With the "erection" of the super-ego, "instinctual renunciation" no longer liberates; rather, a "threatened external unhappiness—loss of love and punishment on the part of external authority—has been exchanged for a permanent internal unhappiness, for the tension of the sense of guilt."[75]

A distinctly psychoanalytical portrayal of the relationship between the ego and super-ego, or, more exactly, between renunciations of instincts and the phenomena of conscience, emerges out of this understanding. The traditional view of conscience held that conscience was the *cause*, and one's moral renunciations were the *effects*. That is, one's instinctual renunciations were generally understood as the results or effects of one's conscience, informed by the moral code and encouraging individual behavior in conformity with this code. Yet the psychoanalytic model claims that this causal relationship becomes inverted as the super-ego gains strength. "Every renunciation of instinct now becomes a dynamic source of conscience and every fresh renunciation increases the latter's severity and intolerance." In this manner Freud suggested the seemingly paradoxical notion that "conscience is the result of instinctual renunciation, or that instinctual renunciation (imposed on us from without) creates conscience, which then demands further instinctual renunciation."[76]

REVIEW OF THE BASIS OF THE PSYCHOANALYTIC SUPER-EGO

Most basically, the psychoanalytic conscience is conceived as one particular expression of the super-ego. The super-ego, as the agent seeking to realize the ego-ideal,[77] is an exacting master, evoking moral ideals and enforcing their demands through the often persistent goading of symptoms, primarily guilt, but also moral promptings that may appear, superficially, virtuous in nature. In this sense then, the super-ego has a dual nature, both "cruel" and "super moral."[78]

There is, according to Freud, no "original, as it were *natural*, capacity to distinguish good from bad."[79] Rather, the super-ego is a precipitate of the ego as it emerges, adapts, and develops. The ego, seeking to moderate instinctual expression in accord with the reality principle and in conformity with its own ideal, "strives to be moral," and is considered by Freud to be the seat of moral constraints. But invariably the ego fails to attain, and yet desires nonetheless to support, its ego ideal, and thus the super-ego arises with, and is constituted by, the identification of the ego with the Oedipal object relations. These Oedipal object relations are themselves expressions of the most primal of instincts emanating from the *id*. The *id* is conceived as "nonmoral," for it is the source of the instincts themselves, or, rather, it *is* the psychic exponent of a composite of instincts,[80] and seeks to satisfy the "instinctual needs of the subject" in accord with the "pleasure principle."[81] The process of the ego's identification with its Oedipal objects results in the *id*'s aggressive instincts, previously directed at the objects, being turned inward and focused on the ego itself in the form of self-recriminations and feelings of guilt.

The super-ego is understood reductively as a product of both individual and collective developmental, evolutionary dynamics. The regressive nature of Freud's thought—"*the aim of all life is death*"[82]—translated into a conservative view of morality and, specifically, conscience. Our "higher nature" does not reflect a genuine impulse or aspiration on the part of humans to be truly virtuous, but rather deceptively serves the narrow interests of the *id*. Because the *id* is chaotic and amoral, the ego's adaptive attitude toward it is one of control and the imposition of regulating order. The moral life thus consists in the strengthening of one's reason and analytical insight, and the effective application of these insights to one's conduct. Morality, in sum, is a matter of instinctual control.[83]

PSYCHOANALYTIC PRACTICE AND THE REVISIONING OF THE SUPER-EGO

On the surface one may conclude that the reductive methods of psychoanalysis would support the notion of conscience as solely reflecting the biologically driven internalization of social *mores*. Yet the impact of depth psychology, and in particular its clinical practice, on moral theory has in fact been complex and potentially subversive of the "modern" notion of conscience. Freudian theory and practice advance certain claims regarding psychodynamics and structures that have a direct bearing on one's understanding of moral agency. It is possible that concepts derived from the field of depth psychology may serve as a resource for a revival of the traditional notion of conscience, though now modified and qualified through alternative psychological models and expressed through the language of critical epistemology. Weiner develops the argument that if we successfully challenge the root psychoanalytic assumption that the *id* and the instincts that comprise it are chaotic and amoral, then the superstructure built on this foundation could take a very different turn. It is just such a "turn" that I will attempt to develop in the remainder of this study. But before doing so I will outline Weiner's arguments regarding both the positive contributions and theoretical constraints of psychoanalysis.

Weiner frames his discussion of conscience by distinguishing between what he terms the "traditional" conscience, and the "modern" variant of conscience. In short, the traditional conscience is compatible with a therapeutic, or transformational view of ethics. It is an ethics less concerned with obedience to laws than with the moral state of the agent. Overt behavior is of secondary importance compared to the nature of the motivation underlying one's actions. For example, being a truly generous person is not to be equated with simply giving alms. Therapeutic ethics has as its goal the transformation of the subject so that one may be, insofar as it is humanly possible, both good and happy in a harmonious whole. In contrast to this transformational view of ethics and the traditional conscience that supports it, there is another significant strain of Western moral tradition—the "legalistic tradition" and the "modern" variant of conscience—

that stresses conformity to laws rather than the development of virtue. Elements of the Hebrew scriptures and the Stoic tradition, social contract theory, and duty-bound Kantian theory fit this description. Yet, Weiner adds:

> The truly modern variant of it [legalistic ethics] can be said to begin when, in the name of a principled and consistent empiricism, the possibility of a hidden, morally ordered, happiness-bearing human nature is no longer taken seriously. It begins when, without apology or reluctance, the natural, the normal, and the average are taken to be the same, and when, consequently, the nature of human desire is felt to be exactly what it seems to be—at best a confusing mixture of good and bad without moral rhyme or reason, and at worst a wild and violent thing—disordered, self-destructive, cruel and bloody, held in check only by the fear of punishment.[84]

Weiner observes that this "modern attitude" emerged not as a result of a change in human nature, nor through enhanced observational capabilities of what had once been obscure—indeed, "the unhappy facts were always known"—but, rather, it reflected a new interpretive "paradigm." This new framework, as the previous passage conveys, is predicated on a very definite portrayal of the interior life. Specifically, it is based on one's felt desires as having no inherent relationship to the moral dimension of one's life, other than that which is subsequently imputed to them or, often, denied them. That is, the "modern attitude" conceives of human desires as expressions of amoral instincts, that is, instincts that reflect, express, or embody nothing other than the basic physiological functions that they ostensibly serve. In this manner, human desires are depersonalized; that is, desires are severed from both moral claims and moral obligations. While on one hand this objectification may rationally liberate one from the claims of biology, it may also alienate one from a sense of natural purpose and cast doubt in the mind about the nature of any passionate desire or "quest" one believes oneself to be pursuing. When "laws of nature," and the related laws of one's being, are believed to be without moral basis, then "it becomes necessary to build one's ethics on some other foundation."[85]

Weiner describes how this has happened in the history of the West. Natural law theories were closely associated with notions of "health" as a primary and natural good, and "virtues" as primary expressions of "moral health." "Health" was considered "the clearest possible example of fulfilled natural purpose." The concept of "health" thus served to bridge the gap between fact and value within this moral tradition.[86] Yet variants of natural law theory (broadly defined) have been steadily supplanted by narrowly conceived rational theories that refuted claims of "natural goods." "It appears that one or another variant on the medical model [i.e., "health" conceived as a, or *the*, natural good] held general sway until the scientific revolution accustomed people to the artifice of a nonteleological anthropology."[87]

Within this "modern" sensibility "the idea of healthy behavior seemed [merely] metaphorical." At the heart of this modern attitude is the reductive causalism that I critiqued throughout part 1 of this study. And, as I have outlined earlier in this chapter, Freud's super-ego may be seen as an exponent of this "modern" anthropology. Yet, Weiner claims, the theorizing and modeling of the psyche undertaken by Freud and other depth psychologists— guided and informed by the practical imperative of healing mental illness—may serve an unexpected role in providing new plausibility structures and enriched interpretations of the traditional notion of conscience.[88]

Weiner believes that, contrary to the common view of psychoanalysis as pure proponent of this modern attitude, "Freud and his humanistic followers were step by halting, unintentional step, renewing in modern form the most ancient foundation of ethics."[89] That is, psychoanalytic practice contradicts psychoanalytic theory such that it may provide resources for a constructive moral psychology. By "ancient foundation" Weiner means several things. First, he refers to an anthropology in which the teleology of "health" provides a natural good, sufficiently meaningful within any relevant context: "If there is any value that can be described as natural, surely it is health."[90] Weiner claims that through the "semiscientific language" of psychotherapy, in pursuit of mental health, "many elements of the old teleology have re-emerged, at least at a semipopular level," and that "the language of therapy has to a large extent taken over the language of virtue."[91]

Second, by "ancient foundation" he refers to an anthropology based on a complex notion of the self that allows for internal conflict and self-deception—as well as the possibility of unknown structures of order and harmony. And, Weiner continues, it is precisely the findings of depth psychology, through its concern for the repressed and the not-yet, the background and the underground, that have advanced the notion of a complex self or, as he phrases it, "the notion of a hidden structure of the soul (the unconscious), a structure that humanistic psychology has suggested might yet be a harmony."

Weiner concludes that the theoretical elements for a revival of the traditional sense of conscience have been provided by psychoanalytic practice. At its most basic level, a viable notion of conscience in the "traditional sense" requires that there be (1) some meaningful notion of responsible moral agency, (2) that "moral goods" may in some manner be said to be real, and (3) that these moral goods may be understood as discernible in part through the cooperation of an inward faculty, or inner processes, outside of normal consciousness. Each of these three factors—responsibility implying a human will, moral goods positing an aim, and discernment providing requisite knowledge—is necessary for conscience to be meaningful as a palpable experience of the most urgent and vital concern.

In Weiner's view, the historical development of these basic concepts in the direction of the Freudian super-ego is a result of a very specific, and unnecessary, portrayal of the informing instincts themselves. Weiner argues that we may accept Freudian moral theory as contingently valid, that is, acceptable as a regional ontology and thus adequate for specific cases, combined with the recognition that a more comprehensive and adequate model may be built upon select elements of its theoretical foundation. I quote at length his summation of the Freudian viewpoint, which will provide a transition to our exploration of how a very different model of conscience may be developed employing Jung's conception of the unconscious and the instincts.

Now, the Freudian superego most certainly is an example of the modern notion of conscience. Indeed, everyone must acknowledge that there is a kind of guilt that stems from childhood subservience to authority, but there is no danger to the traditional theory in the reification of the superego as the locus of that particular species of guilt. The problem lies in the second point (the amorality of instinct), and it quickly vanishes if one merely replaces the (entirely unempirical) Freudian theory of instinct with the one advocated here. Then instinct has sufficient moral content to constitute the ground of the traditional voice of conscience, and also sufficient ambivalence and vagueness to explain the obscurity of that voice.[92]

THE JUNGIAN CONSCIENCE: BASIC STRUCTURAL MODEL

When tracing the roots of Freud's theory of the super-ego I began with an examination of his hypothesis regarding the ego's formation. Then, as I followed the sequencing of Freud's own reasoning, I considered his representation of the *id* out of which the psychoanalytic ego emerged. This examination of the *id* brought me to the seminal foundation of Freud's theory of conscience. In a parallel manner, in order adequately to grasp Jung's conception of conscience, I will need to follow the logical thread backward into Jung's foundational principles. I will first discuss the nature of the Jungian unconscious and its conscious exponent, the ego. I will then explore the dynamic relationship that exists between these two most basic of psychic structures, for it is in the context of this dynamic relationship that Jung understood the manifestations of conscience. Or, rather, conscience is one form of this dialectical relationship.

Unlike the Freudian ego, which is at least in part unconscious and is largely defined in terms of its structural relationships and dynamic functions, the Jungian ego is defined by its relationship to consciousness. Jung wrote, "We understand the ego as the complex factor to which all conscious contents are related. It forms, as it were, the centre of the field of consciousness…[and] the relation of a psychic content to the ego forms the criterion of its consciousness, for no content can be conscious unless it is represented to a subject."[93] This ego subject "appears to possess a high degree of continuity and identity"[94] and, "in so far as this comprises the empirical personality, the ego is the subject of all personal acts of consciousness."[95]

The ego is "acquired, empirically speaking, during the individual's lifetime. It seems to arise in the first place from the collision between the somatic factor and the environment, and, once established as a subject, it goes on developing from further collisions with the outer world and the inner."[96] This depiction—with the exception of the implied meaning contained in Jung's qualifying phrase "empirically speaking"—is in basic agreement with the psychoanalytic model. Yet a critical distinction was made when Jung described the inner world upon which the ego "rests" as having *both* somatic and psychic bases that consist of stimuli of which one may or may not be conscious.[97] The distinction between somatic and psychic, and the inclusion of both in the foundation of the ego, reflects Jung's aversion to reductive materialism, and provided him with the conceptual means to articulate his viewpoint. By using the term *rests* Jung was suggesting a relationship wherein the ego is both informed and limited by, but does not consist of, these somatic and psychic factors.[98] In this manner, then, the ego is defined by consciousness and yet is related to that which is unconscious. Jung described the *somatic basis* of the ego as follows:

> The somatic basis is inferred from the totality of endosomatic perceptions, which for their part are already of a psychic nature and are associated with the ego, and are therefore conscious. They are produced by endosomatic stimuli, only some of which cross the threshold of consciousness. A considerable proportion of these stimuli occur unconsciously, that is, subliminally. The fact that they are subliminal does not necessarily mean that their status is merely physiological, any more than this would be true of a psychic content. Sometimes they are capable of crossing the threshold, that is, of becoming perceptions. But there is no doubt that a large proportion of these endosomatic stimuli are simply incapable

of consciousness and are so elementary that there is no reason to assign them a psychic nature.[99]

And as the somatic basis is comprised of factors of which we
are both conscious and unconscious, so too is the *psychic basis* of
the ego only partly conscious:

> On the one hand the ego rests on the *total field of consciousness*,
> and on the other, on the *sum total of unconscious contents*.
> These [i.e., unconscious or "subliminal" contents] fall into
> three groups: first, temporarily subliminal contents that can
> be reproduced voluntarily (memory); second, unconscious
> contents that cannot be reproduced voluntarily; third, con-
> tents that are not [currently] capable of becoming conscious
> at all. Group two can be inferred from the spontaneous
> irruption of subliminal contents into consciousness. Group
> three is hypothetical; it is a logical inference from the facts
> underlying group two. It contains contents which have *not yet*
> irrupted into consciousness, or which never will.[100]

Several points warrant emphasis. First, the Jungian ego
stands in an inseparable, symbiotic relationship to the body, such
that the boundary between the physiological and the psychic is
not precise but rather a living continuum. Further, Jung claimed
that the unconscious psychic basis of the ego is comprised of more
than repressed or forgotten contents (the "second group"), but in
fact includes a "third group" that he calls the "not yet" or "never
will be" conscious. This claim that there is a generative nature to
certain unconscious contents was at the core of Jung's portrayal of
the psyche. "Although it is a not unimportant fact that man evades
everything unpleasant, and therefore gladly forgets whatever does
not suit him, it nevertheless seems to me far more important to
find out what really constitutes the *positive* activity of the unconscious."[101]

While Jung described the ego as "never more and never less
than consciousness as a whole," it is not superfluous to emphasize
that this does not mean that the psyche itself is never more and
never less than consciousness. Jung himself felt compelled to make
this point repeatedly in the face of rationalist opposition to
acknowledging the reality of the unconscious and the correspon-

ding relativity of the ego. As the passage above portrays, Jung stressed that conscious contents comprise only a portion of the psyche's totality. "Clearly, then, *the personality as a total phenomenon* does not coincide with the ego, that is, with the conscious personality, but forms an entity that has to be distinguished from the ego." Jung called this "total personality" the *"self."* The relationship of the ego to the self is that of a "part to the whole," as "the moved to the mover," and "as object to subject."[102] In fact, "the self, like the unconscious, is an *a priori* existent out of which the ego evolves. It is, so to speak, an unconscious prefiguration of the ego."[103]

These quotations may suggest an ego that is lacking in autonomy, epiphenomenal to the point of lacking genuine agency and significance, and determined such that moral responsibility is absent. But these citations represent only "half the psychological truth" as Jung saw it.

> If it [the predetermined ego] were the whole truth it would be tantamount to determinism, for if man were merely a creature that came into being as a result of something already existing unconsciously, he would have no freedom and there would be no point in consciousness. Psychology must reckon with the fact that despite the causal nexus man does enjoy a feeling of freedom, which is identical with autonomy of consciousness. However much the ego can be proved to be dependent and preconditioned, it cannot be convinced that it has no freedom.…By stating these facts we have, it is true, established an antinomy, but we have at the same time given a picture of things as they are.[104]

While acknowledging the logical antinomy, elsewhere Jung sought to avoid philosophical conundrums by adopting a phenomenological stance. "Inside the field of consciousness it [the ego] has, as we say, free will. By this I do not mean anything philosophical, only the well-known psychological fact of 'free choice,' or rather the subjective feeling of freedom." Yet this feeling (and exercise) of freedom is constrained through our encounters with the necessities and vicissitudes of the external world, as well as "limits" encountered "outside the field of consciousness in the subjective inner world, where it comes into conflict with the facts of the self."[105] One of these "facts of the self" is conscience.

Jung describes conscience as "a special instance" of the "transcendent function."[106] By "transcendent" Jung means nothing metaphysical but rather a "crossing over" or "connecting" of previously separated factors. In the course of individuation, the transcendent function "facilitates a transition from one attitude to another,"[107] achieved through the "discursive co-operation of conscious and unconscious factors."[108] It enables individuation by "bridging the yawning gulf between conscious and unconscious" factors, between the "real and 'imaginary,' or rational and irrational data."[109] The transcendent function both arises from, and results in a reduction of, the "tension of opposites" in the psyche. It is "a natural process, a manifestation of the energy that springs from the tension of opposites," that "creates individual lines of development which could never be reached by keeping to the path prescribed by collective norms."[110] As discussed in chapter 3, the "tension of opposites," as I broadly defined it, refers to "the insistent demand of the psyche as a whole to impel the conscious mind toward a recognition and integration of previously unrecognized, undeveloped, and even denigrated parts of one's own personality."[111] As a particular instance of the transcendent function, conscience exemplifies this experience of the "opposites."

> There is scarcely any other psychic phenomenon that shows the polarity of the psyche in a clearer light than conscience. Its undoubted dynamism, in order to be understood at all, can only be explained in terms of energy, that is, as a potential based on opposites. Conscience brings these ever-present and necessary opposites to conscious perception.[112]

The "transcendent function"—a "discursive cooperation of unconscious and conscious factors"—is integral to, if not synonymous with, Jung's portrayal of the psychodynamics of individuation. Indeed, the cumulative effect of the "transcendent function" may be nothing less than altering one's basic self-identity and conscious attitude toward the external world and one's own self. It is Jung's distinct portrayal of the unconscious, as generative matrix, that makes intelligible his claims that positive, expansive transformations of the personality may be realized through such "discursive cooperation." Jung, as with other key concepts of his psychology, developed a complex and nuanced portrayal of the unconscious that was marked by both similarities and crucial distinctions relative to other competing theories. In broad agreement with psychoanalytic theory, Jung clearly understood and asserted that the unconscious psyche bears the distinct marks of humanity's natural history. Responding to those who would see the psyche in idealistic, ahistorical, or overly rational terms—as a *tabula rasa* of one form or another—he asked rhetorically, "Why should we assume, then, that man is the only living being deprived of specific instincts, or that his psyche is devoid of all traces of evolution?"[113] For Jung the answer was that the human psyche *is* in fact instinctive. Yet, in fundamental contrast to the theories of psychoanalysis and evolutionary psychology, Jung argued that the instinctual manifestations of the unconscious are not properly understood as being ultimately reducible to the purely physiological. That is, both mind and body are informed and animated by instincts, and, conversely, psyche and soma each give their particular expression to instincts.

As outlined in chapter 2, Jung attempted to articulate a "third way" that recognized the substantial reality of both psychic and physical processes.[114] This holistic viewpoint enabled Jung to include certain basic psychic processes in his notion of what is to be considered "instinctive." Yes, Jung acknowledged, "instincts are physiological urges, and are perceived by the senses." Yet "at the same time they [the instincts] also manifest themselves in fantasies and often reveal their presence only by symbolic images. These manifestations are what I call the archetypes."[115]

The archetype itself is, by Jung's definition, unconscious and is known indirectly through its manifestations and influences. The archetype may manifest, stated simply, as a "collective thought pattern"[116] or an "instinctive trend" as basic as "the impulse of birds to build nests, or ants to form organized colonies."[117] Archetypes are not personally acquired, but rather are innate and inherited.[118] Jung explained the archetype in the following manner:

The concept of the archetype has been misunderstood so often that one can hardly mention it without having to explain it anew each time. It is derived from the repeated observation that, for instance, the myths and fairytales of world literature contain definite motifs, which crop up everywhere. We meet the same motifs in the fantasies, dreams, deliriums, and delusions of individuals living today. These typical images and associations are what I call archetypal ideas. The more vivid they are, the more they will be coloured by particularly strong feeling-tones. This accentuation gives them a special dynamism in our psychic life. They impress, influence, and fascinate us. They have their origin in the archetype, which in itself is an irrepresentable, unconscious, pre-existent form that seems to be part of the inherited structure of the psyche and can therefore manifest itself spontaneously anywhere, at any time. Because of its instinctual nature, the archetype underlies the feeling-toned complexes and shares their autonomy.[119]

The archetypes comprise the operative structural elements of what Jung called the *collective unconscious*, which, within his framework, is distinct from the *personal unconscious*. This distinction is important, for it speaks directly to the question of whether the deep unconscious may somehow be seen as intelligible and as a source of nonegoistic knowledge—knowledge such as that which conscience has traditionally been understood to convey. For Jung, the personal unconscious was comprised of materials that are "of a personal nature in so far as they have the character partly of acquisitions derived from the individual's life and partly of physiological factors which could just as well be conscious." If one looks backwards into the development of consciousness, one sees that this "personal layer ends at the earliest memories of infancy." Before that, prior to this personal layer, is the collective unconscious that "comprises the pre-infantile period, that is, the residues of ancestral life."[120] These "residues" are precisely the "primordial ideas," or the archetypes.[121]

The question may be asked how Jung's archetypal stratum compares to the Freudian *id*, since, topographically, the two spheres are roughly analogous, falling just below the personal unconscious and the preconscious, respectively. Asking this question may clarify wherein lie the actual points of division between Freudian and Jungian theory. Not surprisingly, both theorists tended to paint the other in extreme terms that tended to distort or, at least, to not encourage mutual understanding. For instance, Jung wrote,[122]

> In Freud's view, as most people know, the contents of the unconscious are reducible to infantile tendencies which are repressed because of their incompatible character. Repression is a process that begins in early childhood under the moral influence of the environment and continues throughout life. By means of analysis the repressions are removed and the repressed wishes made conscious again. Theoretically the unconscious would thus find itself emptied and, so to speak, done away with.[123]

In this portrayal, Jung acknowledged the inclusion of "infantile tendencies" in psychoanalytic theory yet emphasized the dynamic of repression and its central role in providing content to the unconscious. Jung's conclusion about being able to "empty" the unconscious does not, however, seem consistent with his recognition of the "infantile tendencies" which "continue right into old age."[124] Jung continued this presentation of the psychoanalytic unconscious in the following paragraph, where he began to advance his own positive theory, stating:

> Although from one point of view the infantile tendencies of the unconscious are the most conspicuous, it would none the less be a mistake to define or evaluate the unconscious entirely in these terms. The unconscious has still another side to it: it includes not only repressed contents, but also all psychic material that lies below the threshold of consciousness.[125]

This "other side" of the unconscious would be the Jungian collective unconscious, which, it is implied, is missing from Freudian theory. Jung often spoke of the collective unconscious as if it had no structural counterpart in psychoanalytic theory—as if his concept represented the discovery and announcement of a *terra incognito*. While in fact Jung was making a fundamental break from Freudian thought in his articulation of the concept of the collective unconscious, I feel that his presentation misrepresented Freud's thought and thus confused important theoretical issues.

While in fact there are real and significant differences between the two schools of thought, the way to illuminate the differences is not to present an absolute choice between a supposedly Darwinian-based science and a purportedly mystically driven spirituality. This choice is false in that it misrepresents the underlying issues. Regarding the present problem, I believe the real questions are not, Is there a collective unconscious? or Are there archetypes? Nor is the question, Are we instinctive creatures? The answer to all of these is yes. Rather, the real questions regarding the depths of the human psyche are, What is the nature of our instincts? and How do these instincts manifest themselves psychically?

I say these are the real questions because they admit of common discourse across schools of thought and thus offer the possibility of fruitful dialogue. These questions—focusing on how one understands instincts—also ground the conversation in an embodied phenomenology and away from the conceptual abstractions of the *id* and the collective unconscious. By saying this I do not mean to suggest that these abstractions are not highly significant. In fact I think they are, for they represent metaphors for primal conceptions of the ground of reality. There *is* a real choice here. But I likewise hold that one's commitment to a singular, guiding metaphor should come as a conclusion and not an initial point of argumentation. By focusing on the conception of instincts—and *not* theoretical superstructures—one may remain open to the phenomena themselves, thereby facilitating a flexible, evolving understanding of the theoretical choices before oneself. It is for this reason that I have emphasized throughout this work the way in which Jung *is* grounded in an evolutionary viewpoint, and how this is compatible with his conviction regarding the essential reality of the psyche.

JUNG, INSTINCTS, AND THE COLLECTIVE PSYCHE

Both Freud and Jung incorporated within their own distinctive theories the notion of an inherited, genetic foundation of the human species. Within both psychological models this inherited, instinctual substrate continues to animate the psyche throughout the whole of one's life. The critical difference, however, lies in the way the two theorists answered the final question asked above: How do these instincts manifest themselves psychically?

Freud held that the "first psychical expressions" (in "forms unknown") occur within the *id*, arising from the instincts, which in turn "originate from the somatic organization."[126] As earlier discussed, Freud conceived of the instincts as chaotic, amoral, conflicted, and governed by the pleasure principle.[127] Order, rationality, judgment, and logic are all properties of consciousness alone. To impute these properties, and other so-called virtues of our "higher nature," to any realm of existence outside of consciousness and its by-products was, for Freud, to engage in fanciful, if not infantile, projection.[128]

Jung, however, portrayed the character of the instinctive energies that inform and, in some sense, constitute the psyche in terms very different from psychoanalysis. This had a direct and radical impact on Jung's conceptualization of conscience. Within the Jungian framework an instinct was defined as "an *impulsion* towards certain activities."[129] It is through the archetypes of the collective unconscious that the instincts impel our psychic activity within definite forms and dynamics that, as Jung claimed, resist reductive interpretation. Jung claimed that reductive theories "break down at the point where the dream symbols [and other unconscious products] can no longer be reduced to personal reminiscences or aspirations, that is, when the images of the collective unconscious begin to appear."[130] Jung held that if one interpreted certain psychic material in purely personalistic (i.e., reductive) terms, the phenomena were distorted and the meaning lost.

> I had first to come to the fundamental realization that analysis, in so far as it is reduction and nothing more, must necessarily be followed by synthesis, and that certain kinds of psychic material mean next to nothing if simply broken down, but display a wealth of meaning if, instead of being broken down, that meaning is reinforced and extended by all the conscious means at our disposal—by the so-called method of amplification.[131]

As discussed in chapter 3, Jung believed that the "final point of view" was a necessary complement to the reductive perspective, and it is through the dynamism of the archetypes that we experience the purposeful nature of the unconscious psyche. "Archetypal forms are not just static patterns. They are dynamic factors that manifest themselves in impulses, just as spontaneously as the instincts."[132] The archetypes inform one's sense of imaginative narrative, symbolic import, and creative impulse—in short, a sense of direction and meaning.

THE JUNGIAN UNCONSCIOUS

This formal and dynamic nature of the archetypes yields a very different picture of the unconscious from that of psychoanalysis with direct implications for one's understanding of conscience. Two basic differences distinguish the Jungian unconscious from that of psychoanalysis. First, the unconscious has a creative dimension to it. Second, the unconscious is not portrayed as chaotic, but rather as a source of order. Regarding the creative aspect of the unconscious, Jung wrote that "the unconscious is no mere depository of the past, but is also full of germs of future psychic situations and ideas," and "in addition to memories from a long-distant conscious past, completely new thoughts and creative ideas can also present themselves from the unconscious—thoughts and ideas that have never been conscious before."[133] Jung contrasted this view with that of Freud's in the following manner:

> From this point of view [Freudian] unconscious psychic activity, or what we call the unconscious, appears chiefly as a receptacle of all those contents that are antipathetic to consciousness, as well as of all forgotten impressions. On the other hand, one cannot close one's eyes to the fact that these same incompatible contents derive from unconscious instincts, which means that the unconscious is not just a receptacle but is the matrix of the very things that the conscious mind would like to be rid of. We can go a step further and say that the unconscious actually creates *new* contents. Everything that the human mind has ever created sprang

from contents which, in the last analysis, existed once as unconscious seeds. While Freud lays special emphasis on the first aspect, I have stressed the latter, without denying the first. From this point of view the unconscious appears as the totality of all psychic contents *in statu nascendi.*[134]

This creative dimension of the unconscious was understood by Jung to be the transformative source that both broke down old psychic structures and created new forms and order:

> By acknowledging the reality of the psyche and making it a co-determining factor in our lives, we offend against the spirit of convention which for centuries has regulated psychic life from outside by means of institutions as well as by reason. Not that unreasoning instinct rebels of itself against firmly established order; by the strict logic of its own inner laws it is itself of the firmest structure imaginable and, in addition, the creative foundation of all binding order. But just because this foundation is creative, all order which proceeds from it—even in its most "divine" form—is a phase, a stepping stone.[135]

By describing the unconscious in creative and ordering terms, Jung was *not* suggesting that the unconscious psyche is somehow of the same nature as our consciousness. Nor did he naively suggest that the unconscious is "moral" as the term is normally understood. Rather, he recognized the significant qualitative and operative differences between the conscious and unconscious components of the personality. For example, Jung observed:

> The subliminal [i.e., unconscious] state retains ideas and images at a much lower level of tension than they possess in consciousness. In the subliminal condition they lose clarity of definition; the relations between them are less consequential and more vaguely analogous, less rational and therefore more "incomprehensible."[136]

Jung described the operative differences between consciousness and the unconscious in the following manner:

> In fact, the unconscious seems to be able to examine and to draw conclusions from facts, much as consciousness does.

But as far as one can tell from dreams, the unconscious makes its deliberations instinctively. The distinction is important. Logical analysis is the prerogative of consciousness; we select with reason and knowledge. The unconscious, however, seems to be guided chiefly by instinctive trends, represented by corresponding thought forms—that is, by the archetypes.[137]

This view of the nature of the unconscious informed Jung's attitude toward its manifestations. Rather than view unconscious products as deliberately deceptive, he instead put the onus on consciousness to attempt to discern the peculiar language and symbolism of the unconscious. For example:

The form that dreams take is natural to the unconscious because the material from which they are produced is retained in the subliminal state.... Dreams do not guard sleep from what Freud called the "incompatible wish." What he called "disguise" is actually the shape all impulses naturally take in the unconscious.[138]

These descriptions present unconscious processes as distinct from, yet in some ways analogous to, consciousness. Most significant, however, is the fact that Jung perceived in unconscious manifestations something recognizably intelligible and not devoid of what we might call "human concerns." That is, unconscious processes may seem, particularly when taken as a whole, intentional in a manner that suggests or parallels one's own conscious concerns, conveyed in the manner and quality of experience described above. Therefore, basic to Jung's interpretive approach to the unconscious was the conviction that a "reductive approach" is inadequate if one is to prehend the full significance of unconscious phenomena. By "reductive approach" Jung meant "a method of psychological interpretation which regards the unconscious product not as a *symbol* but *semiotically*, as a *sign*, or *symptom* of an underlying process."[139] Reduction "leads back to the primitive and elementary."[140] This method has a "disintegrative effect on the real significance of the unconscious product, since this is either traced back to its historical antecedents and thereby annihilated, or integrated once again with the same elementary processes from which it arose."[141] Jung recognized that dreams or any other product of the unconscious *could be* employed reductively to "free associate" one's way back to neurotic complexes.[142] But simply that one *can* discover pathogenic effects through hindsight exploration does not prove that the primary significance of unconscious phenomena is in the role of symptom to a recollected trauma.

Jung eschewed the exclusive use of reductive analysis, seeking instead something "more far-reaching than the discovery of complexes," that is, "to know and understand the psychic life-process of an individual's whole personality."[143] Such a pursuit required a method other than the reductive alone, namely, the "constructive method." The "constructive method is concerned with the elaboration of the products of the unconscious (dreams, fantasies, etc.). It takes the unconscious product as a symbolic expression which anticipates a coming phase of psychological development."[144] The constructive method "tries to synthesize, to build up, to direct one's gaze forward."[145] The rationale for this approach, based on an "energic" conception of the psyche, are empirical, epistemological, and practical in nature, as outlined in chapter 3.

Jung considered both the constructive and reductive approaches as appropriate to particular circumstances. Generally, the neuroses of the young are most amenable to treatment via reduction, where the maladjustment is a case of "illusions, fictions, and exaggerated attitudes."[146] And, conversely, the constructive, or synthetic, approach is most often appropriate with adults whose current task is not that of liberation from historical influence but rather the apprehension of one's own meaning. Jung stated that he often commenced clinical treatment with a reductive approach, but would turn toward synthesis when nonpersonal, that is, archetypal, imagery began to appear in the dreams and fantasies of his patients—imagery not to be reduced to merely "personal reminiscences or aspirations."[147]

REDUCTIVE AND CONSTRUCTIVE
METHODS OF INTERPRETING CONSCIENCE

This question of whether one interprets the products of the unconscious reductively or constructively has a direct and central bearing on one's understanding of conscience. Jung, in a 1951 essay, "Fundamental Questions of Psychotherapy," explicitly relates the issues of psychopathology and interpretive procedures to that of morality in the following manner. Jung recognized the ubiquitous presence of socially inculcated moral norms, comparing and relating the factors comprising the "super-ego" to the "collective representations" of Lucien Lévy-Bruhl. "What Freud calls the super-ego is the operation of a complex which from ancient times has found expression in the moral code."[148] Jung described the "super-ego" as "another psychic system within us" that "governs and moulds our lives," and which is constituted by the "general beliefs, views, and ethical values in accordance with which we are brought up and by which we make our way in the world." This super-ego "intervenes almost automatically in all our acts of choice and decision," and, "with a little reflection we can practically always tell why we do something and on what general assumptions our judgments and decisions are based." If one is able to "live with these [moral] premises without friction" one will be able to fit and function smoothly within society.[149]

This much is compatible with Freud's own thinking. Yet Jung believed that a more complex model of conscience and moral theory was needed. He illustrated this thinking by claiming that there are two basic types of neuroses—analogous, as I will discuss, to two types of conscience—that may emerge as a result of, or at least in connection with, a conflict with society's morals. Jung's observations, discussed below, are interesting not only because they emphasized the significant role that the moral factor plays in mental health, but, more importantly, because they illuminated the fact that moral conflicts—and the attendant promptings of conscience—take different forms and require a differentiated discernment dependent on individual circumstances. In short, the concept of a socially inculcated super-ego, though an adequate heuristic device much of the time, may require supplementation in order for a more adequate picture of conscience to emerge.

Jung observed that "when an individual ceases to conform to the canon of collective ideas, he will very likely find himself not only in conflict with society, but in disharmony with himself, since the super-ego represents another psychic system within him. In that case he will become neurotic."[150] In such cases, where the maladjustment is a result of some personal "anomaly" or "weakness" ("congenital or acquired"), issuing in a fallacious attitude that promotes poor judgment and erroneous beliefs, a personalistic interpretation is sufficient. That is, a cure is effected through the "demolition of the subject's false conclusions and wrong decisions," and *not* a critical alteration of relevant moral principles or "collective representations."[151] In such cases the super-ego may be expected to promote society's norms and interests, and adaptation to its promptings is conducive to mental health. Jung termed this form of conscience the "moral" conscience.

However, a second type of neurosis may arise, also related to a conflict with society's norms, and which has broad implications for the way we may understand the varied expressions of conscience. Jung described in the following passage this second type of neurotic conflict.

> The second type [of neurotic person] is represented by individuals who *could* be adjusted without too much difficulty, and who have also proved their aptitude for it. But for some reason or other they cannot or will not adjust themselves, and they do not understand why their own particular "adjustment" does not make normal life possible for them, when in their estimation such a life should be well within the bounds of possibility. The reason for their neurosis seems to lie in their having something above average, an overplus for which there is no adequate outlet. We may then expect the patient to be consciously or—in most cases—unconsciously critical of the generally accepted views and ideas.[152]

The conflict in this second type of neurosis, as Jung described it, is at its core related to the process of individuation (in contrast to an individualistic rejection of collective norms).[153]

That is, this second type of neurotic conflict is best understood in a constructive manner, as arising from the conscious mind's attempt to conform to *both* societal standards and the unconsciously animated urge to individuate. In this form of neurosis the societal norms are largely conscious, and it is one's criticisms of these norms, at least initially, that are largely unconscious. These critical reflections and judgments, and a corresponding devotion to another moral good (i.e., following one's vocation), however vague and inchoate this other "good" may initially be, constitute the dynamic content of conscience in this form of conflict. In these cases conscience is experienced as a "conflict of duties," that is, a conflict of loyalties to the established norms of society and the inner impulses of individuation (itself a moral good). As earlier discussed, Jung argued that ultimately the process of individuation is conducive to the social welfare, yet initially the course of individuation often requires a violation of collective expectations, standards, and *mores*. It is in the context of a "conflict of duties" that the "ethical conscience" may manifest. Jung distinguished the "ethical conscience" from the "moral conscience" in the following manner:

> In the great majority of cases conscience signifies primarily the reaction to a real or supposed deviation from the moral code, and is for the most part identical with the primitive fear of anything unusual, not customary, and hence "immoral." As this behavior is instinctive and, at best, only partly the result of reflection, it may be "moral" but can raise no claim to being *ethical*. It deserves this qualification only when it is reflective, when it is subjected to conscious scrutiny. And this happens only when a fundamental doubt arises as between two possible modes of moral behavior, that is to say in a conflict of duty.[154]

This distinction brings to light the fact that the heeding of the "ethical conscience" almost always requires a violation of, or at least relativization of one's tribal *mores*, that is, the super-ego, the moral conscience, the canon of collective ideas, and so on. Jung observed that "individuation is always to some extent opposed to collective norms, since it means separation and differentiation from the general and a building up of the particular—not a particularity that is *sought out*, but one that is already ingrained in the psychic constitution." The conflicts that do arise between the collective norm and the person pursuing, or yielding to, the course of individuation were seen by Jung to be "only apparent," that is, not "*antagonistic* to it [i.e., the norm], but only *differently oriented*."[155] By arguing for the existence of an "ethical" conscience that supersedes the merely "moral" conscience, Jung was arguing for an enlargement of both the moral context in which one's conscience applies and the human responsibility to listen to the "voice" that speaks for this larger framework.

REVIEW OF THE BASIS OF THE JUNGIAN CONSCIENCE

I have argued that both psychoanalysis and Jungian theory were developed upon a definite conception of the nature of human instincts. Freud, in accord with the reductive materialism of his era, conceived of instincts in physiological terms. In contrast, Jung argued for a conception of instincts that included psychic manifestations. That is, he held that the psyche is "a natural organ,"[156] and that it is structured and impelled by instinctive properties as much as any other component of the human person. Jung used the term *archetypes* to describe the ordering and dynamic properties of the instincts as expressed psychically. The symbolic manifestations of the archetypes were called by Jung "images of instincts."[157] Taken together, the instincts and archetypes "form the 'collective unconscious.'" Jung called it "'collective' because, unlike the personal unconscious, it is not made up of individual and more or less unique contents but of those which are universal and of regular occurrence."[158]

Jung conceived of this collective unconscious as being the generative "matrix" out of which psychic phenomena originated. Jung variously portrayed this deep psychic substratum as potentially creative, purposive, and structurally ordered. This view of the unconscious yields the possibility that psychic phenomena should be interpreted "constructively" and pertain to matters other than the merely—that is, wholly reducible to—biological.

This relatively positive characterization of the unconscious informed Jung's understanding of the causes and cures of psychopathology. If one ignores or represses the unconscious, "and its products can find no outlet in consciousness, a sort of blockage ensues, an unnatural inhibition of a purposive function....As a result of the repression, wrong psychic outlets are found."[159] These "wrong outlets" are the painful and distorted symptoms of psychopathology. The pathology itself is the attitude of the conscious personality, resulting in a disordered relationship between the conscious and unconscious poles of the psyche. In contrast to Freudian theory, which characterized our psychic core, the *id*, as a "cauldron" and "chaos," Jung argued that the depths of the psyche appear as such only when the "normal unconscious psyche" is prevented from expressing its "natural tendencies" because of an inappropriate conscious attitude. Jung wrote the following passage regarding dream interpretation, but it pertains as well to other manifestations of the unconscious, including those of conscience:

> So, by means of dreams (plus all sorts of intuitions, impulses, and other spontaneous events [e.g., conscience]), instinctive forces influence the activity of consciousness. Whether that influence is for better or worse depends upon the actual contents of the unconscious. If it contains too many things that normally ought to be conscious, then its function becomes twisted and prejudiced; motives appear that are not based upon true instincts, but that owe their existence and psychic importance to the fact that they have been consigned to the unconscious by repression or neglect. They overlay, as it were, the normal unconscious psyche and distort its natural tendency to express basic symbols and motifs.[160]

Thus, the ego's task in relating to the unconscious was characterized by Jung as primarily a matter of integrating, as opposed to controlling and, when necessary, sublimating. As I argued in part 1 of this work, Jung, in stark contrast to Freud, eschewed dualisms and sought a holistic portrayal of the human person. Freud dualistically posited Reason[161] against the instincts, hoping that the former, through education, could come to modulate or subjugate the latter. Such an appeal to the strength of, and investment of hope in Reason, seems to me the pinnacle of rational idealism, despite its framing in biological language. Jung, on the other hand, would have been loath to portray the ego-self relationship in such a hostile manner, nor would he have suggested that the further strengthening of the ego was a satisfactory response to our more intractable moral conflicts.

Rather, Jung's predilection for holism and his depiction of the unconscious as purposive in nature were to inform his understanding of the psychology of moral conflict and, specifically, conscience. While in fact the "moral" conscience is to be understood as the internalization of collective values, there is another form of conscience—the "ethical" conscience—that expresses what Jung called the "moral reaction" or "moral impulse" of the psyche. The difference between the moral code and conscience becomes poignantly evident when confronted with what Jung called "conflicts of duty." This distinction—between social code and inner voice—is crucial if one is to accept the potential existence and significance of an innate, autonomous moral function of the psyche, denoted by the term "conscience."

> So, too, our moral reactions exemplify the original behavior of the psyche, while moral laws are a late concomitant of moral behavior, congealed into precepts. In consequence, they appear to be identical with the moral reaction, that is, with conscience. This delusion becomes obvious the moment a conflict of duty makes clear the difference between conscience and the moral code.[162]

Jung acknowledged that one must sometimes violate an element of collective standards, expressed through the "moral conscience," if one listens and responds to the "voice" of the "ethical conscience," that is, the promptings of individuation or, simply, one's "vocation." Discerning what is the moral course of action when faced with a conflict of duty requires not only logical and cognitive capacities but moral fortitude as well. Jung's portrayal of the instinctive base of the psyche affords the possibility that one's conscience may constitute a genuine moral relationship that takes place with, and within, one's own interior. That is, a relationship may arise that is governed by a sense of mutual respect, if not reverence, that is nothing less than personal, an instantiation of an I–Thou reality.[163] Often, and not without paradox, the source of the moral courage needed to heed the call of the ethical conscience is the I–Thou encounter itself. The ethical conscience is this encounter as well as a means of dialogue within the ever-emergent I–Thou relationship.

Chapter 6

JUNG AND THE RELATIVITY OF CONSCIENCE

In the introduction to the previous chapter, I stated that the plausibility of conscience had been eroded in contemporary culture through two basic currents of thought—what I called "nodal points"—that infuse the current Western mind-set. The first of these nodal points—a *reductive naturalization* of reality—is based on a very specific ontology and has informed a pervasive critical perspective of conscience, namely, that of being (merely) the exponent of introjected external authorities. In the current chapter, I will build on this recognition of how ontological premises impact one's view of conscience. I will do so by critically engaging a widespread epistemological temper—*perspectivalism*—that arose, in significant ways, as a radical response to the naturalistic worldview outlined in the previous chapter. Perspectivalism offers a penetrating critique of conscience, approaching it from the direction of the epistemological nodal point, which I will seek to refute—though embracing it in a qualified form—through the concepts of Jung's analytical psychology.

POSTMODERN EPISTEMOLOGY AND CONSCIENCE

In simple terms, epistemology refers to the study of knowledge (Gk. *epistēmē*, "understanding, knowledge"), particularly in reference to its limits and validity. Yet when one moves beyond basic definition and begins to deepen the epistemological inquiry, these simple beginnings tend to quickly ramify. For example, one may focus, from a variety of methodological and theoretical angles, on the act or process of "knowing" (as verb). Or one may explore the nature of "knowledge" (as noun). Or one may reflect on "reason" (as both verb and noun). And so on. Since knowing and knowledge are as human—or, more specifically human—a process as breathing, nearly every field of inquiry may contribute its perspective on the subject. In the contemporary climate—at least within broad swaths of the academic world—epistemology has taken on a decidedly political connotation, such that one's questions—or accusations—are often *Whose* truth? And the subtext is, And for what purpose do you hold, and advance, this viewpoint? In short, What is your agenda?

This line of politically informed epistemological inquiry—based on a functional view of knowing and a perspectival theory of knowledge—epitomizes what may be called a "postmodern temper," which strikes at the heart of the traditional claims of conscience. As outlined in chapter 5, the "traditional conscience" is conceived as a faculty, possessed by all, capable of discerning, or yielding, moral truth with intersubjective validity. The traditional conscience achieves this "in part through a sense of guilt, but it is not coextensive with *all* feelings of guilt and is, therefore, harder to discern than its modern analogue."[1] Its veracity and interpersonal authority are conceived as being derived through a transpersonal source of moral authority, whether this be God, the gods, a form of natural law, or in the capacities of reason itself. The fact that the "voice" of the traditional conscience is so hard to hear and difficult to discern does not necessarily translate into a discrediting of its moral claims. Rather, given the fact that "attempts of different people to consult it will sometimes yield different results,"[2] the fallibility of discerning one's conscience is critical to the ongoing belief in the existence of this moral faculty. Neal O. Weiner addressed the relationship between the fallibility of one's consultation with conscience and its continuing plausibility.

> Given the world as we know it, the infallibility of conscience (based perhaps on a Cartesian notion of a person's privileged access to the contents of his own moral consciousness) is a guarantee of its relativity. By the same token, the fallibility of

conscience (the very feebleness of its voice) is a condition for the possibility of its interpersonal validity.[3]

Postmodernism and its perspectival theory of knowledge radically challenges this traditional view of conscience. Postmodernism is derived from (and issues into) a particular mood and disposition of discontent and criticism, oriented toward "liberation" of one form or another. The term, as I use it in this work, refers to a general development of thought characterized by a pervasive opposition to the fundamental assumptions, effects, and goals of the Enlightenment and modernity. In short, the whole structure of modernity, from metaphysical foundations to the metanarrative roof, is seen as hollow, decadent, and no longer capable—or desirable—to serve as our metaphorical dwelling. Some of the basic assumptions of modernity that fall under the postmodern critique include, but are not limited to, notions of the unitive self, subject-centered reason, philosophies of consciousness, substance, truth, purpose, being, hierarchy, form metanarratives—foundations of all sorts that are the basis of objective truth claims. Conscience, if conceived either as a foundation itself, or as a medium that conveys moral objectivity, falls most definitely under this critique. From a perspectival theory of knowledge, conscience is neither source nor medium of morally significant claims. Instead, conscience, and moral claims in general, are seen as serving more elementary needs and drives of the individual or the group for whom they apply. Traditional moral frameworks—codified in laws, customs, and norms—are thereby seen as deceptive and false, and in this sense immoral if held to be literal.

In order to address the challenge of postmodern epistemology I will engage the ideas of a seminal theorist of postmodernism, Friedrich Nietzsche.[4] As with my discussion of Freud, my engagement with Nietzsche is not intended to provide a comprehensive review of his theories, but rather is employed as a critical foil to clarify the significance of Jung's thought. I will focus on salient features of Nietzsche's theories that have contributed to the development of the current moral climate, specifically those that pertain to the relativization of conscience. While Nietzsche is certainly worthy of exhaustive study himself, my purpose in this chapter is to consider specific aspects of his thought and the resulting impact of his theories on the development of contemporary culture. My intention is not to provide absolute statements about Nietzsche's direct contribution to postmodern culture, but rather to employ him to clarify Jung's ideas regarding conscience and the nature of moral truth. By returning to a seminal source of perspectivalism the root causes of its repercussions and the contrasts with Jung will be made more evident.

NIETZSCHE: THE DEATH OF GOD AND PERSPECTIVALISM

Though in fact Nietzsche's thought may be cited as a generative source of much of the postmodern temper, his own attitude toward criticism and attendant disillusionment was complex. While in fact Nietzsche is properly understood as being dismissive of those who uncritically claim as "true" any established set of moral values or principles, it is equally true that he held the loss of moral values that accompanied the decline in religious belief to be a catastrophic event that his philosophy attempted to address.[5] This complex ambiguity holds true for his attitude regarding conscience as well.

Famously, Nietzsche's mature philosophy began with the proclamation that "God is dead."[6] Nietzsche perceived that the defining characteristic of his time—in both the gravest and greatest sense—was the loss of belief in the Christian God—or, more exactly, the loss of the *possibility* of belief in any god or gods that would sanction the value and meaning of human life. This demise of religious plausibility was described by Nietzsche as "*The greatest change.—*The illumination and the color of all things has changed."[7]

Nietzsche made this declaration of God's demise not in a spirit of celebration, nor in the tone of cool, rational detachment; rather, it was proclaimed more as a frantic lament by the prophetic hysteric in his parable:

> The madman jumped into their midst and pierced them with his eyes. "Wither is God?" he cried; "I will tell you. *We have*

killed him—you and I...." How shall we comfort ourselves, the murderers of all murderers? What was holiest and mightiest of all that the world has yet owned has bled to death under our knives: who will wipe this blood off us?[8]

By "death of God" Nietzsche was using religious language to describe the impact of the scientific worldview on the mythological framework of the Judeo-Christian tradition. As a result of cumulative scientific discovery and philosophical criticism, most recently the Darwinian revolution—"the 'true but deadly' nihilism from across the Channel"[9]—the "sacred canopy" of the Western religious tradition had collapsed.[10] With this collapse Nietzsche was confronted with his "greatest and most persistent problem,"[11] that is, the search "to escape nihilism"—described by Nietzsche as the "why?" finding no answer.[12] Unlike liberal Christians of his (and the contemporary) day, Nietzsche recognized that the *moral authority* of a religion—or *any* worldview—*cannot be separated* from the entirety of its framework, including historical, practical, and epistemological elements, but most significantly, its ultimate *ontological foundation*. Nietzsche made this point in the following manner:

> Christianity is a system, a consistently thought out and *complete* view of things. If one breaks out of it a fundamental idea, the belief in God, one thereby breaks the whole thing to pieces: one has nothing of any consequence left in one's hands....It possesses truth only if God is true—it stands or falls with the belief in God.[13]

Nietzsche responded theoretically to this death of god in what may be described as both a positive and a negative manner. That is, he accepted and embraced the relative truth—that is, the utility and expressive worth—of the scientific critique of traditional religious beliefs. Accordingly, many of his assertions could be readily embraced by those who identify themselves with the "scientific worldview," particularly those embedded in Darwinism such as evolutionary psychology. For example, he stated that "morals may be understood as the doctrine of the relations of supremacy under which the phenomenon of 'life' comes to be."[14] Yet this positive appropriation of the scientific framework was merely the beginning of Nietzsche's theorizing. More radically, Nietzsche developed and employed a hermeneutical form of criticism that is now called "perspectivalism."

As discussed in the introductory chapter, perspectivalism is a defining characteristic of the postmodern temper and presents a far-reaching challenge to *any* effort to establish the plausibility of what we may recognize as a meaningful life and the moral values that inform it. While Nietzsche's "project" was presented in negative, critical terms—as the smashing of idols with a philosophical hammer[15]—the criticism was intended to serve the positive function of preparing the way for Nietzsche's alternatives to traditional theism and morality. Nietzsche considered himself, by his very nature, affirming and positive,[16] and it was this constitutional temper that drove his quest somehow to affirm the meaning of human life.[17] He expressed this aspiration, as a response to the "death of God," through various concepts—the *will to power*, the *Übermensch*, the *eternal recurrence*—and, specific to our purpose, something he called the "revaluation of values." In the preface of *On the Genealogy of Morals*, Nietzsche describes this revaluation as a "demand" for a new kind of knowledge and awareness:

> Let us articulate this *new demand*: we need a *critique* of moral values, *the value of these values themselves must first be called in question*—and for that there is needed a knowledge of the conditions and circumstances in which they grew, under which they evolved and changed (morality as consequence, as symptom, as mask, as tartufferie, as illness, as misunderstanding; but also morality as cause, as remedy, as stimulant, as restraint, as poison), a knowledge of a kind that has never yet existed or even been desired.[18]

The pervasive and central conviction, and the root ontological principle guiding Nietzsche's revaluation of values, was the final and ultimate reality of *this*, and *only* this, actual world in which we currently live. Nietzsche viewed the positing of "another" world somehow "behind" or "above" this natural world as having the inevitable effect of inhibiting, if not negating, the affirmation of one's current existence.

In Christianity neither morality nor religion come into contact with reality at any point. Nothing but imaginary *causes...effects...natural science...psychology...teleology*. Once the concept of "nature" had been devised as the concept antithetical to "God," "natural" had to be the word for "reprehensible"—this entire fictional world has its roots in *hatred* of the natural (—actuality!—).[19]

Nietzsche was aware, however, of the persistent and recurring tendency for theorists—even those explicitly avowing a naturalistic philosophy—to furtively attempt to superimpose upon reality a substitute deity in various guises. For although the Judeo-Christian god had died, the "shadows of God" continue "to darken our minds."[20] Accordingly, Nietzsche attempted to criticize and refute all attempts to posit a form of order, or intention, or moral quality to the cosmos.

Let us beware of thinking that the world is a living being....Let us even beware of believing that the universe is a machine....The total character of the world, however, is in all eternity chaos—in the sense not of a lack of necessity but of a lack of order, arrangement, form, beauty, wisdom, and whatever other names there are for our aesthetic anthropomorphisms. Let us beware of attributing to it heartlessness and unreason or their opposites: it is neither perfect nor beautiful, nor noble, nor does it wish to become any of these things; it does not by any means strive to imitate man. None of our aesthetic and moral judgments apply to it.[21]

This criticism of applying aesthetic or moral standards to the nature of physical processes was extended and applied by Nietzsche to the habit of conceptualizing and interpreting temporal processes, in one's own life and in general history, as morally governed. His purpose here, as with his refutation of the cosmological argument, was to reject without remainder *any* attempt to seek the basis of life affirmation in a rationally imposed construct that served, in fact, to distance oneself from reality. He refuted what amounts to different forms of the teleological argument in the following manner:

> Looking at nature as if it were proof of the goodness and governance of a god; interpreting history in honor of some divine reason, as a continual testimony of a moral world order and ultimate moral purposes; interpreting one's own experience as pious people have long enough interpreted theirs, as if everything were providential, a hint, designed and ordained for the sake of the salvation of the soul—that is *all over* now, that has man's conscience *against* it, that is considered indecent and dishonest by every more refined conscience—mendaciousness, feminism, weakness, and cowardice.[22]

Nietzsche believed that this death of god was now the "presupposition" of the way philosophical, moral problems must be framed and that an "unconditional and honest atheism" was the "locus" of a newfound "integrity." This development was, at its heart, "a triumph achieved finally and with great difficulty by the European conscience, being the most fateful act of two thousand years of discipline for truth that in the end forbids itself the *lie* in faith in God."[23] This rigorous atheism was the starting point of Nietzsche's criticism of all received moral traditions—but it was not the end. Even the relative comforts afforded by what may be termed a "bourgeois atheism"—living in a world of known physical entities and lawful operations, perhaps conceived as "progressing" in some form—is subject to Nietzsche's critical hammer. Before I engage this critical element of his thought, however, several preliminary points must be developed. I will begin by exploring the development of his functional view of moral codes and related hermeneutical critique of foundationalism, which will then lead to the conceptual basis of his reformulation of values, that is, the "will to power." Nietzsche understood the "genealogy" of morals in light of this monistic, operative principle. In his theory conscience played an integral role in the ongoing expression—and repression—of the will to power, and it is through the will to power that we may understand the Nietzschean conscience.

NIETZSCHE'S MORAL FUNCTIONALISM

One of the devices through which Nietzsche developed his functionalist view of morals is the quasi-historical positing of two groups, the "masters" and the "slaves," that he employed in his genealogical reflections. My intention here is not to debate the anthropological veracity of his descriptions of these two types, but rather to appreciate their heuristic value as types of moral character and modes of moral process in which individuals participate to varying degrees. Briefly stated, Nietzsche portrayed "master morality" as "value-creating" and affirmative in nature, and as reflecting the emergence of important capabilities of humans to willfully commit themselves over time. Conversely, Nietzsche described "slave morality" as utilitarian and skeptical in nature and reflective of a deceptive, protective, and resentful character. Nietzsche's sentiments clearly resided with the former group when he wrote:

> There are *master morality* and *slave morality*....In the first case, when the ruling group determines what is "good," the exalted, proud states of the soul are experienced as conferring distinction and determining the order of rank. It should be noted immediately that in this first type of morality the opposition of "good" and "*bad*" means approximately the same as "noble" and "contemptible."[24]

Conversely, slave morality was described in the following manner:

> It is different with the second type of morality, *slave morality*. The slave's eye is not favorable to the virtues of the powerful: he is skeptical and suspicious, *subtly* suspicious, of all the "good" that is honored there—he would like to persuade himself that even their happiness is not genuine. Conversely, those qualities are brought out and flooded with light which serve to ease existence for those who suffer: here pity, the complaisant and obliging hand, the warm heart, patience, industry, humility, and friendliness are honored—for here these are the most useful qualities and almost the only means for enduring the pressure of existence. Slave morality is essentially a morality of utility.[25]

In broad terms, Nietzsche believed that established moral codes and concepts of what is good and what is bad were originally derived *not* from the public recipients of moral favors but rather through the powerful ones who actually performed "good" acts:

> The judgment "good" did not originate with those to whom "goodness" was shown. Rather it was "the good" themselves, that is to say, the noble, powerful, high-stationed and high-minded, who felt and established themselves and their actions as good, that is, of the first rank, in contradistinction to all the low, low-minded, common and plebeian. It was out of this *pathos of distance* that they first seized the right to create values and to coin names for values—what had they to do with utility?[26]

However, Nietzsche believed that the dominant moral values of *his* day reflected those of the "slave," and were the result of resentment. *Resentment* was a term used by Nietzsche to describe a process whereby the weak and disempowered—particularly the early Jews and Christians—had successfully sought to "radically revalue," for personal advantage, the "truly good" moral norms of the "noble aristocracy." Nietzsche described this revaluation in ferocious terms, drawing sharp lines of distinction:

> It was the Jews who, with awe-inspiring consistency, dared to invert the aristocratic value-equation (good = noble = powerful = beautiful = happy = beloved of god) and to hang on to this inversion with their teeth, the teeth of the most abysmal hatred (the hatred of impotence), saying "the wretched alone are the good; the poor, impotent, lowly alone are the good; the suffering, deprived, sick, ugly alone are pious, alone are blessed by God, blessedness is for them alone—and you, the powerful and noble, are on the contrary the evil, the cruel, the lustful, the insatiable, the godless to all eternity; and you shall be in all eternity the unblessed, accursed, and damned!"...One knows *who* inherited this Jewish revaluation.[27]

The significance of the distinction between moralities of "slave" and "master" is that Nietzsche, through the genealogical method, viewed the nature of each group's morals as derivative of more basic, primary functions or drives. That is, a value was explained in naturalistic terms.[28] The establishment—the declaration—of what is good and bad, was not in any way perceived by Nietzsche to be a product of discerning genuine moral properties or structures or laws—whether natural or supernatural in origin—but rather was the expression of one's subjective interests, needs—one's agenda. In the context of "slave and master" moralities, one's morals appear as devices for attaining and maintaining some form of physical and/or psychological dominance over others. In the hands of Nietzsche, this functional critique itself often resulted in statements that expressed a radical form of relativism that inverted the established moral order: "One holds that what is called good preserves the species, while what is called evil harms the species. In truth, however, the evil instincts are expedient, species-preserving, and indispensable to as high a degree as the good ones; their function is merely different."[29]

Yet Nietzsche's critique of moral codes and conscience—and the attempt at their positive revaluation—is more radical than simply a hermeneutic of suspicion regarding one's intentions. This becomes evident when one begins to examine how Nietzsche's functionalism becomes unmoored from what may be considered its "normal" conceptual bases and dynamic structures. By this I mean: functionalist or utilitarian ethics are generally characterized by the existence of a "good" toward which moral endeavor is directed, and by which it is measured, and upon which it is based. In short, there is a foundation of some sort to one's ethical theory and practice, whether this foundation be relatively demonstrable and concrete—for example, survival, power, progress—or more subjective and abstract—for example, happiness, health, truth. Nietzsche attacked all such forms of functional ethics and the reality claims of the "foundations" upon which they are constructed.

NIETZSCHE'S CRITIQUE OF FOUNDATIONS

Nietzsche's interpretive critique of moral valuations became more far-reaching when he engaged in an analysis of the basic logical and linguistic building blocks of regnant worldviews. The implications of some of his critical statements are not always immediately apparent, for his statements, when first encountered and without an understanding of the fullness of his critique, may be read as locating rational processes within a familiar physiologically grounded, naturalistic universe. Yet to assume such a metaphysical foundation in Nietzsche's philosophy is—as he may have said derisively—to fall prey to "mythological thinking."[30] The Nietzschean reader may be forgiven, however, for initially assuming such familiar philosophical terrain, for many of Nietzsche's comments suggest a naturalistic viewpoint. Two examples follow, one pertaining to philosophy in general, the other to the foundations of philosophy, the field of logic:

> By far the greater part of conscious thinking must still be included among instinctive activities, and that goes even for philosophical thinking.[31]

> Behind all logic and its seeming sovereignty of movement, too, there stand valuations or, more clearly, physiological demands for the preservation of a certain type of life.[32]

Yet the full significance of these statements emerges when it becomes clear that the referents of these phrases—"instinctive activities" and "preservation of a certain type of life"—are not as substantial and stable as one would normally expect. For example, "Life is no argument. The conditions of life might include error."[33] And, the notion of "health," a "good" that in practice seems simple and unproblematic, and that clearly guides a myriad of our normal actions, is likewise called into question: "For there is no health as such, and all attempts to define a thing that way have been wretched failures. Even the determination of what is healthy for your *body* depends on your goal, your horizon, your energies, your impulses, your errors, and above all on the ideals and phantasms of your soul."[34]

Yet Nietzsche did not limit his critique to what may be termed biological or temporal process terms. Rather, for Nietzsche, the most basic of terms by which one orients oneself in life are not self-evident, but are constructs themselves, and as such have no claim to "truth" or moral authority. "It is *we* alone who have devised cause, sequence, for-each-other, relativity, constraint, number, law, freedom, motive, and purpose; and when we project and mix this symbol world into things as if it existed 'in itself,' we act once more as we have always acted—*mythologically.*"³⁵ This "mythological thinking" was to Nietzsche the source of innumerable errors and the cause—and effect—of much human decadence. Nietzsche's critique of the most basic of our terms and assumptions about the substantial reality we believe we live in was central to his effort to provide a revaluation of values. His radical criticism of the reality of such basic terms as *substance*, *cause and effect*, and, psychologically, the *ego* and *will* was designed to clear the conceptual space in order to allow for a new way of seeing and living.

In *The Twilight of the Idols*, Nietzsche isolated two fundamental "idiosyncrasies of philosophers" that he believed had plagued the entirety of Western intellectual history, and to which we are just now awakening and responding appropriately. First, Nietzsche claimed that philosophers had heretofore lacked a "historical sense"; that is, they had practiced the pernicious habit of denigrating the "idea of becoming." He claimed that a pervasive "Egyptianism" creates "conceptual mummies," that is, reified constructs that served to deaden and distort. Rather than penetrating to the actual nature of things, philosophers had habitually made the mistake of believing that "what is, does not *become*; what becomes, *is* not."³⁶ Philosophers, seeking to explain this phenomenon, blamed the senses as the source of deception and made the further error of seeking to escape the body in order to attain what they believed to be the really real. "Moral: escape from sense-deception, from becoming, from history, from falsehood....And away, above all, with the *body*, that pitiable *idée fixe* of the senses!"³⁷

Continuing his critique of these "philosophical idiosyncrasies," Nietzsche lifted up Heraclitus as a bright spot in the tradition—as a philosopher to be applauded for his affirmation of *becoming*, and his assertion that *being* is a fiction. However, in Nietzsche's view, Heraclitus nonetheless made the error of blaming our senses for presenting a certain unity to perceived phenomena. According to Nietzsche the error resided not with the senses but with *reason* and its falsification of the data of the senses. "It is what we *make* of their evidence that first introduces a lie into it, for example the lie of unity, the lie of materiality, of substance, of duration."[38] In spite of this error, however, Heraclitus was right in asserting that "being is an empty fiction. The 'apparent' world is the only one: the 'real' world has only been *lyingly added*...."[39]

The second pervasive idiosyncrasy of philosophers that Nietzsche identified "consists in mistaking the first for the last," and, relatedly, establishing what is last as the first in their theoretical formulations. By this Nietzsche meant that philosophers (before himself) mistakenly denied the possibility of the evolution of form and creative development of content. Thus, in this fallacious pre-Darwinian mind-set, "everything of the first rank must be *causa sui*," and, because of the logical principle of noncontradiction, there must be one (and one only) primal cause, that is, God. This inverted thought process was described by Nietzsche as "brain-sick fancies of morbid cobweb-spinners!"[40]

This decadent philosophical attitude holds that that which is real is "Being," and, conversely, that which is "Becoming" is not real. Searching for an explanation for this undesirable quandary, philosophers have traditionally blamed the senses and, relatedly, the body for their inability to realize Being within the realm of existence. Moral: escape the body. For Nietzsche this meant a nay-saying attitude toward life that reflected decline and weakness. Further, this philosophical temperament had become embedded in language so that language supported this mythology of transcendence and being. At the root of it all was the fallacious belief that there was a substantial ego that served as agent of its own deeds. This root error—the objectification of oneself—had been projected onto the world and now permeated everything from religious doctrine to colloquial language. Within the religious sphere, this world negation had often been construed by the weak to their own advantage. Out of resentment the weak developed a morality, based on otherworldliness and motivated by a desire for revenge, that overturned the values of the strong. The effect, manifested in today's hypocritical Christianity, has likewise been a diminishment of life affirmation.

It should be understood that through this critique Nietzsche was *not* simply attempting a more cogent or truthful moral exposition *within* the context of philosophical tradition. Rather, he was attempting to *critique the entire* philosophical program. His fundamental criticism of the philosophical enterprise was that the very means by which it has operated—its language, logic, and the mythology it conveys—are themselves part of the problem:

> It is self-deception on the part of philosophers and moralists to imagine that by making war on *décadence* they therewith elude *décadence* themselves. This is beyond their powers: what they select as an expedient, as a deliverance, is itself only another expression of *décadence*—they *alter* its expression, they do not abolish the thing itself.[41]

As an example of this recurring philosophical error—in this case those in the Cartesian tradition who seek certitude through immediacy of introspective experience, grounded on the seemingly solid foundation of the rational subject—Nietzsche wrote:

> I shall never tire of emphasizing a small terse fact, which these superstitious minds hate to concede—namely, that a thought comes when "it" wishes, and not when "I" wish, so that it is a falsification of the facts of the case to say the subject "I" is the condition of the predicate "think."[42]

But then, immediately following this statement, Nietzsche demonstrated his broader point of just how difficult, if not impossible, it is to think and communicate outside of the "foundationalist mythology" so deeply embedded in our language:

> One has even gone too far with this "it thinks"—even the "it" contains an *interpretation* of the process, and does not belong to the process itself. One infers here according to grammatical habit: "Thinking is an activity; activity requires an agent; consequently—"[43]

Nietzsche's linguistic, hermeneutical analysis has potentially far-reaching implications when applied to psychological phenomena such as conscience. Most significantly, the ability to conceive, or *reconceive*, of conscience as a dialectical process between the conscious subject and unconscious factors that are experienced as intelligible, intentional, and, in some sense, "personal," is challenged in a radical way by Nietzsche's views. This is because his critique of foundations applied not only to the physical world but to the foundations of the personality as well. "There is no 'being' behind doing, effecting, becoming; the 'doer' is merely a fiction added to the deed—the deed is everything."[44] Nietzsche explicitly applied this critical perspective to Kant's philosophy, denying that there is anything "real" beyond the epistemological barrier. "Our entire science still lies under the misleading influence of language and has not disposed of that little changeling, the 'subject' (the atom, for example, is such a changeling, as is the Kantian 'thing-in-itself')."[45]

THE POSITIVE FUNCTION OF NIETZSCHE'S CRITICISMS

I began my exposition of Nietzsche with the observation that "to escape nihilism"—described by Nietzsche as the "why?" finding no answer[46]—was his "greatest and most persistent problem."[47] For Nietzsche, the loss of God, resulting from the emergence of historical and scientific consciousness, found no meaningful substitute in this enlightened, rational worldview. The new demand that he thus faced was to find a new means—not a method, not a foundation, but a perspective that would liberate—for a meaningful life in this world. His critical analysis of moral values had two basic aspects, both of which are employed, as it were, to wipe the slate clean and "open the sea before us."[48] The first aspect of his criticism is characterized by a naturalistic, utilitarian critique of established moral traditions. Nietzsche attempted to demonstrate how "our morality is, *by its own standards*, poisonously immoral: that Christian love is the mimicry of impotent hatred; that most unselfishness is but a particularly vicious form of selfishness; and that *ressentiment* is at the core of our morals."[49] This dimension of his thought *could* fall within a typical scientific critique of our morals, as, for example, through the theories of an evolutionary psychologist.

Yet Nietzsche recognized that any naturalistic revaluation was unable to provide the means of overcoming nihilism. Therefore, the second aspect of his critical method was directed at any and all forms of foundationalism, for example, reductive scientism, that could—and would—attempt authoritatively to define the nature of human beings. His persistent critique of "mummification" was motivated by the recognition that a world-view based solely on an objectified view of reality would be one in which the "why?" would still find no answer. His interpretive, hermeneutical analyses prepared the way—or sharpened the need—for his "revaluation of values." This revaluation sought to penetrate beneath the "foreground" of our morals to uncover the actual processes in operation, which then, perhaps, could serve as the basis of a new standard of valuation. The principles that artic-ulate the heart of Nietzsche's revaluation are "the will to power" and its corollary, "sublimation."

THE WILL TO POWER AND SUBLIMATION

As Walter Kaufmann observed in his authoritative biography of Nietzsche, "The [concept of] will to power did not spring from Nietzsche's head full grown."[50] Rather, it evolved in both expressed form and theoretical significance during the course of Nietzsche's life. The basis of the concept appears to have been a combination of introspection and the observational study of psy-chological processes that reach overt expression through varied cultural phenomena. Originally (in notes from the late 1870s), the "will to power" appeared as "one of two significant psychological phenomena." For example, "Fear (negative) and will to power (positive) explain our strong consideration for the opinions of men."[51] Yet even in these early formulations, where the will to power was but one of several significant psychological forces, its significance resided in the fact that through it Nietzsche was able to explain a moral value through what may be considered a natu-ral process. For example, from *Human, All-Too-Human* (1878), we read how the moral duty of gratitude actually masks an underly-ing will to power:

> The reason why a powerful person is grateful is this: his benefactor has…intruded into…[his] sphere. Without the satisfaction of gratitude, the powerful man would have shown himself powerless and would hence be considered so. Therefore every society of the good, i.e., originally powerful, posits gratitude as one of the first duties.[52]

This theoretical move of explaining the genealogy of certain morals through the dynamics of the will to power became exponentially more significant when the concept was applied to the entirety of human culture. According to Kaufmann, it was when Nietzsche associated the will to power with Greek culture—which Nietzsche viewed as the "acme of humanity"—that the breadth of the concept's explanatory power became fully apparent to him: "Now it occurred to him that the contest *(agon)* itself was a manifestation of the will to power...[and that] the will to power may now be envisaged as the basic drive of all human efforts."[53]

This grandiose claim of Nietzsche's was driven by his belief that he had in fact penetrated deeper into the reality of things than had all the systematic philosophers and moralists preceding him. They had, so he believed, all been constrained and diverted from truly incisive analysis through the moral presuppositions that informed their thought.[54] According to Nietzsche, "all psychology so far has got stuck in moral prejudices and fears: it has not dared to descend into the depths," and "it is permissible to recognize in what has been written so far a symptom of what has so far been kept silent."[55] What has been kept silent is the will to power.

Upon this belief in the revelatory nature of his insights, and the conclusions he had reached regarding the singular role of the will to power in shaping human culture, Nietzsche extended his analysis—in the mode of a thought experiment—until the will to power was understood as the basic force of a monistic metaphysics. In *Beyond Good and Evil* Nietzsche articulated his logic and the presuppositions behind this viewpoint.

> Suppose nothing else were "given" as real except our world of desires and passions, and we could not get down, or up, to any other "reality" besides the reality of our drives—for thinking is merely a relation of these drives to each other: is it not permitted to make the experiment and to ask the question whether this "given" would not be *sufficient* for also understanding on the basis of this kind of thing the so-called mechanistic (or "material") world? I mean, not as a deception, as "mere appearance," and "idea" (in the sense of Berkeley and Schopenhauer) but as holding the same rank of

reality as our affect—as a more primitive form of the world of affects in which everything still lies contained in a powerful unity before it undergoes ramifications and developments in the organic process (and, as is only fair, also becomes tenderer and weaker)—as a kind of instinctive life in which all organic functions are still synthetically intertwined along with self-regulation, assimilation, nourishment, excretion, and metabolism—as a *pre-form* of life.

In the end not only is it permitted to make this experiment; the conscience of *method* demands it. Not to assume several kinds of causality until the experiment of making do with a single one has been pushed to its utmost limit (to the point of nonsense, if I may say so)—that is a moral of method which one may not shirk today.

Suppose, finally, we succeeded in explaining our entire instinctive life as the development and ramification of *one* basic form of the will—namely, of the will to power, as *my* proposition has it; suppose all organic functions could be traced back to this will to power and one could also find in it the solution of the problem of procreation and nourishment—it is *one* problem—then one would have gained the right to determine *all* efficient force univocally as—*will to power*. The world viewed from inside, the world defined and determined according to its "intelligible character"—it would be "will to power" and nothing else.[56]

The foregoing passage may be summarized in the following manner: that what is real (because "given," and not merely rationalized after the fact) is one's "world of desires and passions." "Thinking" is itself "merely a relation of these drives to each other." So too is the "mechanistic (or 'material') world" understood in terms of drives, albeit in a "more primitive" form, or *"pre-form"* of life. Further, the rules of logic—and "the conscience of *method*"—demand that one attempts to assume a single kind of causal force, as opposed to a multiplicity of explanations. Following this procedure, one will then conclude, as did Nietzsche, that the world—insofar as we may determine its "intelligible character"—is the "'will to power' and nothing else."[57] In this manner, then, Nietzsche argued that the most fundamental motive force driving human behavior, and all of existence, to which we can penetrate, is the "will to power." It is through the hermeneutical lens of the will to power that Nietzsche interpreted the genealogy of morals and, specifically, the nature of conscience.

It is important that this will to power *not* be understood as either a simple expression of a psychological function or as simply "power over" in a sociological sense. As just described—but warranting repetition—the will to power was understood by Nietzsche to be a cosmic principle, an inward force that manifested in all forms of existence and, importantly, did not exist outside these forms. As discussed earlier, for Nietzsche the cosmos was a Heraclitean flux, yet one, in his final formulation, that does not tend toward a final goal but rather eternally recurs back upon itself. The human person is a particular manifestation of this general life process that continually seeks to affirm and yet transcend itself. The human being is, as it were, a "rope, tied between beast and overman," stretched over an abyss.[58] It is this dynamic quality of "self-overcoming" that informed the complementary concept of the will to power, that is, the process of "sublimation."[59]

The process of "sublimation" is marked by a complex inner dynamic whereby one simultaneously preserves, cancels, and lifts up oneself. That which is preserved is the basic drive of the will to power. That which is canceled is the immediate aim through its overcoming. And that which is lifted up is the being in a new state of greater power, now directed toward a new challenge and goal that will in turn need to be overcome.[60] Throughout the many iterations and incarnations of this process of sublimation, however, what remains is the will to power. And by sublimating (not repressing) this will to power through disciplined action, a certain greatness can be attained by the individual, marked by a life "strengthened by war and victory, for whom conquest, adventure, danger, and even pain have become needs;…habituation to the keen air of the heights, to winter journeys, to ice and mountains in every sense;…[requiring] a kind of sublime wickedness, an ultimate, supremely self-confident mischievousness in knowledge that goes with great health."[61]

This Nietzschean will to power should not be confused as willfulness or, simply, the will.[62] Indeed, since the will to power is the single principle animating reality, *all* psychological phenomena may—and *must* be—reducible to this force. As quoted above, Nietzsche held that "our entire instinctive life" was to be explained by this force, ranging from the nutritive functions, to sexuality, to rationality, and, of course, to one's morality. Walter Kaufmann observes that Nietzsche's "doctrine [of the will to power] is not, properly speaking, 'irrationalism.' It *is* 'irrationalistic' insofar as the basic drive is not reason; it is *not* 'irrationalistic,' however, insofar as reason is given a unique status."[63] Kaufmann contrasts rationality with sexuality to make his point.

> Reason and the sex drive are both forms of the will to power. The sex drive, however, is an impulse, and in yielding to it in its unsublimated form, man is still the slave of his passions and has no power over them. Rationality, on the other hand, gives man mastery over himself....Reason is the "highest" manifestation of the will to power, in the distinct sense that through rationality it can realize its objective most fully.

Further, rationality holds an esteemed place in Nietzsche's thought because it "is *sui generis*" and thus—unlike the sublimation of sexual impulses in which the immediate sexual objective is canceled—it "cannot be similarly canceled in the process of sublimation."[64]

The quality or character of the will to power is one of necessity, strife, urge, and aspiration. The will to power—the essence of life—is the basis of the "spontaneous, aggressive, expansive, form-giving forces" in the universe.[65] It is, as Kaufmann describes it, "always at war with itself," manifesting not only in the human "battle between reason and impulse" but in "all natural events, all history," seeking to "transcend itself and thus engage in a fight against itself."[66] This constant seeking of self-expression and transcendence entails a certain quality of necessity before which the concept of moral agency disappears as mere linguistic illusion:

> To demand of strength that it should *not* express itself as strength, that it should *not* be a desire to overcome, a desire to throw down, a desire to become master, a thirst for enemies and resistances, is just as absurd as to demand of weakness that it should express itself as strength. A quantum of force is equivalent to a quantum of drive, will, effect—more,

it is nothing other than precisely this very driving, willing, effecting and only owing to the seduction of language (and of the fundamental errors of reason that are petrified in it) which conceives and misconceives all effects as conditioned by something that causes effects, by a 'subject,' can it appear otherwise....But there is no such substratum; there is no 'being' behind doing, effecting, becoming; 'the doer' is merely a fiction added to the deed—the deed is everything.[67]

NIETZSCHEAN CONSCIENCE AND THE REVALUATION OF VALUES

How then, within the framework of the will to power, did Nietzsche understand conscience, both its genealogy and current expressions? Nietzsche discussed conscience within the context of the "revaluation of values." The revaluation of values is a process in which one may—free from theological and moral prejudice—reframe the way one approaches ethical inquiry. One no longer "looks for the origin of evil *behind* the world," but rather asks the question, "under what conditions did man devise these judgments good and evil? *and what value do they themselves possess?*"[68] Nietzsche's basic answer to this question was that moral codes arose under the conditions of the will to power, and that the value of moral values was determined by their ability to facilitate the manifestation of this will to power. Nietzsche concluded that morals serve a more fundamental purpose than what they purport to serve. In *Thus Spake Zarathustra*, Nietzsche poetically portrayed how all moral codes are creations of, tools of, the will to power:

> A table of virtues hangs over every people. Behold, it is the table of its overcomings; behold, it is the voice of its will to power. Praiseworthy is whatever seems difficult to a people; whatever seems indispensable and difficult is called good; and...the rarest, the most difficult—that they call holy.[69]

The problem, however, as Nietzsche saw it, was that the dominant moral norms of the Judeo-Christian tradition tend to thwart the expression of this will to power, turning the will's force inward in acts of self-negation, or even self-torture. We have briefly discussed Nietzsche's distinction between master and slave morality, and I would now like to continue that discussion in terms of how it affects Nietzsche's conception of conscience.

Nietzsche distinguished between what may be called a "good" or "healthy" conscience, and a "bad" conscience. The basis of determining whether one's conscience is good or bad is the degree to which conscience facilitates the manifestation and degree of will to power. Nietzsche associated the good conscience with the human capacity to make promises, which, in his framework, is a landmark of human development. Nietzsche observed (or speculated) how "forgetting"—not as mere *"vis inertiae,"* but as a "positive faculty of repression"—was (and is) necessary for humans to function in the most basic of senses: "There could be no happiness, no cheerfulness, no hope, no pride, no *present*, without forgetfulness."[70] Yet this "forgetfulness," though functional in these limited ways, "has bred in itself an opposing faculty, a memory, with the aid of which forgetfulness is abrogated in certain cases—namely in those cases where promises are made." The existence of this capacity to make promises—to make commitments over time—reflects a tremendous evolution in humanity's capacity to manifest the will to power. This is so because the capacity to make promises reflects a heightened form of selfhood, of self-awareness, of capacities of the self that may be sustained over time. The person's self-image, based on real capacities, must have "become calculable, regular, necessary," in which one is able "to stand security for his own future, which is what one who promises does!"[71] Our "good" conscience was understood as the term succinctly denoting this heightened sense of self-governance, if not self-mastery:

> The proud awareness of the extraordinary privilege of *responsibility*, the consciousness of this rare freedom, this power over oneself and over fate, has in his [i.e., the "sovereign" individual] case penetrated to the profoundest depths and become instinct, the dominating instinct. What will he call this dominating instinct, supposing he feels the need to give it a name? The answer is beyond doubt: this sovereign man calls it his *conscience*.[72]

197

Yet, Nietzsche asked, "how did that other 'somber thing,' the consciousness of guilt, the 'bad conscience,' come into the world?"[73] Nietzsche's answer is that our bad conscience arose "under the stress of the most fundamental change" humanity ever experienced, that is, the process of civilization wherein we became "enclosed within the walls of society and of peace."[74] Nietzsche painted a grand evolutionary picture wherein the process of civilizing humanity was compared to the progression that sea animals experienced when they were "compelled to become land animals or perish." The early, predomesticated humans—what Nietzsche called "semi-animals"—were "well adapted to the wilderness, to war, to prowling, to adventure." In this environment, supposedly, the will to power, the "instinct for freedom,"[75] was allowed unconstrained, though limited, expression. Then, "suddenly," through the impact of civilization, "all their instincts were disvalued and 'suspended.'"[76] Thus "began the gravest and uncanniest illness, from which humanity has not yet recovered, man's suffering *of man, of himself*—the result of a forcible sundering from his animal past, as it were a leap and plunge into new surroundings and conditions of existence, a declaration of war against the old instincts upon which his strength, joy, and terribleness had rested hitherto."[77] This "illness" is the "bad conscience." Nietzsche described the emergence of our bad conscience (as well as one's sense of self, or "soul") through the psychodynamics of *inhibition* or *repression*, engendered through conflict with the social environment.

> All instincts that do not discharge themselves outwardly *turn inward*—this is what I call the *internalization* of man: thus it was that man first developed what was later called his "soul." The entire inner world, originally as thin as if it were stretched between two membranes, expanded and extended itself, acquired depth, breadth, and height, in the same measure as outward discharge was *inhibited*. Those fearful bulwarks with which the political organization protected itself against the old instincts of freedom—punishments belong among these bulwarks—brought about that all those instincts of wild, free, prowling man turned backward *against man himself*. Hostility, cruelty, joy in persecuting, in attacking, in change, in destruction—all this turned against the

possessors of such instincts: *that* is the origin of the "bad conscience."[78]

This "political organization" that established the "bulwarks" against the free expression of our instincts was none other than the "masters." Nietzsche was quick to say that while the "masters" did not themselves develop the "illness" of the bad conscience, "it would not have developed *without them*, this ugly growth, [and] it would be lacking if a tremendous quantity of freedom had not been expelled from the world, or at least the visible world, and made as it were *latent* under their hammer blows and artists' violence."[79]

Yet, although the bad conscience is "the gravest of illnesses," it is "an illness as pregnancy is an illness."[80] One's bad conscience, viewed through the interpretive lens of the will to power, may be seen as a useful step in the human history of moral development. Nietzsche observed that "the existence on earth of an animal soul turned against itself, taking sides against itself, was something so new, profound, unheard of, enigmatic, contradictory, *and pregnant with a future* that the aspect of the earth was essentially altered. Indeed, divine spectators were needed...."[81] Thus, in accord with Nietzsche's conception of the will to power and its dynamic corollary, sublimation, one's bad conscience may be seen as a fiction that facilitated the achievement of certain states of power—for example, heightened awareness of self—but which now is in need of replacement, for its general effect is that of being hostile to life. For example, Christian morality has "taught moral skepticism very trenchantly and effectively, accusing and embittering men, yet with untiring patience and subtlety; it destroyed the faith in his 'virtues' in every single individual."[82] Thus, our bad conscience may be seen as serving the purpose of heightening our awareness of the complexities of self and the world. While the bad conscience may in fact be antithetical to life, by deceiving us of its true relations and facilitating repressions, it may become a means itself to the furtherance of the will to power.

Nietzsche lifted up the possibility that the bad conscience "is the same active force that is at work on a grander scale in those artists of violence and organizers who build states," but is here "directed backward, in the 'labyrinth of the breast.'" But with the bad conscience the "material" to be worked is "the whole ancient animal self—and *not*, as in that greater and more obvious phenomenon, some *other* man, *other* men." The possible yield of this work is nothing less than the emergence of a "new abundance of beauty and affirmation," born out of an awareness of its opposite.

> This secret self-ravishment, this artists' cruelty, this delight in imposing a form upon oneself as a hard, recalcitrant, suffering material and in burning a will, a critique, a contradiction, a contempt, a No into it, this uncanny, dreadfully joyous labor of a soul voluntarily at odds with itself that makes itself suffer out of joy in making suffer—eventually this *active* "bad conscience"—you will have guessed it—as the womb of all ideal and imaginative phenomena, also brought to light an abundance of strange new beauty and affirmation, and perhaps beauty itself.— After all, what would be "beautiful" if the contradiction had not first become conscious of itself, if the ugly had not first said to itself: "I am ugly"?[83]

One's conscience thus *may* serve an educative function—yet *only* when it "eventually" becomes an *"active"* conscience, that is, a conscience that is itself self-reflective, and in which its moral presuppositions are seen in the context of the will to power. Conscience in this Nietzschean sense is a form of self-consciousness that may either facilitate or impede the immediate demands of the will to power, depending on whether it is an exponent for this will to power or its opposite. This positive aspect of conscience may or may not manifest in the life of any given individual. Certainly, in Nietzsche's view, for many it did not. In the broader phylogenetic picture, however, the bad conscience has served to strengthen humans through the development of our self-consciousness and related assessments regarding the nature of reality. Thus, Nietzsche claimed that what has "really triumphed over the Christian god" is "Christian morality itself, the concept of truthfulness that was understood ever more rigorously, the father confessor's refinement of the Christian conscience, translated and sublimated into a scientific conscience, into intellectual cleanliness at any price."[84]

Yet today—because the Christian god has died, because humanity has reexamined the nature of itself, because humanity has grown in its profundity—has humanity not "reached the necessity of once more resolving on a reversal and fundamental shift in values? Don't we stand at the threshold of a period which should be designated negatively, to begin with, as *extra-moral?*"[85] Rather than look to mere consequences, or even to root intentions, humanity is now called to an "overcoming," or "self-overcoming of morality," in which its moral values are interpreted in light of the will to power.

> Moral judgment is never to be taken literally: as such it never contains anything but nonsense. But as *semiotics* it remains of incalculable value: it reveals, to the informed man at least, the most precious realities of cultures and inner worlds which did not *know* enough to "understand" themselves. Morality is merely sign-language, merely symptomatology: one must already know *what* it is about to derive profit from it.[86]

This "self-overcoming" of morality is today achieved through a "more refined conscience," the "most malicious conscience," the "scientific conscience."[87] This intellectually clean conscience, self-reflective, aware that its moral presuppositions are reflections of the will to power, arrives at a simple moral formula:

> What is good?—All that heightens the feeling of power, the will to power, power itself in man.
> What is bad?—All that proceeds from weakness.
> What is happiness?—The feeling that power *increases*—that a resistance is overcome.[88]

JUNG'S ALTERNATIVE TO PERSPECTIVALISM

Nietzsche was motivated by a desire to overcome the nihilism that accompanied the "death of God."[89] Nietzsche recognized that if one accepts the Enlightenment conception of reason, and the standards of knowledge and truth associated with empirical science, it was impossible for him rationally to justify moral values that would infuse life with meaning. In short, the "why?"

found no answer within the objectified worldview of science. Nietzsche's response was the radical relativism outlined above, which sought to dissolve all theoretical foundations that might be used to establish an objective claim that, he believed, would in its turn be reduced to impersonal forces, rendering the world meaningless for human aspirations.

Carl Jung, born a generation after Nietzsche, responded in a different manner to the challenges posed by reductive scientism, particularly that of Darwinian-based biology. An examination of two key conceptual categories guides my critical dialogue between Jung and Nietzschean perspectivalism: (1) operative definitions of "truth" and "knowledge," and (2) the ontology of self that underlies one's associated epistemology. The significance and relationship of these two concepts are as follows: If one adopts an operative definition of truth that is relational, receiving, experiential—in contrast to the objectifying, controlling, and experimental conception of truth that perspectivalism critiques[90]—then the essential problem of ethical knowledge is *not* the inability rationally to justify moral truth claims, but rather the challenge of explaining why such a justification is not possible without falling into relativism.[91] In other words, if one's criteria for what constitutes valid ethical knowledge change, then one's practical focus may likewise shift from frustration at the inability to clearly and cleanly articulate absolute moral truth, to an exploration of how moral discernment and choice of contextual, relative moral truths are an ineluctable—and essential—feature of the human condition. If the redefining of this problem is to be plausible, then the second conceptual category identified above—the ontology of the self—must support a conception of the psyche that admits of relative, complex, and evolving truth claims is necessary. Jung's psychology advances just such a psychological model. Conscience, within this model, is one of the means by which a degree of sufficient, practical ethical certitude may be attained.

Jung's ethical reflections, as publicly conveyed during his lifetime in the *Collected Works*, occurred in the context of his psychological practice and methodology. I use the qualifier "as publicly conveyed" because Jung drew an important distinction between what he as a private individual experienced in his practical life, and what he as a theorist of personality would formulate and publicly express. As a private individual, Jung believed it important, even necessary, for persons to construct an operative *Weltanschauung* to the best of one's ability. "Nobody is more convinced of the importance of the search for truth than I am." Moreover, "it is ethically indispensable that one give all the credit to one's subjective truth, which means that one admits to being bound by one's conviction and to apply it as a principle of one's actions."[92] Yet, though it is certainly important to seek truth and to act upon its implications, Jung held that it was equally important to recognize one's propensity to error regarding (1) matters that could, in theory, be verified, and (2) awareness of the more profound limitations on knowing imposed by inherent epistemological constraints. "Any human judgment, no matter how great its subjective conviction, is liable to error, particularly judgments concerning transcendental subjects." For Jung, these "transcendental" subjects included assertions about metaphysical beings and claims about absolute moral truths. Thus, Jung's practical epistemological attitude was one that advocated the attempt to formulate a working *Weltanschauung* and ethical principles by which to live, and yet with the caveat that one acknowledge the subjective nature of one's understanding. "Moral judgment is human, limited, and under no condition metaphysically valid." It is "obvious hubris" to think otherwise.[93]

The theoretical basis of this viewpoint was grounded in Kantian epistemology, particularly its delineation of the *phenomena* from the *noumena*, with the associated claim that humans are unable to cross the "barrier" from the former to the latter.[94] The "thing in itself" is forever beyond direct knowledge. Jung identified science, and particularly his analytical psychology, as a disciplined methodology to explore *observable* phenomena, mindful of the epistemological barrier that distinguishes science from non-empirical disciplines such as philosophy and theology.

> Psychology to me is an honest science that recognizes its own boundaries, and I am not a philosopher or a theologian who believes in his ability to step beyond the epistemological barrier. Science is made by man, which does not mean that there are not occasionally acts of grace permitting transgression

into realms beyond. I don't depreciate or deny such facts, but to me they are beyond the scope of science as pointed out above.[95]

Thus, in his "private capacity as a man" Jung could concur with the view that the unconscious is a "portcullis of God," but even with "the best will in the world" he could not "maintain that this is a verifiable assertion, which is what science is all about in the end. It is a subjective confession which has no place in science."[96] This is not to deny that "there is an original behind our images, but it is inaccessible."[97]

Though this epistemological position may seem entirely negative in nature, that is, as establishing impassable boundaries to one's ability to know objectively what is absolutely true, it serves, possibly, the positive function of opening oneself to forms of knowing other than strict objectivism. That is, the epistemological limits that Jung applied to his psychology pertained most significantly and directly to what Tillich termed "controlling" knowledge. Therefore, if one acknowledges that one is simply unable, because of inherent limits, to gain objective control over the subject of one's inquiry such that one may claim to possess truth (i.e., "controlling" knowledge), *then* one is presented with the choice of either skepticism (or, more acutely, nihilism), or the recognition of different modes of knowing and resulting forms of understanding. "Receiving" knowledge is one such form of knowing, which neither seeks nor wants control, but rather freely acknowledges its "relativity." In fact, this relativity—in the sense of "relational"—is the very basis of receiving knowledge. Thus, the Kantian recognition of human epistemological finitude serves not only to constrain the reach of reason but also to redirect this very same reason away from its fixation on the project of control and experimental verification and toward receptivity and experiential confirmation. It was in this manner that Jung adopted Kant's epistemology.

Nietzsche, in spite of his emphasis on the perspectival nature of knowledge, did accept the relative validity and applicability of the standards of knowledge as defined by the reductive science of his era, that is, strictly controlling, as, for instance, when he grasped and yielded to the implications of an orthodox Darwinian anthropology. It was when this epistemological standard was applied rigorously to the "spheres of value"—ethics, theology, philosophy—that Nietzsche concluded that God was dead and that humans lived in a meaningless world—as defined by controlling reason. Nietzsche's subsequent philosophy may be seen as a radical repudiation of the very epistemological standards that led him into his nihilistic quandary in the first place. He rejected objectivism because, to one "intellectually honest" such as himself, it was seen to be illusory in nature and, perhaps of greatest motivational import, ultimately unable to satisfy humanity's deepest longings.

Yet, looked at from a different angle, Nietzsche's guiding metaphors never quite moved beyond the quest for control. His descriptive term for the monistic principle that characterizes the intelligible structure of the world was, tellingly, the "will to power." This phrase does not, despite its misuse by some, refer to simple notions of physical or political power only, but rather to more subtle and complex dynamics of self-overcoming, and so on. But the essential character of this principle—through which Nietzsche formulated his revaluation of values and his theory of conscience—is one of control, subsuming dominance, and mastery. I state this not as a moral criticism of Nietzsche, but rather to make the point that his moral psychology was governed by an epistemological temper that predetermined, or at least strongly governed, how he understood the nature of conscience and the value of its promptings.

Jung's response to the nihilistic challenges of reductive scientism was quite different from Nietzsche in terms of both his psychological theories and his epistemological commitments. For example, although Jung, in agreement with Nietzsche, recognized the dynamic, process nature of reality, he did not conclude from this basic observation that our human experience of relative solidity, continuity, and identity in everyday life was illusory and pernicious. Rather, Jung sought to articulate a view of human reality that did justice to both the inescapable change that continuously erodes and transforms self and world and the relative permanence—as measured by a human life—of the objects and subjects that comprise our world of experience. For example, when he discussed the relativity of human reason, and the permeability and fluidity of the ego, he did so in the context of broader psychodynamics and structures that provide a narrative framework of meaning that encompasses the individual human life in a manner that may soften the need of the ego to be its own sense and source. That is, "change" is perceived by Jung not singularly, nor primarily, in its destructive and disintegrative aspects but rather as a potentially transformative process. For example, at the core of Jung's psychology was a relativization of the ego, particularly in the second half of life, to the more encompassing "self." Further, exemplifying this practice of incorporating the realities of multiplicity and relativity within a more encompassing, unifying framework, Jung placed at the center of his theories the concept of psychological types and the four functions, which served to relativize the hegemonistic claims of the "thinking" function.

The effect of this theoretical typology was a broadening of what was considered to be "rational" to include *both* the "feeling" and "thinking" functions, and an embracing of the epistemological significance of the "irrational" ("sensation" and "intuition").[98] Jung recognized that controlling reason, in the form of "intellectualism," is in ways antithetical to a moral attitude because it is devoid, or dismissive, of feelings—the very means by which one relates to and grasps the moral significance of an event, a choice, a moment. "Feeling always binds one to the reality and meaning of symbolic contents, and these in turn impose binding standards of ethical behavior from which aestheticism and intellectualism are only too ready to emancipate themselves."[99] Thus, by arguing that feelings are an indispensable source of ethical understanding, Jung is opening the way for the claims of alternative forms of knowing other than a narrowly strict, controlling form of reason.

Jung argued further that in the varied spheres of moral relationship—that is, between persons and all that is seen as "personal," including one's own depths—one must not only "judge," but one must "perceive" as well if one wishes to genuinely understand. That is, one must not only control and grasp, but one must receive and yield as well.

Hence an attitude that seeks to do justice to the unconscious as well as to one's fellow human beings cannot possibly rest on knowledge alone, in so far as this consists merely of thinking and intuition. It would lack the function that perceives value, i.e., feeling, as well as the *fonction du reel*, i.e., sensation, the sensible perception of reality.[100]

By arguing that noncognitive experiences—feelings, intuitions, the "heart," fantasies, visions, and all manner of unconscious products, including conscience—yield ethical knowledge, Jung is striking at the heart of both the positivist's and perspectivalist's critique of the meaning of moral valuation and, specifically, conscience. By arguing that feelings and the like convey real moral content, he is putting in place, within his theories, a framework in which non-egoistic moral insight and knowledge may be inwardly derived. What is needed to complete this line of reasoning is that these "noncognitive" phenomena are not only *able* to express moral content, but that the source, ground, or animating nature from which they arose is in some sense "moral." For Jung, conscience was seen, in its "ethical" manifestations, as an exponent for just such a moral realm. As discussed in the last chapter, Jung conceived of the instincts not as merely blind and compulsive, but as having potential moral "content"—purposeful, ordered, creative, "personal"—and as expressing themselves not only physically but psychically as well via the archetypes and the more generalized "moral impulse." Thus, the basis of Jung's claim that conscience may yield genuine moral understanding is the corollary belief that it is potentially expressive of psychic substrata of such rootedness and depth that substantive, ontological ramifications, and resulting epistemological claims of a moral nature, are at least implicit.

In contrast to Jung, Nietzsche applied his deconstructionist criticisms to the notion of a human subject of relative continuity without offering either a practical means by which one may live out of such a perspective, or a broader worldview in which "becoming" and "the many" may be balanced with "being" and "the one." Perhaps Jung's context as a practicing therapist, unlike the relatively solitary life of Nietzsche, compelled him to theorize with the practical demands of psychic healing always at the forefront of his mind. Nonetheless, Nietzsche's psychological models may be criticized not only practically but theoretically as well. Practically, within the parameters of one's actual life as a sentient creature, one assumes relative continuity of identity for oneself and others. To lose this continuity is a psychological disaster. Jung, as a practicing psychiatrist, was prone to recognizing this. Nietzsche, as an autonomous philosopher, was afforded the luxury of imagining the absolute. Theoretically, the notion of the personality as existing, or "being," in a state of radical flux is rendered problematic by the manifest human ability to construct, or recognize, structures of meaning (fictions) within a cosmos that is itself—according to Nietzsche—radically in flux. Nietzsche's theories are unable to account for the emergence of intelligible structures and purposes in a cosmos of radical becoming.

Jung, in an attempt to find the right language and concepts to talk about a psychological foundation that could adequately account for the full range of our experience, made a crucial distinction between "one's own unconscious" and the "collective unconscious." This distinction, based on his *ur*-commitment to "psychic reality," is the determining point of whether one sees unconscious products, such as conscience, as grounded in more than one's own personhood and thus, potentially, expressive of a suprapersonal moral realm. Nietzsche, for example, rejected the meaningfulness of belief in "metaphysical" beings because such beliefs were seen as illusory projections of one's own psychodynamics. Jung concurred that metaphysics was in fact nonempirical and projective in nature, and yet this did not equate with the idea that such ideas had no suprapersonal significance. Jung held that a third way was possible between uncritical metaphysics and reductive naturalism. This third way, *esse in anima*, is decisive in determining how Jung interpreted unconscious phenomena. Responding to a critic of his treatment of the spiritual experiences of "Brother Klaus," Jung wrote:

> Your alternative is either "metaphysical God" or Brother Klaus' "own unconscious." This is the *caput draconis*! Unwittingly and unawares you impute to me a theory which I have been fighting against for decades, namely Freud's theory. As you know, Freud derives the religious "illusion" from

the individual's "own" unconscious, that is, from the personal unconscious. There are empirical reasons that contradict this assumption. I have summed them up in the hypothesis of the collective unconscious.[101]

By distinguishing between one's "own" unconscious and the "collective" unconscious Jung attempted to establish an epistemological framework that overcame the dualistic choice between "absolute objectivity" and "radical subjectivity." That is, through inward immediacy one potentially encounters elements of experience that have suprapersonal significance that relate oneself to frameworks of meaning and value. Through such experiences—personally and as recounted by others—Jung believed that he had discovered an "objective" psyche, that is, a psychological stratum of relative stability independent of conscious, human construction, and to which one is able to relate and to conceptually grasp in linguistic, imaginal approximations. These approximations may serve as guiding and orienting metaphors for the life lived in relation to both an inner and an outer world.

The recognition of the epistemological significance of the unconscious is dependent on a receptive attitude on the part of the ego, in contrast to a demand for control.

> The psyche is a phenomenon not subject to our will; it is nature, and though nature can, by skill, knowledge, and patience, be modified at a few points, it cannot be changed into something artificial without profound injury to our humanity. Man can be transformed into a sick animal but not moulded into an intellectual ideal.[102]

For Jung, unconscious phenomena—including conscience—were the means by which the conscious ego remained in contact with the instinctual foundations of the personality. When the connection between consciousness and the unconscious was atrophied or occluded because of neglect, lack of understanding, or repression, the ego became enervated. The role of the unconscious as the ground of conscious certitude was basic to Jung's understanding of how conscience functions within the broader personality. In the following passage Jung was referring to the loss of plausibility of religious beliefs, but the ideas pertain as well to ethical principles and the metaphors that support them:

> If, however, certain of these images become antiquated, if, that is to say, they lose all intelligible connection with our contemporary consciousness, then our conscious acts of choice and decision are sundered from their instinctive roots and a partial disorientation results, because our judgment then lacks any feeling of definiteness and certitude, and there is no emotional driving-force behind decisions.[103]

In this way the unconscious may be a basis of experiential verification of one's understandings, choices, and actions. Jung recognized, however, that there is difference between a purely subjective, private experience—"inspiration," one's mood, or a hunch—and what one may properly call knowledge or truth. Jung, while clearly valuing the unconscious as generative source of consciousness, nonetheless held that what was optimal was an ongoing cooperation between consciousness and its unconscious foundations. Consciousness is able to apply rational norms and rules to unconscious phenomena, enabling a controlled and contained realization that is able to be applied in practical ways and communicated interpersonally.

> Imagination and intuition are vital to our understanding...[yet] the safe basis of real intellectual knowledge and moral understanding gets lost if one is content with the vague satisfaction of having understood a "hunch." One can explain and know only if one has reduced intuitions to an exact knowledge of facts and their logical connections.[104]

Particularly in the realm of moral judgment, the active, conscious participation of the ego is vital in responsibly engaging the unconscious and allowing it to manifest overtly. The need for conscious discernment of one's animating moral presuppositions is made acute in Jung's psychology considering the paradoxical nature of the unconscious. "As the general manifestations of the unconscious are ambivalent or even ambiguous ('It is a fearful thing to fall into the hands of the living God,' Heb. 10:31), decision and discriminating judgment are all-important."[105]

210

Jung portrayed the ethical conscience as the means by which the conscious personality engaged in such a discernment, or what he called a "dialogue," with unconscious promptings pertaining to conflicts of duty. Jung held that resulting decisions of the person represent a form of moral "truth" that was valid insofar as it was based on the "discursive cooperation" between conscious and unconscious factors. The ethical conscience reflects neither rational reason alone nor blind submission to unconscious impulses, and yields a receptive form of knowledge that is experientially verified.

> Only the creative power of the ethos that expresses the whole man can pronounce the final judgment. Like all the creative faculties in man, his ethos flows empirically from two sources: from rational consciousness and from the irrational unconscious. It is a special instance of what I have called the transcendent function, which is the discursive co-operation of conscious and unconscious factors or, in theological language, of reason and grace.[106]

Jung used the terminology of "truth" in a very particular way. As discussed in chapter 2, Jung claimed to adhere to a form of empiricism that conformed to scientific standards. This form of empiricism was phenomenological and not strictly experimental in nature. Thus, he argued that for the science of psychology "the best we can achieve is true expression. By true expression I mean an open avowal and detailed presentation of everything that is subjectively observed." This means that it is "best to abandon the notion that we are today in anything like a position to make statements about the nature of the psyche that are 'true' or 'correct.'"[107] And yet there is another form of "truth" that Jung acknowledged—a "subjective truth" that he described in this manner:

> Can our experience of the objective world ever save us from our subjective bias? Is not every experience, even in the best of circumstances, at least fifty-per-cent subjective interpretation? On the other hand, the subject is also an objective fact, a piece of the world; and what comes from him comes, ultimately, from the stuff of the world itself, just as the rarest and strangest organism is none the less supported and nourished

211

by the earth which is common to all. It is precisely the most subjective ideas which, being closest to nature and to our own essence, deserve to be called the truest.[108]

This notion of "truth" and "truest" informed Jung's ideas about the nature of moral values. Jung acknowledged the practical relativity of moral judgment. "The formulation of ethical rules is not only difficult but actually impossible because one can hardly think of a single rule what would not have to be reversed under certain circumstances."[109] And, theoretically, in accord with Nietzsche and perspectivalism in general, Jung acknowledged that one's moral judgments may claim no absolute metaphysical basis. "Moral judgment is human, limited, and under no condition metaphysically valid."[110] Yet for Jung the relativity of one's moral judgments was not cause to lapse into nihilistic despair. Rather, the relativity of moral values was seen in the context of the dynamic evolution of human consciousness. On the individual level, Jung made the simple observation that an individual's understanding of what is moral is likely to evolve over time. This does not mean that ethical choices need to be made solely in the context of the immediate present; rather it demonstrates the role of human judgment in determining what is good and evil in any given context.

> As a therapist I cannot, in any given case, deal with the problem of good and evil philosophically but can only approach it empirically. *But because I take an empirical attitude it does not mean I relativize good and evil as such.* I see very clearly: this is evil, but the paradox is just that for this particular stage of development it may be good. Contrariwise, good at the wrong moment in the wrong place may be the worst thing possible. If it were not like this everything would be so simple—too simple.[111]

Thus, by accepting the transitory and evolving nature of moral standards, Jung heightened the significance of conscience in one's practical life. His portrayal of the collective unconscious is the basis by which he believed that conscience was able to facilitate genuine moral insight and understanding—a form of subjective truth that is experientially verified through feelings of moral infidelity or affirmation. "We can refuse to obey this command [of conscience] by an appeal to the moral code and the moral views on which it is founded, though with an uncomfortable feeling of having been disloyal."[112] For Jung, the contextual, evolving nature of morals does not negate their "truth" or relative claims upon our lives. For although a moral claim may be—if the phrase is permissible—only relative in an absolute sense, such a claim on an individual, at a definite time and place, may be, paradoxically, absolutely binding on that individual. In fact, this relativity of morals, as humanly perceived, is to be not only expected but embraced. It is to be expected because of the inherent epistemological limits discussed above, but also because moral judgments are commensurate—for good and ill—to the level of consciousness of the knower. This last point—alluding to the evolving nature of a person's moral capacities—is the basis of how and why Jung held that the relativity of morals ought to be both acknowledged and embraced. The relativity of morals is to be affirmed—in a cognitive and moral sense—precisely because the human discernment of moral goods lies at the heart of the "coming to consciousness" that is the very raison d'être of human beings. It is within this context of evolving consciousness that Jung advocated that we acknowledge the illusory nature—not of our morals themselves—but of our aspirations for absolute moral truth. Instead of such questionable ambitions, Jung advocated that one should attempt to foster an ongoing relationship with one's interior moral sources, including one's conscience. Permanence is to be sought not in fixed ideas—whatever their nature—but in the continuity and dependability of an ever-present relationship.

> I know too well how transitory and sometimes even futile our hypotheses are, to assume their validity as durable truths and as trustworthy foundations of a *Weltanschauung* capable of giving man sure guidance in the chaos of this world. On the contrary, I rely very much on the continuous influx of the *numina* from the unconscious and from whatever lies behind it.[113]

Jung believed that recognizing the relativity of one's knowledge—moral and otherwise—was important not only in order to open oneself to other forms of understanding but also because the acknowledgment of one's epistemological limits tended to facilitate understanding between persons. In contrast to such beneficent results, claims of objective truth tend, according to Jung, to generate conflicts born of self-righteousness and, relatedly, misunderstandings founded on projections.

Late in his life Jung engaged the theologian Martin Buber, through professional journals and third-party correspondence, in a debate that, on the surface, centered on the question of whether Jung was a gnostic (a charge Jung vehemently denied).[114] Underlying this charge of Buber's were important epistemological issues that profoundly affect one's understanding of theology and resulting ethical commitments. I will address in broad outline these issues of epistemology, theology, and ethics in the next chapter as a means of exploring the significance of conscience for understanding, and appreciating, the whole of Jung's thought.

PART III

Conscience and Jung's
Moral Vision

Chapter 7

FROM ID TO THOU

Even if one is persuaded that Jung's theory of conscience is plausible and persuasively refutes, or at least qualifies, other competing theories, the question still remains whether his psychology as a whole may help us to understand, and address, our contemporary moral problems. I will engage this broader question by responding to the recurring accusation that Jung was a modern-day gnostic.[1] This debate about Jung's theological location is relevant not simply to the religious scholar, but will serve to illustrate the defining characteristics and suitability of Jung's ethic. This argument about whether Jung was a gnostic will allow me to summarize—and amplify—much of the preceding discussion by drawing out in sharp relief Jung's epistemological convictions, attitudes toward community and creation itself, and, informing it all, his root anthropological assumptions. For this discussion I will draw primarily on Jung's writings and correspondence during the 1950s, a period when these accusations were topical following his publication of *Answer to Job*.[2] Following this critical exposition of Jung's relationship to gnosticism, I will outline the most significant implications of his theory of conscience for understanding the far-reaching importance of his thought as a whole. That is, I will explore how conscience is at the heart of Jung's *Weltanschauung*—which is not a religion and not quite a myth—and it is conscience that in fact makes Jung so un-gnostic, for it is our conscience that binds us to the goodness and meaning of this life, this reality.

GNOSTICISM: GENERAL CHARACTERISTICS

Hans Jonas, in *The Gnostic Religion*, states that "the *name* 'Gnosticism,' which has come to serve as a collective heading for a manifoldness of sectarian doctrines appearing within and around Christianity during its critical first centuries, is derived from *gnosis*, the Greek word for 'knowledge.'"[3] For the gnostics, knowledge was "the means for the attainment of salvation, or was even the form of salvation itself." Not surprisingly, this salvific knowledge was believed by the gnostics to be contained in their own "articulate doctrine."[4] This doctrine typically appealed to the authority of esoteric ("hidden") texts in which the resurrected Jesus Christ revealed to the apostles the hidden meaning of the events of his life. This secret "knowledge" was transmitted via esoteric initiatory rites and rituals to "a limited number of adepts." Yet, according to Mircea Eliade, it was not the esotericism nor the syncretism that defined gnosticism—for these were common features of the Hellenistic period and the early centuries of Christianity.[5] It was the peculiarity of their beliefs. By "citing the authority of an oral and secret apostolic tradition" individual gnostics could "introduce into Christianity" both beliefs and practices antithetical to "the ethos of the Gospel." Eliade described these beliefs as resulting from "the daring, and strangely pessimistic, reinterpretation of certain myths, ideas, and theologoumena" widely available during the period. The central ideas include: "The dualism of spirit/matter, divine (transcendent)/ antidivine; the myth of the fall of the soul (= spirit, divine particle), that is, incarnation in a body (assimilated to a prison); and the certainty of deliverance (salvation) by virtue of gnosis."[6]

Hans Jonas provided an abstract of major gnostic tenets (which I have futher extracted below), focusing on the points relevant to our discussion of Jung's psychology:

> *Theology:* The cardinal feature of gnostic thought is the radical dualism that governs the relation of God and world, and correspondingly that of man and world. The deity is absolutely transmundane, its nature alien to that of the universe, which it neither created nor governs and to which it is the complete antithesis: to the divine realm of light, self-contained and

remote, the cosmos is opposed as the realm of darkness. The world is the work of lowly powers [the Archons] which, though they may mediately be descended from Him, do not know the true God and obstruct the knowledge of Him in the cosmos over which they rule.

Cosmology: The universe, the domain of the Archons, is like a vast prison whose innermost dungeon is the earth, the scene of man's life.

Anthropology: [Humans are] composed of flesh, soul, and spirit. But reduced to ultimate principles, [their] origin is twofold: mundane and extra-mundane. Not only the body but also the "soul" is a product of the cosmic powers [Archons]. Enclosed in the soul is spirit, or "pneuma,"…a portion of the divine substance from beyond which has fallen into the world.

Eschatology: The radical nature of the dualism determines gnosticism's doctrine of salvation. As alien as the transcendent God is to "this world" is the pneumatic self in the midst of it. The goal of gnostic striving is the release of the "inner man" from the bonds of the world and his return to his native realm of light. The necessary condition for this is that he *knows* about the transmundane God and about himself, that is, about his divine origin as well as his present [imprisoned] situation.

Morality: In this life the *pneumatics*, as the possessors of gnosis called themselves, are set apart from the great mass of mankind. The immediate illumination [of gnosis] not only makes the individual sovereign in the sphere of knowledge … but also determines the sphere of action. Generally speaking, the pneumatic morality is determined by hostility toward the world and contempt for all mundane ties. From this principle, however, two contradictory conclusions could be drawn, and both found their extreme representatives: the ascetic and the libertine. The former deduces from the possession of gnosis the obligation to avoid further contamination by the world and therefore to reduce contact with it to a minimum; the latter derives from the same possession the privilege of absolute freedom.[7]

JUNG AND GNOSTICISM:
HOLISM AND DUALISM

The reasons for associating Jung with gnosticism date to his early professional days and pertain to more than any supposed theoretical affinities. I will briefly identify these associations and offer Jung's defensive rebuttals as to why these do not in fact make him a gnostic. Perhaps first and foremost of the reasons for linking Jung with the gnostics is the fact that he avidly read gnostic literature and cited it frequently in his own writings. Yet Jung argued that simply studying a subject does not make one a "believer" in the subject.

> The people who call me a Gnostic cannot understand that I am a psychologist, describing modes of psychic behavior precisely like a biologist studying the instinctual activities of insects. He does not *believe* in the tenets of the bee's philosophy. When I show the parallels between dreams and Gnostic fantasies I *believe* in neither. They are just facts one does not need to believe or hypostatize.[8]

Jung's avowed motivation for studying the gnostics was his enthusiastic "discovery that they were apparently the first thinkers to concern themselves (after their fashion) with the contents of the collective unconscious."[9] In order to broaden the empirical basis of his observations and hypotheses regarding contemporary culture, Jung sought throughout his career historical precedents for his ideas (hence his equally enthusiastic "discovery" of the alchemists, which he viewed as a significant historical link between the gnostics and the psychology of the unconscious[10]), and he believed gnosticism provided this lineage.

In addition to simply studying the gnostics, Jung, near the resolution (1916) of his "creative illness,"[11] personally wrote a short (twelve pages) "poem in Gnostic style," titled "Seven Sermons of the Dead" *(Septem Sermones ad Mortuos)*.[12] If taken as an expression of his personal, literal beliefs, this peculiar, mythopoetic piece would suggest some affinities between Jung's worldview and that of the gnostics. Jung, in a late-life letter, apologetically and defensively described this text as "a poetic paraphrase of the psychology of the unconscious" that he had written "for a friend's birthday celebration (a private print!)."[13]

Beyond these textual, scholarly reasons for linking Jung with the gnostics are the more substantive issues of his theoretical formulations and commitments that were sustained throughout his life. Most basically, Jung is *not* gnostic in the manner of his dispositional devotion to holistic ways of understanding, in contrast to the radical dualism that permeated gnostic metaphysics, anthropology, and ethics. In part 1 of this work I discussed Jung's moral framework within the contours of three fundamental presuppositions and rationale, all of which advocate nondualistic ways of conceiving human experience. This holistic commitment is as significant in shaping the "ethos" of Jung's psychology as the radical dualism is in defining the gnostic spirit. While the gnostics believed in the negative nature of creation and its immediate source in an evil creator god, Jung was radically affirming of the value of creation and the human role therein. For example, speaking broadly about his ethical commitment to one's immediate, everyday life: "The meaning of human development is to be found in the fulfillment of *this* life—it is rich enough in marvels— and not in detachment from this world."[14]

Ethically, Jung advocated a moral commitment to human relationships that recognized the inherent intertwining of one's welfare and fate with that of one's fellow human beings. This commitment is antithetical to the elitist, escapist gnostic temperament. In a letter to a pastor, Jung expressed his conviction that individual illumination is never a satisfactory "end-state," but rather always entails an ethical responsibility toward others:

> You could indeed rejoice over this [achieving a degree of personal liberation] did not your "joyfulness" crassly conflict with the suffering of the world and your fellow man....It falls to the lot of anyone who has overcome something or detached himself from something to bear in the same measure the burden of others....I know these moments of liberation come flashing out of the process, but I shun them because I always feel at such a moment that I have thrown off the burden of being human and that it will fall back on me with redoubled weight.[15]

This does not mean that Jung did not value and recognize the indispensable role of introversion in facilitating psychological transformation. But he believed that a life lived in isolation from others is suitable, that is, moral, only as a phase necessary for preparing one for a return to communal life.

> Although the anchorite does not represent a model for living, the solitude of religious experience can be, and will be, an unavoidable and necessary transitional phase for everyone who seeks the essential experience, that is to say the *primordial* religious experience. This alone forms the true and unshakable foundation of his inner life of belief. But once he has attained this certitude, he will in the normal course of things be unable to remain alone with it. His fulfillment spills over in communication.[16]

Jung recognized that individuation itself could be achieved only in deep relationship with others. Rather than viewing the world and one's fellow humans as fallen, evil, unclean, Jung urged an ethic of empathic, mutual understanding:

> Nobody can become aware of his individuality unless he is closely and responsibly related to his fellow beings, he is not withdrawing to an egoistic desert when he tries to find himself. He can only discover himself when he is deeply and unconditionally related to some, and generally related to a great many, individuals with whom he has a chance to compare and from whom he is able to discriminate himself.[17]

From the above passages I believe it is evident and demonstrable that Jung's basic anthropology and ethics are essentially different from that of the gnostics. His thinking is, at its core, permeated with a holistic affirmation of the created world and of the goodness, and necessity, of extending one's ethical commitments to one's fellow human beings. This is in sharp contrast to the gnostic pessimistic dualism and elitist ethic outlined above.

Yet, although the above arguments are perhaps significant enough themselves to counter the claim that Jung was gnostic, there is another issue, with broad ethical implications, that is raised by the debate about Jung's theology and to which we now turn. This issue—epistemological in nature, yet also existential, theological, psychological, and, if one so chooses, metaphysical—is perhaps *the* problem, *the* question around which so many other conflicts and quandaries have arisen throughout history. Elaine Pagels, in her book *The Gnostic Gospels*, describes how the defining question for the early Christian theologian Justin Martyr—a question that was central to his conversion from Platonism to Christianity—was whether "the human mind could find God within itself, or whether it needed instead to be enlightened by divine revelation—by means of the Scriptures and the faith proclaimed by the church."[18] I would argue that whether Jung is to be considered essentially gnostic or not rests on this issue of how one conceives of the human–divine relationship and the role of the psyche therein. Or, more simply, does one accept or reject his epistemological stance? This epistemological viewpoint is another expression of what I have called Jung's "third way," a hermeneutical outlook that seeks to mediate between apparently contradictory positions in a variety of contexts.

JUNG AND GNOSTICISM: THE EPISTEMOLOGICAL DIVIDE

Jung's own understanding of his theoretical distinction from the gnostics focused on essential epistemological differences. "There is a difference between hypothesis and hypostasis. The Gnostic, which Buber accuses me of being, makes no hypothesis, but a hypostasis in making metaphysical statements."[19] And whereas the gnostic uncritically engaged in elaborating mythic doctrine, Jung conceived of his work more modestly. He saw himself not as a mystical proclaimer of *gnosis* but as an empiricist who remained carefully within epistemological barriers.

> Why is so much attention devoted to the question of whether I am a Gnostic or an agnostic? Why is it not simply stated that I am a psychiatrist whose prime concern is to record and interpret his empirical material? I try to investigate facts and make them more generally comprehensible.[20]

This "investigation of facts" included archetypal content of the unconscious that was plainly and distinctly of a religious nature. Jung explained that because of the centrality of the religious factor in human psychic life this inclusion of the mythic and metaphysical was unavoidable—not to say most desirable—in any adequate general psychology. "Since views and opinions about metaphysical or religious subjects play a very great role in empirical psychology, I am obliged for practical reasons to work with concepts corresponding to them. In so doing I am aware that I am dealing with anthropomorphic ideas and not with actual gods and angels."[21] In this manner—by explicitly disavowing that individual subjective experience may merit the status of literal, objective truth claim for the public community—Jung attempted to refute the charge that his statements had crossed the threshold of reducing God to one's own unconscious. As discussed in the last chapter, Jung rejected what he felt was a dualistic choice between either "one's own" unconscious or a "metaphysical being,"[22] and instead attempted to articulate a synthetic, mediating alternative. He sometimes pursued this project constructively, and sometimes critically, as when he claimed that in fact it was not *he* who was engaging in the gnostic practice of hypostatizing metaphysical beings, but rather his accusers. "You overlook the facts and then think that I hypostatize ideas and am therefore a 'Gnostic.' *It is your theological standpoint that is a gnosis, not my empiricism*, of which you obviously haven't the faintest inkling."[23]

Jung believed that the failure to acknowledge epistemological limits not only resulted in erroneous theoretical claims but also had the socially pernicious effect of alienating us from others through self-righteous claims and misunderstandings founded on projections.

> We shall never be able to understand other philosophies or religions if everyone thinks his conviction is the only right one. Thus Buber blandly assumes that everyone thinks the same as he does when he says "God." But in reality Buber means Yahweh, the orthodox Christian means the Trinity, the Mohammedan Allah, the Buddhist Buddha, the Taoist Tao, and so on....This leads to no understanding between people, of which we stand in such dire need today. My appar-

ent skepticism is only a recognition of the epistemological barrier, of which Buber doesn't seem to possess the ghost of an idea. When I say that God is first and foremost our conception, this is twisted into God is "nothing but our conception." In reality there is a background of existence which we can intuit at most but cannot transpose into the sphere of our knowledge.[24]

As discussed in chapter 2, at the core of Jung's form of empiricism is his commitment to what he termed "psychic reality." From the above discussion I believe it is fair to conclude that whether or not one judges Jung's psychology to be essentially gnostic rests on whether one accepts or rejects the suprapersonal epistemological and ontological significance of the products of the collective unconscious. Finally, one's judgment of the significance of the phenomenon of conscience is likewise determined by one's epistemological position regarding the nature of inwardly derived knowledge.

CONSCIENCE AND JUNG'S PSYCHOLOGY

I began this study by observing that there were difficulties in understanding the moral significance of Jung's psychology owing to problems in his own presentation of ideas and distorted readings of him by advocates and detractors alike. My thesis was that by adequately understanding the nature and role of conscience in Jung's psychology, one might gain a new appreciation of his psychology as a whole. I have described the moral presuppositions of Jung's thought that grounded and framed his thinking regarding conscience, and I have described in various ways how his theory of conscience is different from alternative theories. I will now briefly consider how Jung's ideas regarding conscience can shed new light on the way one understands two cardinal features of his psychology, namely, individuation and his psychology of religion. These remarks are not exhaustive or comprehensive in nature, but are intended to identify what I consider to be the most critical, relevant issues and to offer provisional conclusions.

Through the lens of conscience the process of individuation assumes a more relational, conflicted, and morally driven character than when conceived in terms of alternative concepts such as "greater consciousness" or "self-realization." While individuation *was* characterized by Jung as often necessitating, or precipitating, an isolation from the external world, the process is also constituted by engagement with others. While analysis and other introspective methods are integral to individuation, Jung claims that these are "only the preparatory part. The main analysis is what to do with the things that have emerged from the unconscious."[25] The "what to do" element of individuation refers directly to one's moral reflections and the ethical decisions that emerge in dialogue with conscience.

Relatedly, conscience may be seen as keeping the process of individuation closer to one's everyday reality by forcing encounters with one's shadow. That is, individuation without the moral element forced upon oneself by an examination of conscience is more prone to becoming ungrounded and introverted. Jung wryly observed that there was a tendency among "foolish Jungians" to attempt to "avoid the shadow and make for the archetypes."[26] Conscience, as the function par excellence for examining one's motives—the salutary and unsavory alike—is essential to this difficult process of recognizing one's shadow. Jung described the relationship between conscience, the shadow, and the broadening of consciousness in the following manner:

> If a man is endowed with an ethical sense and is convinced of the sanctity of ethical values, he is on the surest road to a conflict of duty. And although this looks desperately like a moral catastrophe, it alone makes possible a higher differentiation of ethics and a broadening of consciousness. A conflict of duty forces us to examine our conscience and thereby to discover the shadow. This, in turn, forces us to come to terms with the unconscious.[27]

In this convoluted manner, moral conflicts, and the encounter with one's ethical conscience in particular, facilitate the process of individuation. This much, in fact, may be readily apparent. But it is important to recognize that not only does conscience "serve" the process of individuation, but the process of individuation serves a larger ethical purpose. That is, individuation itself is an ethically infused process that serves larger ethical ends. Conscience, as an integral factor in the process of individuation, is an indispensable element in realizing this larger ethical aim. As discussed earlier, Jung described the unconscious as a natural phenomenon that is not "moral," or "immoral," as we normally understand the term when we pass moral judgment on ourselves and others. Rather, it is "morally neutral." For example, "a dream never says 'you ought' or 'this is the truth.' It presents an image in much the same way as nature allows a plant to grow, and it is up to us to draw conclusions. If a person has a nightmare, it means he is either too much given to fear or too exempt from it."[28] Thus, it is our conscious attitude and reflective discernment that ultimately determine how the unconscious phenomena are allowed or enabled to manifest, and whether they "will be conducive to good or evil."[29] Conscience, as a dialectical process between consciousness and the unconscious, is the means by which these moral evaluations are made.

As Jung was quite quick to point out, individuation may, and often does, lead to a conflict with established norms. If one is to remain "true to one's innermost nature and vocation," that is, if one is to continue on the path of individuation, then an encounter with the ethical conscience will most likely arise, unless one is blessed with a most benign family and social context that allows for the harmonious realization of the individual personality. Jung described how, paradoxically, this encounter with conscience is both the locus of acute ethical conflict and the means of resolution.

> Without wishing it, we human beings are placed in situations in which great "principles" entangle us in something, and God leaves it to us to find a way out. Sometimes a clear path is opened with his help, but when it really comes to the point one has the feeling of having been abandoned by every good spirit. Then it may turn out that he can no longer keep to the letter of the law. That is where his most personal ethics begin: in grim confrontation with the Absolute, in striking out on a path condemned by current morality and the guardians of the law. And yet he may feel that he has never been truer to his innermost nature and vocation, and hence

never nearer to the Absolute, because he alone and the
Omniscient have seen the actual situation as it were from
inside, whereas the judges and condemners see it only from
outside.[30]

Conscience is thus at the heart of individuation, for it both
precipitates the conflicts that make us aware of our shadow, drawing us into relational engagement, and is the means whereby differentiation of the moral quality of unconscious forces occurs. But
even more importantly, individuation itself, when informed by a
strong ethical sense, was seen by Jung in the context of a wider
range of issues. Yes, by consciously engaging the manifold moral
conflicts that one confronts in life one may develop a refined conscience, which in turn may yield greater self-awareness. And this
greater consciousness may, in turn, yield greater moral freedom.[31]

In spite of, or because of, this relatively positive portrayal of
human moral capacities, Jung was clear to distinguish individuation from other disciplines or processes that lay claim to the
salvific benefits of one's efforts. "It is equally out of place to say
that individuation is *self-redemption*. This is precisely what it is
not."[32] Conscience, by way of forcing a recognition of the limits of
rational reflection, may serve to lead a person from the ethical to
the religious spheres of life. In this sense, conscience is thus not
only the means of infusing individuation with ethical content, but
is also that which places individuation itself in a greater context
that gives it an ultimate rationale.

> For people with religious sensibilities this [ethical] rational-
> ism is not enough; they have a dim suspicion that ethics
> needs a different foundation from the one which Janus-faced
> reason grants it. "Reason" is, notoriously, not necessarily eth-
> ical any more than intelligence is. These people sense in reli-
> gion an indispensable I–Thou relationship which is not at
> hand in any rational decisions based on ego-conditioned
> judgments.[33]

Beyond these ethical reflections, conscience sheds light on
certain elements of Jung's psychology of religion, specifically the
question of evil. Jung's theodicy—which, it is easy to forget, was
articulated within the epistemological limits of his analytical psy-

chology—was based on the concept of a creator who was not fully conscious. Jung explained his rationale in the following manner:

> You know that we human beings are unable to explain anything that happens without or within ourselves otherwise than through the use of the intellectual means at our disposal. We always have to use mental elements similar to the facts we believe we have observed. Thus when we try to explain how God has created His world or how He behaves toward the world, the analogy we use is the way in which our creative spirit produces and behaves. When we consider the data of palaeontology with the view that a conscious creator has perhaps spent more than a thousand million years, and has made, as it seems to us, no end of detours to produce consciousness, we inevitably come to the conclusion that—if we want to explain His doings at all—His behavior is strikingly similar to a being with an at least very limited consciousness."[34]

Thus, within his epistemological limits, human experience suggests, by way of analogy, that God is a being of limited consciousness. Though unsatisfactory in certain respects, Jung argues that this portrayal, insofar as reason is able to approach the problem at all, is closer to human experience. Jung offered the following appeal to experience to validate his ideas, as opposed to the ideal hypostasis of God as Summum Bonum:

> It is permissible to assume that the Summum Bonum is so good, so high, so perfect, but so remote that it is entirely beyond our grasp. But it is equally permissible to assume that the ultimate reality is a being representing all the qualities of its creation, virtue, reason, intelligence, kindness, consciousness, *and their opposites,* to our mind a complete paradox. The latter view fits the facts of human experience, whereas the former cannot explain away the obvious existence of evil and suffering. "Whence evil?"—this age-old question is not answered unless you assume the existence of a [supreme] being *who is in the main unconscious.*[35]

Jung objected to the notion of Summum Bonum, and *privatio boni,* on the grounds that it diminished the reality of one's shadow and the depth of moral struggle at the heart of life. "I am afraid of unreflecting optimism and of secret loopholes, as for instance, 'Oh, you can trust in the end that everything will be all right.' *Id est:* 'God is good' (and not beyond good and evil)."[36] Most significantly, however, the idea of a Creator already fully conscious rendered pointless, as Jung saw it, humanity's own participation in creation:

> Since a creation without the reflecting consciousness of man has no discernible meaning, the hypothesis of a latent meaning endows man with a cosmogonic significance, a true *raison d'être*. If on the other hand the latent meaning is attributed to the Creator as part of a conscious plan of creation, the question arises: Why should the Creator stage-manage this whole phenomenal world since he already knows what he can reflect himself in, and why should he reflect himself at all since he is already conscious of himself? Why should he create alongside his own omniscience a second, inferior consciousness—millions of dreary little mirrors when he knows in advance just what the image they reflect will look like?[37]

Bringing to consciousness the "latent meanings" of creation meant for Jung more than a simple self-reflective consciousness. Rather, the significant contribution of humanity is in the conscious discernment of good and evil, which, according to Jung, attain actual existence through the "intervention of human consciousness." *Conscience* is the term used to describe this process of conscious adjudication between good and evil.

> With no human consciousness to reflect themselves in, good and evil simply happen, or rather, there is no good and evil, but only a sequence of neutral events, or what the Buddhists call the Nidhana-chain, the uninterrupted causal concatenation leading to suffering, old age, sickness, and death. Buddha's insight and the Incarnation in Christ break the chain through the intervention of the enlightened human consciousness, which thereby acquires a metaphysical and cosmic significance.[38]

The presupposition that God is "in the main unconscious" thus informed Jung's understanding of the positive, moral purpose of human existence: "Why has God created consciousness and reason and doubt, if complete surrender and obedience to his will is the *ultima ratio*? He was obviously not content with animals only. He wants reflecting beings who are at the same time capable of surrendering themselves to the primordial creative darkness of his will, unafraid of the consequences."[39]

This portrayal of the human–divine relationship informed Jung's description of what the new "form of worship" would look like to those who accepted the responsibility of conscientious living. "Instead of the propitiating praise to an unpredictable king or the child's prayer to a loving father, the responsible living and fulfilling of the divine will in us will be our form of worship of and commerce with God."[40]

Jung's moral psychology places conscience at the center of this process of the responsible incarnation of the unconscious. Conscience then, as Jung portrayed it, was the means by which one may be true to both one's own "innermost nature," and to the Creator that one "worships" as a responsible self. The basis of Jung's conception of conscience is the conviction that the human experience of its own depths *does* represent an encounter with the ontological foundations of reality. Jung's critical epistemology provided the theoretical framework whereby one's inability to objectively grasp and know this ground was not a reason for skepticism, but rather was the basis of acknowledging our finitude and our human task: the ongoing discernment and conscientious expression of the "continuous influx of the *numina* from the unconscious and from whatever lies behind it."[41]

AN EGRESS

Whereas Freud saw a chaotic and amoral *id*, to be dominated when possible and sublimated when necessary, Jung saw a generative matrix out of which psychic life in all of its complexity emerges, from the sublime to the wicked, from the brilliant to the banal. Whereas Nietzsche saw a will to power in a world of self-serving struggle, Jung saw a tremendous yet personal "other" with whom, like Job, one may argue, grapple, and plead, who is both advocate and accuser, and in whom, in the end, one may recognize a superior form of wisdom. Conscience, if one hearkens to its deeper movements, may be the proclaimer and sustainer of one's relationship with this inward *thou*.

Through one's encounters with conscience—once recognized as a dialogue with a suprapersonal source of guidance—one may be inspired to risk following one's deeper desires, shedding the false guilt of heteronomous authorities, hoping and asking for grace to choose what is good and eschew what is bad in this world marked by good and evil. What was once a world of soulless objects, mindless impulse, and selfish drives, may through conscience become the dramatic realm for a quest of cosmogonic significance in which one is called to engage and join the fray. Through conscience the merely "it is" becomes an "I ought." And, through conscience, one's own ground of being, once an *id*, is found to be a *thou*.

This is neither science nor metaphysics but rather the truth of subjectivity, that is, clear discernment and forthright expression of one's most essential, compelling, and immediate inward experience. To this experience many names have been given. Carl Jung called it conscience.

Appendix

A BRIEF HISTORY OF CONSCIENCE

A brief and broad overview of the history of the idea of conscience in the West may be written as follows, demonstrating a diversity of meanings within conceptual unity, constellated around an experiential core:

Although the Hebrew scriptures contain no concept that corresponds directly to the predominant notion of conscience as an inner, moral faculty, we do read of God's omniscient scrutiny and judgment as both exemplar and projection of the human experience of moral self-examination (e.g., Ps 139). For Plato, conscience was understood primarily in its cognitive aspect as the ability to rationally recognize the Good, and it was believed to be, potentially, universally available to all persons. To the Stoics, conscience was an internal moral authority, condemning in its "bad" form and praising in its "good" form. Interestingly, in the writings of Cicero, bad conscience is referred to as consciousness of something (usually an immoral act), while good conscience is referred to without reference to the object of consciousness, but instead refers to a praising of some virtue, some quality of the person.

The specific term *conscience* derives from this period (early common era) from *conscientia* (L) meaning "to know with," and is closely aligned etymologically and functionally with the term *consciousness*. In the writings of Paul, conscience is understood as the law of God, present in the hearts of all humans, which accuses and convicts. The focus of Paul's conscience becomes one's integrity with one's self vis-à-vis one's relationship with God. Given our sinfulness, a good conscience before God requires a bad conscience with one's self. Further, while conscience for Paul was the court of first appeal, the community was to serve as intermediate guide, with God as the final judge. Augustine, expressing a heightened mode of self-reflexivity, spoke of conscience in the context of knowing God through knowing ourselves, or, conversely, knowing ourselves only through knowing God.

Characteristically, the medieval Franciscans spoke of conscience in terms of an affect of the heart, while the Dominicans understood conscience as a form of cognition aligned with reason. Aquinas designated two functions that relate to moral judgment and behavior: *synderesis* orients us to the good, decides, and is infallible; *conscientia* motivates, judges, and is fallible.

The Protestant Reformation saw itself as both an outgrowth of and defender of conscience, exemplified in Luther's "I can do no else." In reaction to the ecclesial management of conscience (through the ritualized "tribunal of conscience" and "care of the soul"), the Reformers invoked Paul's injunction that one's allegiance is not to an external law (and its institutional locus) but to God's law within one's heart, thereby rejecting the notion of salvation through works externally mediated.

Enlightenment philosophers, with their general emphasis on and trust in the powers of reason, tended to align conscience with the autonomous, rational self capable of self-governance. However, as morality and religion became logically differentiated and functionally separated in this period of thought, the authority of conscience was subjected to radical criticism as its supposed divine source was undermined. While Descartes, Locke, Kant, and others believed morality and conscience were inseparable from their religious contexts, the nineteenth century was marked by critics of religion, such as Feuerbach, Marx, and Nietzsche, who believed that the traditional notion of conscience was essentially an internalization of repressive social forces engineered by the powerful to preserve their privilege. As these cultural critics focused on the destructive and constraining aspects of morality, conscience came to be seen in polarized negativity, that is, as supporting either aggrandized self-righteousness or compulsive self-recrimination.

Continuing this iconoclastic work, Freud completed the demolition of the Victorian conscience by vigorously challenging its traditional portrayal as a legitimately authoritative voice. He claimed that, in fact, much of our psychic suffering may be attributed to the tyrannical and compulsive goading of the super-ego—the internalization of familial and social mores—and that full human maturity and satisfaction required precisely that we mitigate this oppressive voice of the old.

Jung advanced the notion of a twofold conscience, the "moral conscience" and the "ethical conscience." The former concept is roughly analogous, operationally though not aetiologically, to Freud's super-ego, while the latter concept represents an example of the transcendent function. The ethical conscience most often arises when critical reflection is brought to bear on a conflict of duties, where society's mores provide no clear answer, and the solution can arise only through the creative ethos of the whole personality, that is, a creative dialogue between consciousness and the unconscious, or, theologically, reason and grace.

Subsequent theorists in the field of developmental psychology, for example, Lawrence Kohlberg and Erik Erikson, have extended psychoanalytic theory to construct more sophisticated understandings of the formation of conscience and the positive role that it may play in enabling social adaptation.

Finally, current thought in biologically rooted areas of psychological inquiry, for example, genetic and evolutionary psychology, accord conscience a positive role in contributing to the survival and evolution of the human species. From these biological perspectives, however, conscience is understood in purely functional, utilitarian terms without traditional reference to a moral authority resting in natural laws, cosmic principles, or the will of the divine, however conceived.

NOTES

Chapter 1

1. Paul Tillich, *Systematic Theology*, vol. 1 (Chicago: University of Chicago Press, 1951), 10, 12–14, etc.

2. Charles Taylor, *Sources of the Self: The Making of the Modern Identity* (Cambridge, MA: Harvard University Press, 1989), 3–52, etc.

3. Don S. Browning, *Religious Thought and the Modern Psychologies: A Critical Conversation in the Theology of Culture* (Philadelphia: Fortress Press, 1987), 18–20, etc.

4. From "Auguries of Innocence," which commences "To see a World in a grain of Sand...." (William Blake, *The Essential Blake*, ed. Stanley Kunitz [New York: Ecco Press, 1987], 62).

5. Tillich uses similar terminology in his essay "Moralisms and Morality: Theonomous Ethics," though with an emphasis not on conscience but rather on the problem of the "relative" and "absolute" in ethical theory and practice, as addressed through his ontological framework of essence and existence (Paul Tillich, *Theology of Culture*, ed. Robert C. Kimball [London: Oxford University Press, 1959], 133–45).

6. This thought represents an extension of Jung's own phrasing: "A dream that is not understood remains a mere occurrence; understood, it becomes a living experience" ("Fundamental Questions of Psychotherapy," in Carl G. Jung, *The Collected Works of C. G. Jung*, vol. 16, *The Practice of Psychotherapy*, trans. R. F. C. Hull [Princeton: Princeton University Press, 1955], 123). It may be noted that this passage of Jung's was paraphrased—uncredited—by James Hillman as "soul refers to that unknown component which...turns events into experiences" (James Hillman, *Re-Visioning Psychology* [New York: HarperPerennial, 1975], xvi).

7. Suggestively, *conscientia* originally meant either "to know with another" or "to know with oneself." Logically, and paradoxically, this

would imply that "oneself" is also, in some sense, "another"—a problem not unfamiliar to the field of psychopathology.

8. For a cursory review of this historical background, see the appendix.

9. I use here the term *conscience* broadly, as "self-referential moral deliberation," without judgment as to the depth, quality or nature of this "conscience," and in this sense I believe the above statement is justified. Regarding the decline in heteronomous sources, see, for example, Donald A. Crosby, *The Specter of the Absurd: Sources and Criticisms of Modern Nihilism* (Albany: State University of New York Press, 1988), or William Barrett, *Death of the Soul: From Descartes to the Computer* (Garden City, NY: Anchor Press, 1986).

10. This basic idea of the declining authority of traditional sources of moral norms permeates many of the sources informing this study, including Peter Berger, *The Sacred Canopy: Elements of a Sociological Theory of Religion* (Garden City, NY: Doubleday, 1967); Taylor, *Sources of the Self*; Crosby, *Specter of the Absurd*; and Carl G. Jung, particularly *The Collected Works of C. G. Jung*, vol. 10, *Civilization in Transition*, trans. R. F. C. Hull (Princeton: Princeton University Press, 1964), and vol. 11, *Psychology and Religion: West and East*, trans. R. F. C. Hull (Princeton: Princeton University Press, 1958).

11. Though it is beyond the immediate scope of this work, it is of interest to note that Nietzsche claimed, "There is no point on which we have learned to think and feel more differently" than that of the primordial transvaluation of conscience, from that of alignment with "the herd" to that of endorsing a consciousness of individuality and related personal responsibility (Friedrich Nietzsche, *The Gay Science*, trans. Walter Kaufmann [New York: Vintage Books, 1974], 175). Although the issue of identification or differentiation with "the herd" is ever present, even to this day, our discussion here commences, in a sense, at the zenith of this "individual conscience"—what Nietzsche called the "scientific conscience" (ibid., 307)—and attempts to contribute to a new transvaluation.

12. The following discussion of conscience during the medieval and Reformation periods is largely derived from Benjamin Nelson, *On the Roads to Modernity: Conscience, Science, and Civilizations: Selected Writings*, ed. Toby E. Huff (Totowa, NJ: Rowman & Littlefield, 1981); and Paul Tillich, *A History of Christian Thought*, ed. Carl E. Braaten (New York: Simon & Schuster, 1967).

13. Nelson, *On the Roads to Modernity*, 43–49.

14. Erik H. Erikson, *Young Man Luther: A Study in Psychoanalysis and History* (New York: W. W. Norton, 1958), 195, 214–18, etc.

15. Van A. Harvey, *A Handbook of Theological Terms* (New York: Collier Books, 1964), 46–47 and 56–58.

16. Frederick Copleston, *A History of Philosophy*, vol. 5 (New York: Image Books, 1959), 171–201; and Nelson , *On the Roads to Modernity*. A specific and poignant instance from our own American history is the quotation from the French book of maxims *The Rules of Civility*, which George Washington memorized, copied, and quoted throughout his life: "Labor to keep alive in your breast that spark of celestial fire known as conscience" (George Washington, quoted in *George* magazine, October 1999, p. 164).

17. Jung, *Collected Works*, 10:447.

18. Neal O. Weiner, *The Harmony of the Soul: Mental Health and Moral Virtue Reconsidered* (Albany: State University of New York Press, 1993), 152.

19. Ibid.

20. Harvey, *Handbook of Theological Terms*, 157.

21. See, for example, Weiner, *Harmony of the Soul*, 158, and Crosby, *Specter of the Absurd*, 1–8.

22. Philip Rieff, *The Triumph of the Therapeutic: Uses of Faith after Freud* (Chicago: University of Chicago Press, 1966), 22–23.

23. Carl G. Jung, *The Collected Works of C. G. Jung*, vol. 18, *The Symbolic Life: Miscellaneous Writings*, trans. R. F. C. Hull (Princeton: Princeton University Press, 1950), 616 (1949). *The Collected Works* of C. G. Jung were compiled by the editors according to both thematic and chronological criteria. Thus, within any given volume there may be texts spanning several decades. In order to facilitate the reading of this study I have placed in parentheses in the notes following page references the original date of publication of the specific text cited from the *Collected Works* volume; if the volume is a single text I identify the original date of publication.

24. Carl G. Jung, *Letters*, vol. 1, *1906–1950*, ed. Gerhard Adler in collaboration with Aniela Jaffé, trans. R. F. C. Hull (Princeton: Princeton University Press, 1973), 375 (1945).

25. Another example, written shortly before Jung's death: "A doctor sees so many things from the seamy side of life that he is seldom far from the truth when he interprets the hints that his patient produces as signs of an uneasy conscience" (Carl G. Jung, *Memories, Dreams, Reflections*, recorded and ed. by Aniela Jaffé; trans. Richard and Clara Winston [New York: Vintage Books, 1961], 27).

26. See, for example, Henri F. Ellenberger, *The Discovery of the Unconscious* (New York: Basic Books, 1970); and Peter Homans, *Jung in Context* (Chicago: University of Chicago Press, 1979).

27. Erich Neumann, *Depth Psychology and a New Ethic*, trans. Eugene Rolfe (Boston: Shambhala, 1990), 80.

28. Ibid., 29.

29. Jung, *Collected Works*, 10:437–55 (1958).

30. Ibid., 456–68.

31. Ibid., 458.

32. Jung, *Collected Works*, 16:180 (1946).

33. Rieff, whose attitude toward Jung is critical yet at times ambiguous, makes an interesting statement relevant to this issue: "No one knows the exact wording of Jung's title to greatness. However it may be explained and qualified, the legitimacy of that title will depend in part upon the success of his attempt to install a psychology where ontology once reigned" (*Triumph of the Therapeutic*, 42).

34. Browning, *Religious Thought*, 8.

35. As one example, Jung's personal secretary, Aniela Jaffé, titled her overview study of Jung *The Myth of Meaning*, trans. R. F. C. Hull (New York: Penguin Books, 1971).

36. Jung, *Collected Works*, 10:446 (1958).

37. Ibid., 437.

38. Ibid., 439.

39. Ibid.

40. Ibid., 449.

41. Ibid., 453.

42. Ibid., 439.

43. Ibid., 454.

44. Ibid., 437.

45. Ibid.

46. Ibid., 454.

47. For example, in discussing Freud's theory of the super-ego, Jung wrote, "Either it was the tyranny of the primal father which created morality, or, if it was already implanted in human nature, it was also present in the primal father, who by his very constitution bore the moral law within him. The question cannot be resolved empirically because it is in the highest degree improbable that a primal father ever existed and, furthermore, we ourselves were not around when the first moral reactions took place" (Carl G. Jung, *Letters*, vol. 2, *1951–1961*, ed. Gerhard Adler in collaboration with Aniela Jaffé; trans. R. F. C. Hull [Princeton: Princeton University Press, 1973], 457 [1958]). This theoretical posi-

tion—the transcendent nature of nonempirical questions—was generally stated in an agnostic tone by Jung, for example, when addressing the question of human freedom: "Nevertheless, it remains a matter of doubt how much his seemingly free decision has a causal, and possibly unconscious motivation. This may be quite as much an 'act of God' as any natural cataclysm. The problem seems to me unanswerable, because we do not know where the roots of the feeling of moral freedom lie; and yet they exist no less surely than the instincts, which are felt as compelling forces" (Carl G. Jung, *The Collected Works of C. G. Jung*, vol. 9, part ii, *Aion*, trans. R. F. C. Hull [Princeton: Princeton University Press, 1959], 26 [1951]). In order to understand this theoretical position—and why it was not simply an abdication of scientific responsibility—it will be necessary for me to articulate Jung's epistemological views within the framework of his psychology as a whole. This task is part of the rationale behind the logical construction of this study.

48. The issue of the origin of conscience and whether it is ultimately reducible to biological or social factors is at the very heart of the subject of this book and as such provide the topics of chapters 5–6.

49. Jung, *Collected Works*, 10:453–54 (1958).

50. Ibid., 450.

51. Ibid., 454.

52. Ibid., 439.

53. Ibid., 443.

54. This statement of mine is a general summation of much of Jung's essay "A Psychological View of Conscience," but its subject matter receives focused articulation in pp. 441–44 in Jung, *Collected Works*, vol. 10 (1958).

55. Ibid., 443–4.

56. Ibid., 454.

57. Ibid.

58. Jung, *Collected Works*, 9.ii:25 (1951).

59. Jung, *Collected Works*, 10:454 (1958).

60. Ibid.

61. Ibid., 455.

62. Ibid., 454–55.

63. Ibid., 446. Jung acknowledges that the "dividing line is fluid" between the concepts of "feelings" and "emotions." Yet "for practical reasons" he conceptually distinguishes the two by describing emotions as "involuntary" and "characterized by a marked physical innervation," while feelings are largely devoid of intense physical innervations and are "a voluntarily disposable function" (Carl G. Jung, *The Collected Works of*

C. G. Jung, vol. 6, *Psychological Types*, A Revision by R. F. C. Hull of the Translation by H. G. Baynes [Princeton: Princeton University Press, 1971], 411–12 [1921], and 433–36).

64. Jung, *Collected Works*, 6:434.

65. I use the phrase "re-personalize" in the sense that Erazim Kohák uses the term, that is, as an effort to reverse the "systematic depersonalization of both our conception of the world and of the world of our ordinary life itself" by conceiving of the world as "personal," that is, "as structured in terms of relations best understood on the model of meaningful relations among persons," guided by "a deep respect for the integrity of their being, conceiving of our interrelation with them as governed by moral law, not simply utility and consent" (Erazim Kohák, *The Embers and the Stars: A Philosophical Inquiry into the Moral Sense of Nature* [Chicago: University of Chicago Press, 1984], 210, 209, and 214, respectively).

66. Jung, *Memories, Dreams, Reflections*, 325.

67. Jung, *Collected Works*, 10:442 (1958).

68. Jung, *Memories, Dreams, Reflections*, 338.

Chapter 2

1. Carl G. Jung, *The Collected Works of C. G. Jung*, vol. 10, *Civilization in Transition*, trans. R. F. C. Hull (Princeton: Princeton University Press, 1964), 311 (1958).

2. By way of contrast, see, for example, Freud's rejection of religious feeling as a valid source of knowledge or apprehension of reality. Freud "cannot discover this oceanic feeling" in himself but instead finds recourse in the "ideational content" associated with the feelings in order to deal with them "scientifically" (Sigmund Freud, *Civilization and Its Discontents*, trans. and ed. James Strachey [New York: W. W. Norton, 1961], 11).

3. Carl G. Jung, *The Collected Works of C. G. Jung*, vol. 18, *The Symbolic Life: Miscellaneous Writings*, trans. R. F. C. Hull (Princeton: Princeton University Press, 1950), 324 (1950).

4. Carl G. Jung, *The Collected Works of C. G. Jung*, vol. 6, *Psychological Types*, A Revision by R. F. C. Hull of the Translation by H. G. Baynes (Princeton: Princeton University Press, 1971), 52 (1921).

5. Carl G. Jung, *The Collected Works of C. G. Jung*, vol. 11, *Psychology and Religion: West and East*, trans. R. F. C. Hull (Princeton: Princeton University Press, 1958), 365–66 (1952); "I shall not give a cool and carefully considered exegesis that tries to be fair to every detail, but a purely subjective reaction. In this way I hope to act as a voice for many who feel

the same way as I do, and to give expression to the shattering emotion which the unvarnished spectacle of divine savagery and ruthlessness produces in us."

6. Ibid., 456.

7. For example, Jung, *Memories, Dreams, Reflections*, recorded and ed. by Aniela Jaffé; trans. Richard and Clara Winston (New York: Vintage Books, 1961), 195.

8. That is, not subject to the conscious will.

9. Jung, *Memories, Dreams, Reflections*, 192.

10. A term used by Henri F. Ellenberger in *The Discovery of the Unconscious: The History and Evolution of Dynamic Psychiatry* (New York: Basic Books, 1970), but which I believe pertains to Jung's own self-understanding as well (see pp. 39, 210, 670–73, etc.).

11. Ibid., 176.

12. Ibid., 192.

13. Ibid., 194–95.

14. A similar point is made by James Olney regarding Plato and the role of "two realms or modes of existence" in shaping the full range of his thought (James Olney, *The Rhizome and the Flower: The Perennial Philosophy, Yeats and Jung* [Berkeley: University of California Press, 1980], 30).

15. "Nothing but" was a favorite English phrase of Jung's derived from William James, whom Jung met at the Clark Conference in 1909. For Jung's recollections of their meeting and subsequent time spent together see Carl G. Jung, *Letters*, vol. 1, *1906–1950*, ed. Gerhard Adler in collaboration with Aniela Jaffé, trans. R. F. C. Hull (Princeton: Princeton University Press, 1973), 530–31 (1949).

16. Carl G. Jung, *The Collected Works of C. G. Jung*, vol. 5, *Symbols of Transformation*, trans. R. F. C. Hull (Princeton: Princeton University Press, 1956), 226 (orig. 1911–12/1952).

17. For example, Freud held in tension (or, if one prefers, incoherence) elements of both positions. An avowed realist, dedicated to scientific materialism, Freud consistently depicted the human mind as sharply constrained, if not determined, by elemental, impersonal forces within. Yet, in spite of this seeming impotence of the ego, Freud continued to consider the rational mind as the basis of a residual optimism for the future of humanity: "We may insist as often as we like that man's intellect is powerless in comparison with his instinctual life, and we may be right in this. Nevertheless, there is something peculiar about this weakness. The voice of intellect is a soft one, but it does not rest until it has gained a hearing. Finally, after a countless succession of rebuffs, it suc-

ceeds" (Sigmund Freud, *The Future of an Illusion*, trans. and ed. James Strachey [New York: W. W. Norton, 1961], 68).

18. Carl G. Jung, *The Collected Works of C. G. Jung*, vol. 8, *The Structure and Dynamics of the Psyche*, trans. R. F. C. Hull (Princeton: Princeton University Press, 1960), 169 (1954).

19. Jung, *Collected Works*, 11:331 (1932).

20. One aspect of Jung's philosophy of science is conveyed in the following passage: "In order to determine, even approximately, the real nature of material things we need the elaborate apparatus and complicated procedures of chemistry and physics. These disciplines are really tools which help the human intellect to cast a glance behind the deceptive veil of images into a non-psychic world" (Jung, *Collected Works*, 8:384).

21. For example, Carl G. Jung, *The Collected Works of C. G. Jung*, vol. 9, part ii, *Aion*, trans. R. F. C. Hull (Princeton: Princeton University Press, 1959), 29–30; and *The Collected Works of C. G. Jung*, vol. 7, *Two Essays on Analytical Psychology*, trans. R. F. C. Hull (Princeton: Princeton University Press, 1953), 71; and *Collected Works*, 18:247.

22. Jung, *Letters*, 1:383 (1945).

23. Carl G. Jung, *Letters*, vol. 2, *1951–1961*, ed. Gerhard Adler in collaboration with Aniela Jaffé, trans. R. F. C. Hull (Princeton: Princeton University Press, 1973), 567 (1960).

24. Ibid.

25. "Most," as opposed to "mostly," is in the original letter as written in English by Jung, presumably as an expressive, colloquial form of speech.

26. Jung, *Letters*, 2:567 (1960).

27. Ibid.

28. Carl G. Jung, *C. G. Jung Speaking*, ed. William McGuire and R. F. C. Hull (Princeton: Princeton University Press, 1977), 410–27 (1959). The phrase "on the frontiers of knowledge" refers to the title of a series of articles by French-Swiss author Georges Duplain for *Gazette de Lausanne* (1959), in which Jung's psychology was discussed, particularly Jung's recent statements regarding flying saucers.

29. Jung, *Collected Works*, 8:382 (1933).

30. Jung, *Collected Works*, 6:306 (1921).

31. Jung, *Letters*, 1:454 (1947). Regarding Jung's use of the word *entelechy*, the editors make the following observation: "[Entelechy is] 'That which carries its goal in itself,' a term used by Aristotle to describe the active force inherent in the organism which turns potentiality into actuality and so leads to the attainment of the pre-existent goal."

32. Browning, *Religious Thought*, 164, 168, etc.

33. Carl G. Jung, M.-L. von Franz, Joseph L. Henderson, Jolande Jacobi, and Aniela Jaffé, *Man and His Symbols* (New York: Doubleday, 1964), 95.

34. Although Jung was avowedly convinced of the purposeful necessity of the continued evolution of human consciousness, he did on occasion speak and write nostalgically about a simpler time when humans lived comfortably within an unassailable mythic framework. For example, after visiting with the American Pueblos, and learning something of the mysterious bases of their religion, Jung wrote, "If we set against this our own self-justifications, the meaning of our lives as it is formulated by our reason, we cannot help but see our poverty. Out of sheer envy we are obliged to smile at the Indians' naiveté and to plume ourselves on our cleverness; for otherwise we would discover how impoverished and down at the heels we are. Knowledge does not enrich us; it removes us more and more from the mythic world in which we were once at home by right of birth....Such a man is in the fullest sense of the word in his proper place" (Jung, *Memories, Dreams, Reflections*, 252–53). This conflict is not resolved logically, but is rather lived forward, seeking a higher unity.

35. Ibid., 144.

36. Ibid.

37. Jung, *Memories, Dreams, Reflections*, 3.

38. Jung, *Jung Speaking*, 287 (1957).

39. It should be noted that Jung was not simply an armchair anthropologist, but rather made numerous and explicit efforts to directly encounter other cultures—in Africa, southwest America, and Asia—at a more "primitive" level than that of Europe. Further, I believe it is worth recalling that the specific language that Jung employed to described these journeys was prior to our era of sensitive political correctness. Beyond specific pejorative words, however, Jung's overall disposition toward these pre-industrial cultures was one of respect, if not nostalgic envy, often accompanied by a corresponding criticism of his own European civilization. See, for example, Jung, *Memories, Dreams, Reflections*, 238–88, or n. 36 above.

40. Jung, *Collected Works*, 8:302 (1920/48).

41. Ibid., 302–3.

42. Jung, *Collected Works*, 5:226 (1911–12/52).

43. Jung, *Collected Works*, 6:307 (1921).

44. Jung, *Letters*, 1:465 (1947).

45. Ibid., 406 (1946).

46. Ibid., 59 (1929).
47. Ibid., 61–62 (1929).
48. For example, "Every statement about the transcendental is to be avoided because it is only a laughable presumption on the part of a human mind unconscious of its limitations" (Jung, *Collected Works*, 11:476 [1939]).
49. Ibid.
50. Ibid.
51. Carl G. Jung, *The Collected Works of C. G. Jung*, vol. 13, *Alchemical Studies*, trans. R. F. C. Hull (Princeton: Princeton University Press, 1967), 54.
52. Ibid.
53. Jung, *Collected Works*, 11:477 (1939).
54. Ibid.
55. Jung, *Collected Works*, 8:328 (1926).
56. Jung, *Collected Works*, 6:45 (1921).
57. Jung, *Collected Works*, 8:327 (1926).
58. Jung, *Collected Works*, 6:52 (1921).
59. Jung, *Letters*, 2:520 (1959).
60. Ibid., 339, 343 (1934).
61. Jung, *Collected Works*, 8:328 (1926).
62. Ibid., 382 (1933).
63. Ibid., 383.
64. Jung, *Collected Works*, 18:33 (1935).
65. Jung, *Letters*, 1:525–26 (1949).
66. Ibid., 415 (1959).
67. Jung, *Jung Speaking*, 414 (1959).
68. Jung, *Collected Works*, 5:xxv (1911–12/1952).
69. Jung, *Collected Works*, 10:93–94 (1931).
70. Jung, *Collected Works*, 6:51 (1921).
71. Jung, *Collected Works*, 8:381 (1927).
72. Jung, *Collected Works*, 10:93–94 (1931).

Chapter 3

1. Erazim Kohák states that "*Prima Philosophy* cannot start with speculation. It must first see clearly and articulate faithfully the sense evidently given in experience" (*The Embers and the Stars: A Philosophical Inquiry into the Moral Sense of Nature* [Chicago: University of Chicago Press, 1984], 12). I believe this method applies as well to any psychological inquiry that seeks general application.

2. Don S. Browning, Don S. Browning, *Religious Thought and the Modern Psychologies: A Critical Conversation in the Theology of Culture* (Philadelphia: Fortress Press, 1987), 8.

3. Ibid., xi, 10.

4. Ibid., 8.

5. Neal O. Weiner, *The Harmony of the Soul: Mental Health and Moral Virtue Reconsidered* (Albany: State University of New York Press, 1993), 1, 2, 18, etc.

6. Ibid., 144.

7. Browning, *Religious Thought*, 50.

8. Salvatore R. Maddi, *Personality Theories: A Comparative Analysis* (Pacific Grove, CA: Brooks/Cole Publishing, 1989), 80.

9. This portrayal of Jung dates from his earliest conflicts with Freud and the psychoanalytic school, following his separation from the movement. Freud, in his *Autobiographical Study*, wrote, "But their [Adler and Jung] strength lay, not in their own content, but in the temptation which they offered of being freed from what were felt as the repellent findings of psycho-analysis without the necessity of rejecting its actual material. Jung attempted to give to the facts of analysis a fresh interpretation of an abstract, impersonal and non-historical character, and thus hoped to escape the need for recognizing the importance of infantile sexuality and of the Oedipus complex as well as the necessity for any analysis of childhood" (Sigmund Freud, *An Autobiographical Study*, trans. and ed. James Strachey [New York: W. W. Norton, 1952], 58–59).

10. Carl G. Jung, *Memories, Dreams, Reflections*, recorded and ed. by Aniela Jaffé; trans. Richard and Clara Winston (New York: Vintage Books, 1961), 325.

11. Carl G. Jung, *The Collected Works of C. G. Jung*, vol. 16, *The Practice of Psychotherapy*, trans. R. F. C. Hull (Princeton: Princeton University Press, 1955), 51 (1929).

12. Carl G. Jung, *The Collected Works of C. G. Jung*, vol. 10, *Civilization in Transition*, trans. R. F. C. Hull (Princeton: Princeton University Press, 1964), 454 (1958).

13. Jung, *Collected Works*, 16:234 (1946).

14. Carl G. Jung, *The Collected Works of C. G. Jung*, vol. 8, *The Structure and Dynamics of the Psyche*, trans. R. F. C. Hull (Princeton: Princeton University Press, 1960), 18–28 (1948).

15. Ibid., 397 (1930/1931).

16. Ibid., 4 (1948).

17. Ibid.

18. It is important to realize that Jung makes no attempt to penetrate to the "final" ontological nature—whatever this would mean anyway—of this "energy," just as he avoids any attempt to reduce or explain consciousness by a more primary reality. "Energy" within the Jungian framework is an irreducible, regulative principle.

19. Jung, *Collected Works*, 8:6 n. 7 (1948).

20. Ibid., 31.

21. Carl G. Jung, *The Collected Works of C. G. Jung*, vol. 4, *Freud and Psychoanalysis*, trans. R. F. C. Hull (Princeton: Princeton University Press, 1961), 296 (1917).

22. Ibid., 24.

23. Ibid., 5.

24. Ibid.

25. Ibid., 295.

26. Kohák, *Embers and the Stars*, 234 n. 38.

27. Ibid., 23.

28. Ibid.

29. Ibid., 24.

30. Ibid.

31. Carl G. Jung, *The Collected Works of C. G. Jung*, vol. 5, *Symbols of Transformation*, trans. R. F. C. Hull (Princeton: Princeton University Press, 1956), 132 (1911–12/1952).

32. The use of "quantitative" and "qualitative" terminology was employed also by Freud in his formulations of libido theory. "We have defined the concept of libido as a quantitatively variable force which could serve as a measure of processes and transformations occurring in the field of sexual excitation. We distinguish this libido in respect of its special origin from the energy which must be supposed to underlie mental processes in general, and we thus also attribute a *qualitative* character to it. In thus distinguishing between libidinal and other forms of psychical energy we are giving expression to the presumption that the sexual processes occurring in the organism are distinguished from the nutritive processes by a special chemistry" (Sigmund Freud, *Three Essays on the Theory of Sexuality*, trans. and ed. James Strachey [New York: Basic Books, 1962; originally published in 1905; this passage added 1915], 83). Not surprisingly, Freud disagreed with Jung's broadening of the definition of libido: "It would be sacrificing all that we have gained hitherto from psycho-analytic observation, if we were to follow the example of C. G. Jung and water down the meaning of the concept of libido itself by equating it with psychical instinctual force in general. The distinguishing of the sexual instinctual impulses from the rest and the consequent

restriction of the concept of libido to the former receives strong support from the assumption which I have already discussed that there is a special chemistry to the sexual function" (ibid., 84–85).

33. Jung, *Memories, Dreams, Reflections*, 208.

34. Ibid., 27.

35. Jung, *Collected Works*, 8:28 (1948).

36. Ibid., 29.

37. Ibid., 9 (emphasis in original).

38. Ibid.

39. Ibid., 9–10.

40. Ibid., 28.

41. Carl G. Jung, *The Collected Works of C. G. Jung*, vol. 6, *Psychological Types*, A Revision by R. F. C. Hull of the Translation by H. G. Baynes (Princeton: Princeton University Press, 1971), 455–56 (1921); and idem, *Collected Works*, 10:446 (1958).

42. Erazim Kohák makes this point in the following manner: "Ontology here refers to an inventory and an ordering of what is taken to be. A general ontology would have to include all that presents itself and functions as real in lived experience, including intentional objects. For the purposes of a special inquiry, however, whether it is chemistry, physics, or psychology, the researcher necessarily restricts the totality of the phenomenal field to the region of whatever is relevant to the inquiry. Such a restriction is essential, but it means that the ontology of that inquiry is regional, a correlate of a particular science (*Embers and the Stars*, 227–28).

43. Jung, *Collected Works*, 8:28 (1948).

44. Ibid., 29–30.

45. Ibid., 18.

46. Ibid., n. 21.

47. It is noteworthy that Jung was opposed to anyone calling themselves "Jungian." For example, "I can only hope and wish that no one becomes 'Jungian'" (Carl G. Jung, *Letters*, vol. 1, *1906–1950*, ed. Gerhard Adler in collaboration with Aniela Jaffé, trans. R. F. C. Hull [Princeton: Princeton University Press, 1973], 405 (1946).

48. Jung, *Collected Works*, 8:25 (1948).

49. Ibid., 8.

50. Ibid., 25.

51. Ibid., 7: "The causal connections existing between psychic facts, which we can observe at any time, contradict the epiphenomenon theory."

52. Ibid., 26.

53. Ibid., 26–27.

54. Jung, *Collected Works*, 5:128–31 (1911–12/1952).

55. Ibid., 135.

56. Ibid., 136.

57. Ibid.

58. Ibid.

59. Jung, *Collected Works*, 6:212 (1921).

60. Jung, *Collected Works*, 5:137 (1911–12/1952).

61. Carl G. Jung, *The Collected Works of C. G. Jung*, vol. 7, *Two Essays on Analytical Psychology*, trans. R. F. C. Hull (Princeton: Princeton University Press, 1953), 52–53, note (1917/1926/1943).

62. Edward F. Edinger, *Ego and Archetype: Individuation and the Religious Function of the Psyche* (New York: Penguin Books, 1972), 5.

63. Carl G. Jung, *The Collected Works of C. G. Jung*, vol. 13, *Alchemical Studies*, trans. R. F. C. Hull (Princeton: Princeton University Press, 1967), 12 (1948).

64. Ibid., 375 (1931).

65. This dismissal of the reality of the unconscious as an effective and powerful force influencing, if not governing, our lives is commonly perceived by both individuals and society at large. Much of the early history of depth psychology was devoted to exploring, and demonstrating to the wider public, the empirical reality of unconscious factors. Although now something of a commonplace in popular culture, the reality and intelligibility of the "unconscious" are still disputed in certain spheres of our culture.

66. Jung, *Collected Writings*, 13:12 (1948).

67. Ibid., 374 (1931).

68. Ibid., 12 (1948).

69. Ibid., 13.

70. Ibid.

71. Jung, *Collected Works*, 6:213 (1921).

72. Carl G. Jung, *The Collected Works of C. G. Jung*, vol. 18, *The Symbolic Life: Miscellaneous Writings*, trans. R. F. C. Hull (Princeton: Princeton University Press, 1950), 449 (1916).

73. Jung, *Collected Works*, 8:358 (1931).

74. Jung, *Collected Works*, 6:414 (1921).

75. Ibid., 416.

76. Ibid.

77. Published in *Collected Works*, vol. 18, from a manuscript dated October 1916, found in the archives of the Psychological Club, Zurich, following Jung's death.

78. Jung, *Collected Works*, 18:449 (1916).

79. Ibid., 450.

80. Jung, *Collected Works*, 8:364 (1928/1931).

81. Jung makes the following statement in a letter from 1957: "Even though assignment to a particular type may in certain cases have lifelong validity, in other very frequent cases it is so dependent on so many external and internal factors that the diagnosis is valid only for certain periods of time. Freud was just such a case." (Jung believed Freud was originally an introverted feeling type, only to later become, neurotically, an extroverted thinker.) Carl G. Jung, *Letters*, vol. 2, *1951–1961*, ed. Gerhard Adler in collaboration with Aniela Jaffé; trans. R. F. C. Hull [Princeton: Princeton University Press, 1973], 347 (1957).

82. Jung, *Memories, Dreams, Reflections*, 209.

83. Jung, *Collected Works*, 10:168 (1934).

84. Carl G. Jung, *The Collected Works of C. G. Jung*, vol. 17, *The Development of Personality*, trans. R. F. C. Hull (Princeton: Princeton University Press, 1954), 105 (1924).

85. Jung, *Collected Works*, 7:59 (1917/1926/1943).

86. Ibid., 60.

87. Ibid., 61.

88. Ibid., 74.

89. Ibid., 60–61.

90. Jung, *Collected Works*, 10:169 (1934); and 7:60 (1917/1926/1943).

91. Jung, *Collected Works*, 8:68 (1948).

92. Jung, *Collected Works*, 7:51–52 (1917/1926/1943).

93. Jung, *Collected Works*, 10:170 (1934).

94. Ibid., 169.

95. Jung, *Collected Works*, 7:53 (1917/1926/1943); and 10:169 (1934).

96. Jung, *Collected Works*, 10:169 (1934).

97. Ibid., 171.

98. Jung described the "feeling-toned complex" as "the *image* of a certain psychic situation which is strongly accentuated emotionally and is, moreover, incompatible with the habitual attitude of consciousness. This image has a powerful inner coherence, it has its own wholeness and, in addition, a relatively high degree of autonomy, so that it is subject to the control of the conscious mind to only a limited extent, and therefore behaves like an animated foreign body in the sphere of consciousness. The complex can usually be suppressed with an effort of will, but not

argued out of existence, and at the first suitable opportunity it reappears in all its original strength" (*Collected Works*, 8:96 [1948]).

99. Ibid., 101.

100. Carl G. Jung, *The Collected Works of C. G. Jung*, vol. 9, part i, *The Archetypes and the Collective Unconscious*, trans. R. F. C. Hull (Princeton: Princeton University Press, 1959), 131 (1950).

101. Jung, *Memories, Dreams, Reflections*, 325.

102. Ibid., 140.

103. Ibid., 144.

104. Ibid.

105. Ibid., 144.

106. This statement applies to empirical science as well, which "posits objects that are confined within rational bounds, because by deliberately excluding the accidental it does not consider the actual object as a whole, but only that part of it which has been singled out for rational observation" (Jung, *Collected Works*, 6:455 [1921]).

107. Ibid.

108. Ibid., 434.

109. Ibid., 411.

110. Ibid., 434.

111. Ibid.

112. Although "feeling" is conceptually distinguishable from the other functions, it is in practice not wholly independent. Jung observes, for example, that there is often an almost "inseparable amalgam" of feeling and sensation (i.e., the receiving of sensory data), particularly where feeling is still an "undifferentiated function." When feeling is mixed like this with other functions, it may take on a "concrete" (or, synonymously, "simple") form. Thus, feeling "can easily become dependent on another function," for example, thinking, and in these circumstances it finds expression only when subordinated to the other, dominant function (Jung, *Collected Works*, 6:435 [1921]). Feeling may also take an "abstract" form in what is typically called a "mood." Moods are abstract in the sense that they so completely shape the feeling state as to "embrace" the multiple and varied individual feeling valuations that may arise, thereby "abolishing" individualized, proportionate reactions that would otherwise normally occur (ibid.).

113. Ibid., 435.

114. Ibid., 458.

115. Ibid., 459.

116. Ibid., 437.

117. Ibid., 434.

118. Ibid., 455.
119. Ibid., 88.
120. Jung, *Collected Works*, 8:361 (1928/1931).
121. Jung, *Collected Works*, 17:173 (1934).
122. Jung, *Collected Works*, 8:361 (1928/1931).

Chapter 4

1. "Through the study of these collective transformation processes and through understanding of alchemical symbolism I arrived at the central concept of my psychology: *the process of individuation*" (Carl G. Jung, *Memories, Dreams, Reflections*, recorded and ed. by Aniela Jaffé; trans. Richard and Clara Winston [New York: Vintage Books, 1961], 209, emphasis Jung's).

2. Carl G. Jung, *The Collected Works of C. G. Jung*, vol. 4, *Freud and Psychoanalysis*, trans. R. F. C. Hull (Princeton: Princeton University Press, 1961), 337 (1929).

3. Carl G. Jung, *The Collected Works of C. G. Jung*, vol. 17, *The Development of Personality*, trans. R. F. C. Hull (Princeton: Princeton University Press, 1954), 179 (1934).

4. Ibid., 167.

5. Charles Taylor, *Hegel and Modern Society* (Cambridge: Cambridge University Press, 1979), 1–14.

6. Ibid., 1.

7. Charles Taylor describes "expressivism" (as advocated by Herder) as a theory committed to a view of humans "as having a unity analogous to that of a work of art, where every part or aspect only found its proper meaning in relation to all the others. Human life unfolded from some central core—a guiding theme or inspiration—or should do so, if it were not so often blocked and distorted" (*Hegel and Modern Society*, 1–2).

8. Erazim Kohák makes the distinction between two ways of seeing reality by posing a question: "Shall we conceive of the world around us and of ourselves in it as *personal*, a meaningful whole, honoring its order as continuous with the moral law of our own being and its being as continuous with ours, bearing its goodness—or shall we conceive of it and treat it, together with ourselves, as *impersonal*, a chance aggregate of matter propelled by a blind force and exhibiting at most the ontologically random lawlike regularities of a causal order? Is the Person or is matter in motion the root metaphor of thought and practice? That answered, all else follows" (Erazim Kohák, *The Embers and the Stars: A*

Philosophical Inquiry into the Moral Sense of Nature [Chicago: University of Chicago Press, 1984], 124–25).

9. Taylor, *Hegel and Modern Society*, 1.

10. Ibid.

11. Ernest Becker, *The Denial of Death* (New York: Free Press, 1973), e.g., 4–7 regarding our "cultural hero-systems."

12. While scientific reductionism may be applied to social as well as individual moral ends, in both theory and practice social goods are often posited as more significant than the individual and as embodying a moral good more enduring than the transient, individual life. For example, utilitarianism, "probably the most famous normative ethical doctrine in the English-speaking tradition of moral philosophy," in its classical formulation by J. S. Mill, is based on the "greatest happiness principle." This basic tenet, as defined by Antony Flew, "holds that the supreme good is the greatest happiness of the greatest number of people" (*A Dictionary of Philosophy* [New York: St. Martin's Press, 1979], 135, 361). And practically, Ernest Becker observes how individuals seek immortality and meaning through "transference objects" within the "cultural hero-system." "It doesn't matter whether the cultural hero-system is frankly magical, religious, and primitive or secular, scientific, and civilized. It is still a mythical hero-system in which people serve in order to earn a feeling of primary value, of cosmic specialness, of ultimate usefulness to creation, of unshakable meaning. They earn this feeling by carving out a place in nature, by building an edifice that reflects human value: a temple, a cathedral, a totem pole, a skyscraper, a family that spans three generations. The hope and belief is that the things that man creates in society are of lasting worth and meaning, that they outlive or outshine death and decay, that man and his products count" (Becker, *Denial of Death*, 4–5, 148–50).

13. Carl G. Jung, *The Collected Works of C. G. Jung*, vol. 10, *Civilization in Transition*, trans. R. F. C. Hull (Princeton: Princeton University Press, 1964), 275 (1957).

14. Ibid., 500 (1934).

15. Carl G. Jung, *The Collected Works of C. G. Jung*, vol. 16, *The Practice of Psychotherapy*, trans. R. F. C. Hull (Princeton: Princeton University Press, 1955), 106 (1946).

16. Jung, *Collected Works*, vol. 10 (1934), 149.

17. Carl G. Jung, *Letters*, vol. 2, *1951–1961*, ed. Gerhard Adler in collaboration with Aniela Jaffé; trans. R. F. C. Hull (Princeton: Princeton University Press, 1973), 207 (1955).

18. Jung, *Collected Works*, 10:305 (1957).

19. Carl G. Jung, *The Collected Works of C. G. Jung*, vol. 3, *Psychogenesis of Mental Disease*, trans. R. F. C. Hull (Princeton: Princeton University Press, 1960), 259 (1958).

20. Carl G. Jung, *Letters*, vol. 1, *1906–1950*, ed. Gerhard Adler in collaboration with Aniela Jaffé, trans. R. F. C. Hull (Princeton: Princeton University Press, 1973), 198 (1935).

21. Ibid., 239 (1937).

22. Ibid., 504 (1948).

23. C. G. Jung (1875–1961).

24. This passage, it should be noted, was written prior to the events of September 11, 2001.

25. Jung, *Memories, Dreams, Reflections*, 4–5. In his privately printed (1916) *Septem Sermones ad Mortuos* ("Seven Sermons to the Dead") in consciously acknowledged gnostic terminology, he speaks of "the pleroma" (reprinted in *Memories, Dreams, Reflections*, 378–90).

26. See, for example, Carl G. Jung, *The Collected Works of C. G. Jung*, vol. 8, *The Structure and Dynamics of the Psyche*, trans. R. F. C. Hull (Princeton: Princeton University Press, 1960), 102 (1934), where he summarizes the emergence in modern thought of the idea of the unconscious; or his *Letters*, 1:87 (1932), where he traces the "intrusion" of Eastern thought into Western philosophy, beginning with Meister Eckhart and concluding with E. von Hartmann. Jung's most extensive elaborations of his intellectual sources occur, not surprisingly, in his autobiography, *Memories, Dreams, Reflections*, e.g., 68–70, 100–103, and 200–202.

27. In a less explicitly autobiographical note, Jung makes this observation about psychological context: "Inner peace and contentment depend in large measure upon whether or not the historical family which is inherent in the individual can be harmonized with the ephemeral conditions of the present" (*Memories, Dreams, Reflections*, 90 and 237, respectively).

28. Jung, *Collected Works*, 17:53 (1923).

29. Carl G. Jung, *The Collected Works of C. G. Jung*, vol. 12, *Psychology and Alchemy*, trans. R. F. C. Hull (Princeton: Princeton University Press, 1953), 50 (1944).

30. "Every civilized human being, however high his conscious development, is still an archaic man at the deeper levels of his psyche. Just as the human body connects us with the mammals and displays numerous vestiges of earlier evolutionary stages going back even to the reptilian age, so the human psyche is a product of evolution which, when

followed back to its origins, shows countless archaic traits" (Jung, *Collected Works*, 10:51 (1931).

31. Jung, *Collected Works*, 4:295 (1916).

32. "As far as we can discern, the sole purpose of human existence is to kindle a light in the darkness of mere being. It may even be assumed that just as the unconscious affects us, so the increase in our consciousness affects the unconsciousness" (*Memories, Dreams, Reflections*, 326). See chapter 7, below.

33. Jung, *Letters*, 2:xlvi (1949).

34. Jung, *Memories, Dreams, Reflections*, 3.

35. Carl G. Jung et al., *Man and His Symbols* (New York: Doubleday, 1964), 85.

36. Carl G. Jung, *The Collected Works of C. G. Jung*, vol. 7, *Two Essays on Analytical Psychology*, trans. R. F. C. Hull (Princeton: Princeton University Press, 1953), 153 (1928). Also, "The individual becomes morally and spiritually inferior in the mass" (Jung, *Collected Works*, 10:276 [1957]).

37. Jung, *Memories, Dreams, Reflections*, 3.

38. Ibid., 209.

39. Jung, *Collected Works*, 7:173 (1928).

40. Carl G. Jung, *The Collected Works of C. G. Jung*, vol. 9, part i, *The Archetypes and the Collective Unconscious*, trans. R. F. C. Hull (Princeton: Princeton University Press, 1959), 275 (1939).

41. Walter Kaufmann, *Discovering the Mind*, vol. 3. (New York: McGraw-Hill, 1980), 372, 433.

42. Anthony Stevens, *On Jung* (London: Routledge, 1990), 260.

43. Related to these questions of a possible "elitism" is the charge that Jung's psychology was in essence a mystical doctrine or secret *gnosis*. I will address this charge in the final chapter as a way of evaluating Jung's ethic, practice, and the metaphysics behind them.

44. Jung, *Collected Works*, 17:173 (1934).

45. Jung, *Collected Works*, 12:52 (1936).

46. Neal O. Weiner, *The Harmony of the Soul: Mental Health and Moral Virtue Reconsidered* (Albany: State University of New York Press, 1993), 164–65.

47. Ibid.

48. Jung, *Collected Works*, 7:116–17 (1917/1926/1943).

49. Late in life, in 1959, Jung was asked by one of his pupils about comments he had made in 1910 regarding Christianity, such as, "[We should encourage] making the cult and the sacred myth what they once were—a drunken feast of joy where man regained the ethos and holiness

of an animal," and other indiscreet remarks. Jung responded to the student: "Best thanks for the quotation from that accursed correspondence. For me it is an unfortunately inexpungable reminder of the incredible folly that filled the days of my youth. The journey from cloud-cuckoo-land back to reality lasted a long time. In my case Pilgrim's Progress consisted in my having to climb down a thousand ladders until I could reach out my hand to the little clod of earth that I am" (Jung *Letters*, 1:19 n. 8 [1959]).

50. Ibid., 442 (1946).

51. Carl G. Jung, *The Collected Works of C. G. Jung*, vol. 6, *Psychological Types*, A Revision by R. F. C. Hull of the Translation by H. G. Baynes (Princeton: Princeton University Press, 1971), 448 (1921).

52. Jung, *Collected Works*, 7:174 (1928).

53. Jung, *Letters*, 1:442 (1946).

54. Jung, *Letters*, 2:324 (1956).

55. Jung, *Collected Works*, 8:394 (1931).

56. Jung, *Collected Works*, 7:174 (1928). When pressed to describe such a person, Jung wrote: "It is perfectly true that I never described an 'individuated person' for the simple reason that nobody would understand why I describe such a case, and most of my readers would be bored to tears. I am also not such a great poet that I could produce a really worthwhile picture. A genius like Goethe or Shakespeare might hope to to be able to describe the lordly beauty and the divine completeness of an individuated old oak-tree, or the unique grotesqueness of a cactus. But if a scientist risked doing the same, nobody would understand or appreciate it. Science is only concerned with the average idea of an oak or a horse or man[/woman] but not with their uniqueness" (*Letters*, 2:323 [1956]). Also of interest in this regard, Jung, *Memories, Dreams, Reflections*, 287.

57. Jung, *Collected Works*, 17:174 (1934).

58. Ibid.

59. Ibid., 175.

60. Ibid.

61. Jung, *Collected Works*, 7:173 (1928).

62. "The only thing that distinguishes [the individual personality] from all others is his[/her] sense of vocation" (Jung, *Collected Works*, 17:178 [1932]).

63. Ibid., 176.

64. Jung, *Collected Works*, 7:173 (1928).

65. Ibid., 173–74.

66. Jung, *Collected Works*, 16:108 (1941).

67. Jung, *Collected Works*, 17:178 (1934).

68. Jung, *Collected Works*, 7:173 (1928).

69. Ibid., 174.

70. Jung, *Memories, Dreams, Reflections*, 325.

71. Ibid., 131.

72. Ibid.

73. Jung, *Collected Works*, 16:70 (1931).

74. A paraphrase of Tillich's first ontological principle (Paul Tillich, *Systematic Theology*, vol. 1 [Chicago: University of Chicago Press, 1951], 163–66).

75. Jung, *Collected Works*, 10:277 (1957).

76. Peter Berger, *The Sacred Canopy: Elements of a Sociological Theory of Religion* (Garden City, NY: Doubleday, 1967), 1–57.

77. Jung, *Collected Works*, 6:448 (1921).

78. Jung, *Collected Works*, 7:193 (1928).

79. Ibid.

80. Ibid., 155.

81. Ibid., 193.

82. Jung, *Collected Works*, 9.i:125 (1940/50).

83. I say "in part" because an expanded consciousness—while a necessary aspect or outcome of individuation—does not exhaustively define the individuating process of self-realization and integration. Speaking of individuation in terms of consciousness alone tends to over-intellectualize the actual nature of the experience, which is marked by matters of the will and moral fortitude. A broad and deep consciousness is realized in its fullness when it internalizes the subjectively intimate experiences of struggle, suffering, courage, and acceptance.

84. Carl G. Jung, *The Collected Works of C. G. Jung*, vol. 13, *Alchemical Studies*, trans. R. F. C. Hull (Princeton: Princeton University Press, 1967), 12 (1929).

85. Ibid., 118 (1942).

86. Ibid., 12 (1929).

87. Jung, *Collected Works*, 10:184 (1936), and 211 (1945).

88. Carl G. Jung, *The Collected Works of C. G. Jung*, vol. 9, part ii, *Aion*, trans. R. F. C. Hull (Princeton: Princeton University Press, 1959), 9 (1951).

89. Jung, *Collected Works*, 13:14–15 (1929).

90. Ibid., 267–68.

91. Carl G. Jung, *The Collected Works of C. G. Jung*, vol. 11, *Psychology and Religion: West and East*, trans. R. F. C. Hull (Princeton:

Princeton University Press, 1958), 584 (1944); and *Collected Works*, 13:14–15 (1929).

92. Jung, *Collected Works*, 13:15 (1929).
93. Jung, *Collected Works*, 9.i:125 (1940/50).
94. Ibid.
95. Ibid., 126.
96. Ibid.
97. Ibid.
98. Ibid., 125.
99. Ibid., 126–27.
100. Jung, *Collected Works*, 10:277 (1957).
101. Ibid.
102. Jung, *Collected Works*, 7:152 (1928).
103. Ibid., 153.
104. Jung, *Letters*, 2:218 (1955).
105. Jung, *Letters*, 1:348 (1944).
106. Jung, *Collected Works*, 7:152 (1928).
107. Ibid.
108. Ibid., 152–53.
109. Jung, *Collected Works*, 9.i:127 (1940/1950).
110. Jung, *Collected Works*, 10:247 (1957).
111. Ibid.
112. Jung, *Collected Works*, 17:179 (1932).
113. Jung, *Collected Works*, 7:153 (1928).
114. Jung, *Collected Works*, 17:179 (1932).
115. Ibid., 178–79.
116. Ibid.
117. Ibid.
118. Ibid.
119. Ibid., 178.
120. Ibid., 180.
121. Jung, *Collected Works*, 10:179 (1936).
122. Jung, *Collected Works*, 7:152 (1928).
123. Jung, *Collected Works*, 8:315 (1920/48).

Chapter 5

1. Philip Rieff makes several references to Jung that are relevant to this point. I cite these quotations not as a form of proof regarding what one's assessment of Jung ought to be, but rather simply as confirmation that ontology *is* at the crux of the matter: "When the theologians will finally catch up with Jung, they might discover in him that particular

psychology for which they have been seeking, in a prolonged agony, a substitute for all those ontologies crumbling at the foundation of theology," and "No one can know the exact wording of Jung's title to greatness. However it may be explained and qualified, the legitimacy of that title will depend in part upon the success of his attempt to install a psychology where ontology once reigned" (*The Triumph of the Therapeutic: Uses of Faith after Freud* [Chicago: University of Chicago Press, 1966], 41–42).

2. For example, Alfred North Whitehead, *Process and Reality: An Essay in Cosmology*, Gifford Lectures, 1927–28, ed. David Ray Griffin and Donald W. Sherburne (New York: Free Press, 1929), 1–74; and Frederick Copleston, S.J., *A History of Philosophy*, vols. 1–3 (New York: Image Books, 1946, 1950, 1953), vol. 1, esp. 72–75, and 124–26.

3. Neal O. Weiner, *The Harmony of the Soul: Mental Health and Moral Virtue Reconsidered* (Albany: State University of New York Press, 1993), 6.

4. Alexandre Koyré, *From the Closed World to the Infinite Universe* (Baltimore: John Hopkins University Press, 1957), 2.

5. Weiner, *Harmony of the Soul*, 7.

6. The term *construct* is used throughout Erazim Kohák's *The Embers and the Stars*, in contrast to what he calls "experiential givens." For example, "It is what we are accustomed to treating as 'objective reality'—the conception of nature as a system of dead matter propelled by blind force—that is in truth the product of a subject's purposeful and strenuous activity, a construct built up in the course of an extended, highly sophisticated abstraction" (*The Embers and the Stars: A Philosophical Inquiry in to the Moral Sense of Nature* [Chicago: University of Chicago Press, 1984], 6).

7. For example, Charles Taylor, Frederick Copleston, Don S. Browning, Paul Tillich, C. G. Jung.

8. Whitehead begins his *Process and Reality* with the following description: "Speculative Philosophy is the endeavor to frame a coherent, logical, necessary system of general ideas in terms of which every element of our experience can be interpreted. By this notion of 'interpretation' I mean that everything of which we are conscious, as enjoyed, perceived, willed, or thought, shall have the character of a particular instance of the general scheme. Thus the philosophical scheme should be coherent, logical, and, in respect to its interpretation, applicable and adequate. Here 'applicable' means that some items of experience are thus interpretable, and 'adequate' means that there are no items incapable of such interpretation" (p. 3).

9. Ibid.

10. Kohák, *Embers and the Stars*, 234 n. 38 (emphasis added).

11. Ibid., 227–28 n. 8 (emphasis added).

12. Robert Wright, *The Moral Animal: Evolutionary Psychology and Everyday Life* (New York: Vintage Books, 1994); also by Robert Wright, *Nonzero: The Logic of Human Destiny* (New York: Vintage Books, 2001), in which the author wrestles with the question of purpose in evolution, concluding that cooperative organisms are the eventual outcome toward which both biological and cultural evolution tend.

13. Wright, *Moral Animal*, 10.

14. Ibid., 4.

15. Ibid., 328.

16. Weiner is not writing explicitly about evolutionary psychology, but his description of "anthropology...naturalistic brackets" describes accurately the ideas and character of Wright's theory (Weiner, *Harmony of the Soul*, 19).

17. Wright, *Moral Animal*, 313–14.

18. Ibid., 148.

19. Ibid., 5.

20. Ibid., 212.

21. Ibid., 328.

22. Ibid., 321.

23. Sigmund Freud, *New Introductory Lectures on Psycho-Analysis*, trans. and ed. James Strachey (New York: W. W. Norton, 1965), 77.

24. Freud also used the terms *ego ideal* and *ideal ego* to refer to "a special psychical agency" that included the function of conscience. According to Peter Gay, "it is as an equivalent to the 'ego ideal' that '*das Über-Ich*' makes its first appearance, though its aspect as an enforcing or prohibiting agency predominates later. Indeed, after *Ego and the Id* and the two or three shorter works immediately following it, the 'ego ideal' disappears almost completely as a technical term" (Peter Gay, "Biographical Introduction," in Sigmund Freud, *The Ego and the Id*, trans. Joan Riviere; rev. and ed. James Strachey [New York: W. W. Norton, 1960], xxxv–xxxvi).

25. Freud, *Ego and the Id* , 30, 33, 51–52, 56.

26. Sigmund Freud, *Beyond the Pleasure Principle*, trans. and ed. James Strachey (New York: W. W. Norton, 1961).

27. Freud, *Ego and the Id*, 30 (emphasis in original).

28. Ibid.

29. Freud, *New Introductory Lectures on Psycho-Analysis*, 93.

30. Ibid., 91–92.

31. Sigmund Freud and C. G. Jung, *The Freud/Jung Letters*, ed. William McGuire, trans. Ralph Manheim and R. F. C. Hull (Cambridge, MA: Harvard University Press, 1988), 140–41.

32. Freud provided the following summary of his theoretical developments at the time of the introduction of his structural model, seeking to explain the new dualism of life-and-death instincts and the transformation of ego instincts from merely self-preservative to libidinal in nature: "With the hypothesis of narcissistic libido and the extension of the concept of libido to the individual cells, the sexual instinct was transformed for us into Eros, which seeks to force together and hold together the portions of living substance. What are called the sexual instincts are looked upon by us as the part of Eros which is directed toward objects. Our speculations have suggested that Eros operates from the beginning of life and appears as a 'life instinct' in opposition to the 'death instinct' which was brought into being by the coming to life of inorganic substance. These speculations seek to solve the riddle of life by supposing that these two instincts were struggling with each other from the very first. [Added 1921:] It is not so easy, perhaps, to follow the transformations through which the concept of the 'ego-instincts' has passed. To begin with we applied that name to all the instinctual trends (of which we had no closer knowledge) which could be distinguished from the sexual instincts directed towards an object; and we opposed the ego-instincts to the sexual instincts of which the libido is the manifestation. Subsequently we came to closer grips with the analysis of the ego and recognized that a portion of the 'ego-instincts' is also of a libidinal character and has taken the subject's own ego as its object. These narcissistic self-preservative instincts had thenceforward to be counted among the libidinal sexual instincts. The opposition between the ego-instincts and the object-instincts, both of a libidinal nature. But in its place a fresh opposition appeared between the libidinal (ego- and object-) instincts and others, which must be presumed to be present in the ego and which may perhaps actually be observed in the destructive instincts. Our speculations have transformed this opposition into one between the life instincts (Eros) and the death instincts" (Freud, *Beyond the Pleasure Principle*, 73–74 note).

33. Ibid., 3: "In the theory of psycho-analysis we have no hesitation in assuming that the course taken by mental events is automatically regulated by the pleasure principle."

34. Ibid., 7: "Under the influence of the ego's instincts of self-preservation, the pleasure principle is replaced by the *reality principle*. This latter principle does not abandon the intention of ultimately

obtaining pleasure." It should be further noted that aggressive instincts, as a result of Freud's clinical and personal experience, as well as reflections on historical and cultural processes, were also acknowledged in later theoretical constructions and were seen as exponents of a destructive or death instinct (*Thanatos*). Freud engaged this subject, for example, in the following manner: "Hate, as a relation to objects, is older than love. It derives from the narcissistic ego's primordial repudiation of the external world with its outpouring of stimuli" (Freud, from *Instincts and their Vicissitudes* [1915], quoted in Anthony Storr, *Freud* [Oxford: Oxford University Press, 1989], 49).

35. Freud, *Ego and the Id*, 15.

36. Freud, *Beyond the Pleasure Principle*, 5.

37. As *Eros* (as love, lust, and ardent desire) and *Thanatos* (as death, aggression, and hate).

38. I do not use the term *speculative* in a pejorative sense, but rather descriptively, as Freud himself acknowledged regarding his polemical process and rhetorical strategies: "What follows is speculation, often far-fetched speculation, which the reader will consider or dismiss according to his individual predilections" (Freud, *Beyond the Pleasure Principle*, 26).

39. Freud, *Ego and the Id*, 58.

40. Freud, *Beyond the Pleasure Principle*, 29.

41. Ibid.

42. *Pcpt.-Cs.* refers to the "perceptual-consciousness system," terminology used in *Interpretation of Dreams* (Freud, *Ego and the Id*, 18–19, 26).

43. Freud, *Beyond the Pleasure Principle*, 30–31 (emphasis in original).

44. Ibid., 32.

45. Whether the conscious mind is conceived of as resting on, and derived from, a dynamic unconscious substrate, or whether the ego and its reasoning capacities are believed to be self-sufficient and the complete master of the psychic house, is the basic distinction between German Idealism and British empiricism, respectively.

46. Freud, *Beyond the Pleasure Principle*, 26.

47. Sigmund Freud, *Civilization and Its Discontents*, trans. and ed. James Strachey (New York: W. W. Norton, 1961), 85.

48. Ibid.

49. Ibid., 86.

50. Following the gradual transformation of primary narcissism to that of object-cathexes.

51. "There is no doubt that this ego ideal is the precipitate of the old picture of the parents, the expression of admiration for the perfection which the child then attributed to them" (Freud, *New Introductory Lectures on Psycho-Analysis*, 81).

52. Ibid., 79.

53. My discussion of the super-ego represents what I consider to be the core elements of this psychoanalytical concept, and, specifically, the heart of the theory as most widely appropriated by our culture. Freud's own theorizing was more complex than that outlined here. For example, he wrote: "The super-ego is, however, not simply a residue of the earliest object-choices of the *id*; it also represents an energetic reaction-formation against these choices. Its relation to the ego is not exhausted by the precept: 'You *ought to be* like this (like your father).' It also comprises the prohibition: 'You *may not be* like this (like your father)—that is, you may not do all that he does; some things are his prerogative.' This double aspect of the ego ideal derives from the fact that the ego ideal had the task of repressing the Oedipus Complex; indeed, it is to that revolutionary event that it owes its existence" (Freud, *Ego and the Id*, 30). Whether this elaboration of Freud's represented a clarification or an obfuscation is beyond the scope of this work.

54. Ibid.

55. Ibid., 80: "the installation of the super-ego can be described as a successful instance of identification with the parental agency."

56. In fact, the ego itself is "formed to a great extent out of identifications which take the place of abandoned cathexes by the *id*" (Freud, *Ego and the Id*, 48).

57. Ibid.

58. Ibid., 32–33.

59. Ibid., 32.

60. Ibid., 49.

61. Freud described this process of precipitate formation in the following manner: "The experiences of the ego seem at first to be lost for inheritance; but when they have been repeated often enough and with sufficient strength in many individuals in successive generations, they transform themselves, so to say, into experiences of the *id*, the impressions of which are preserved by heredity." Whether this explanation is credible in light of today's understanding of evolutionary and genetic processes, or is an example of Lamarkianism, is beyond the critical scope of this work. I cite Freud's rationale in order to make clear that I do not unwittingly embrace his subsequent theorizing based on this operative assumption (*Ego and the Id*, 35).

62. Freud, *New Introductory Lectures on Psycho-Analysis*, 76.
63. Freud, *Ego and the Id*, 32.
64. Ibid.
65. Ibid., 33.
66. Ibid.
67. Ibid.
68. Ibid., 51.
69. Ibid., 50–52.
70. Ibid., 84.
71. Ibid., 56.
72. Ibid., 56–57.
73. Ibid.
74. Freud, *Civilization and Its Discontents*, 90
75. Ibid., 89.
76. Ibid., 91.
77. Freud's use of the two terms *ego-ideal* (as well as *ideal ego*) and *super-ego* was fluid and inconsistent during the course of his life's output. Sometimes the two terms were used as equivalents and at other times as referring to a psychic content and psychic agency, respectively. Other times the use of *ego ideal* disappeared altogether. For a brief discussion of the context, development, and usage of these terms, see Gay's "Biographical Introduction" in Freud, *Ego and the Id*, xxxv–xxxvii.
78. Freud, *Ego and the Id*, 56.
79. Freud, *Civilization and Its Discontents*, 85.
80. Freud, *Ego and the Id*, 56.
81. Freud, *New Introductory Lectures on Psycho-Analysis*, 92.
82. Freud, *Beyond the Pleasure Principle*, 46 (emphasis in original).
83. Freud, *Ego and the Id*, 56.
84. Weiner, *Harmony of the Soul*, 12.
85. Ibid., 13.
86. Ibid., 23; also 14–19 and 24–37.
87. Ibid., 17.
88. Ibid.
89. Ibid.
90. Ibid., 16.
91. Ibid., 15.
92. Ibid., 156.
93. Carl G. Jung, *The Collected Works of C. G. Jung*, vol. 9, part ii, *Aion*, trans. R. F. C. Hull (Princeton: Princeton University Press, 1959), 3 (1951).

94. Carl G. Jung, *The Collected Works of C. G. Jung*, vol. 6, *Psychological Types*, A Revision by R. F. C. Hull of the Translation by H. G. Baynes (Princeton: Princeton University Press, 1971), 425 (1921).

95. Jung, *Collected Works*, 9.ii:3 (1951).

96. Ibid., 5.

97. Most simply stated, by "psychic" Jung referred to phenomena "where there is evidence of a will capable of modifying reflex or instinctual processes." Jung discussed the issue of volition as a defining characteristic of the psychic in *Collected Works*, vol. 8, *The Structure and Dynamics of the Psyche*, part 4, *Instinct and Will*, trans. R. F. C. Hull (Princeton: Princeton University Press, 1960), 3 (1947).

98. Ibid.

99. Ibid.

100. Ibid. (emphasis in original).

101. Jung, *Collected Works*, 8:364 (1928/1931).

102. Carl G. Jung, *The Collected Works of C. G. Jung*, vol. 11, trans. R. F. C. Hull (Princeton: Princeton University Press, 1958), 259 (1942/1954); idem, *Collected Works*, vol. 9.ii:5 (1951).

103. Jung, *Collected Works*, 11:259 (1942/1954).

104. Ibid.

105. Jung, *Collected Works*, 9.ii:5 (1951).

106. Carl G. Jung, *The Collected Works of C. G. Jung*, vol. 10, *Civilization in Transition*, trans. R. F. C. Hull (Princeton: Princeton University Press, 1964), 454 (1958).

107. Jung, *Collected Works*, 6:480 (1921).

108. Jung, *Collected Works*, 10:454 (1958).

109. Carl G. Jung, *The Collected Works of C. G. Jung*, vol. 7, *Two Essays on Analytical Psychology*, trans. R. F. C. Hull (Princeton: Princeton University Press, 1953), 80 (1917/26/43).

110. Jung, *Collected Works*, 6:448–49 (1921).

111. See pp. 76–79 above, regarding the "problem of opposites."

112. Jung, *Collected Works*, 10:447 (1958).

113. Carl G. Jung et al., *Man and His Symbols* (New York: Doubleday, 1964), 75.

114. Particularly pp. 33–39 above.

115. Jung et al., *Man and His Symbols*, 69.

116. Ibid., 75.

117. Ibid., 69.

118. Ibid., 75.

119. Jung, *Collected Works*, 10:449 (1958).

120. Jung, *Collected Works*, 7:77 (1917/1926/1943).

121. Jung used the term *primordial ideas* before adopting the terminology of the *archetype*. I believe Jung adopted the latter term so as to avoid the charge of simple Lamarkianism, while allowing for a more nuanced epistemology that distinguishes between the general form and the specific, manifest content of the archetype. Even late into his life he continued to struggle against a Lamarkian reading of the archetypes, evidenced, for example, in the following footnote: "The concept of the archetype is a specifically psychological instance of the 'pattern of behavior' in biology. Hence it has nothing whatever to do with inherited ideas, but with modes of behavior" (Carl G. Jung, *The Collected Works of C. G. Jung*, vol. 16, *The Practice of Psychotherapy*, trans. R. F. C. Hull [Princeton: Princeton University Press, 1955], 124 [1951]).

122. In fairness to Jung, I should make clear that this quotation comes from a lecture delivered in 1916 to the Zurich School for Analytical Psychology, a forum and a time when Jung may be expected to have engaged in maximum political rhetoric. See Jung, *Collected Works*, 7:269 (1917), for a chronology of the text, which served as the core of his essay "The Relations Between the Ego and the Unconscious," which later became the important second part of his book *Two Essays on Analytical Psychology*, and *Collected Works*, vol. 7 (1917/1926/1943).

123. Jung, *Collected Works*, 7:270 (1917).

124. Ibid.

125. Ibid.

126. Freud (from *SE*, XXIII.145), quoted in Storr, *Freud*, 46.

127. See pp. 112–16 above.

128. As quoted earlier in this chapter, "It is easy to show that the ego ideal answers to everything that is expected of the higher nature of man. As a substitute for a longing for the father, it contains the germ from which all religions have evolved…[etc.]" (Freud, *Ego and the Id*, 33). Whether in fact the ego ideal is somehow a "by-product" of the ego's functioning is an important question and one that will be the basis of one of my critiques of the naturalized conscience in the conclusion of this work.

129. Jung, *Collected Works*, 6:451 (1921) (emphasis in original).

130. Jung, *Collected Works*, 7:80–81 (1917/1926/1943).

131. Ibid., 81.

132. Jung et al., *Man and His Symbols*, 76.

133. Ibid., 38

134. Jung, *Collected Works*, 8:364 (1928/1931).

135. Carl G. Jung, *The Collected Works of C. G. Jung*, vol. 12, *Psychology and Alchemy*, trans. R. F. C. Hull (Princeton: Princeton University Press, 1953), 73 (1936).

136. Ibid., 63.

137. Ibid., 78.

138. Ibid., 64.

139. Jung, *Collected Works*, 6:459 (1921).

140. Carl G. Jung, *The Collected Works of C. G. Jung*, vol. 17, *The Development of Personality*, trans. R. F. C. Hull (Princeton: Princeton University Press, 1954), 105 (1946).

141. Jung, *Collected Works*, 6:459–60 (1921).

142. As well as external objects, such as ink blots, "cyrillic letters, crystal balls, prayer wheels, modern paintings, etc." For an interesting account of how Jung gained insight into the widespread opportunity for free association and its implications for dream interpretation, see Jung et al., *Man and His Symbols*, 27–28.

143. Ibid, 28–29.

144. Jung, *Collected Works*, 6:422 (1921).

145. Jung, *Collected Works*, 17:105 (1946).

146. Ibid.

147. Jung, *Collected Works*, 7:80–81 (1917/1926/1943).

148. Jung, *Letters*, vol. 2, *1951–1961*, ed. Gerhard Adler in collaboration with Aniela Jaffé; trans. R. F. C. Hull (Princeton: Princeton University Press, 1973), 457 (1958).

149. Jung, *Collected Works*, 16:120 (1951).

150. Ibid.

151. Ibid, 120–21.

152. Ibid, 121.

153. See chapter 4, pp. 100–108, for a critical discussion of individuation and individualism.

154. Jung, *Collected Works*, 10:454 (1958).

155. Jung added as clarification: "A real conflict with the collective norm arises only when an individual way is raised to a norm, which is the actual aim of extreme individualism. Naturally this aim is pathological and inimical to life. It has, accordingly, nothing to do with individuation, which, though it may strike out on an individual bypath, precisely on that account needs the norm for its *orientation* to society and for the vitally necessary relationship of the individual to society (Jung, *Collected Works*, 6:449 [1921]).

156. Jung, *Collected Works*, 8:364 (1928/1931).

157. Carl G. Jung, *C. G. Jung Speaking*, ed. William McGuire and R. F. C. Hull (Princeton: Princeton University Press, 1997), 414 (1959).

158. Jung, *Collected Works*, 8:133–34 (1919).

159. Ibid., 364 (1928/1931).

160. Jung et al., *Man and His Symbols*, 64.

161. The capitalization is Freud's: "Our God, Logos, will fulfill whichever of these wishes nature outside us allows...." Freud, *The Future of an Illusion*, 69.

162. Jung, *Collected Works*, 10:444 (1958).

163. This and my subsequent discussion of "personalism" are primarily indebted to Erazim Kohák's *Embers and the Stars*, while my reference to the I–Thou relationship is a direct allusion to Martin Buber's *I and Thou*. The title of this work itself, *The Id and Thou*, is a double reference to Freud and Buber, and suggests that what I seek in this analysis is a revisioning of Freud's moral psychology through a repersonalization of our moral vision in which what was once merely *id* has now become a *thou*. That is, our own interior may become the locus of a reverential dialogue with moral significance. Conscience is a term referring to this internal moral dialogue with an "other." Jung's psychology provides the basic framework for the development of this ontic moral psychology. By "personalism" I do *not* refer to more recent theories pertaining to probability, but rather to the older usage of the term denoting that the individual is the primary category/metaphor and starting point of reflection, and that by way of extension a conception of reality emerges in which the intrinsic dignity of all beings is recognized and incorporated into subsequent theories.

Chapter 6

1. Neal O. Weiner, *The Harmony of the Soul: Mental Health and Moral Virtue Reconsidered* (Albany: State University of New York Press, 1993), 152.

2. Ibid.

3. Ibid.

4. Friedrich Nietzsche (1844–1900).

5. "Nietzsche's difference from other naturalistic philosophers must be sought first in his profound concern whether universally valid values and a meaningful life are at all possible in a godless world, and secondly in his impassioned scorn for those who simply take for granted the validity of any particular set of values which happens to have the sanction of their religion, class, society, or state" (Walter Kaufmann,

Nietzsche: Philosopher, Psychologist, Antichrist [Princeton: Princeton University Press, 1950], 103).

6. First articulated in Nietzsche, *Die Fröhliche Wissenschaft*; Eng. trans., *The Gay Science*, trans. Walter Kaufmann (New York: Vintage Books, 1974), 167.

7. Ibid., 196.

8. Ibid., 181.

9. Nietzsche, quoted in Kaufmann, *Nietzsche*, 167.

10. The "sacred canopy" is Peter Berger's term referring to the socially constructed mythological framework, a nomos, in which societies and individuals make and find meaning during the course of their lives, particularly in "marginal situations" when one is threatened with meaninglessness (Berger, *The Sacred Canopy: Elements of a Sociological Theory of Religion* [Garden City, NY: Doubleday, 1967], 21–23).

11. Kaufmann, *Nietzsche*, 100.

12. Nietzsche, in *The Will to Power* (pp. 1–2), wrote: "What does nihilism mean? *That the highest values devalue themselves.* The goal is lacking; the answer is lacking to our 'Why?'" quoted in Kaufmann, *Nietzsche*, 122.

13. Nietzsche, *The Twilight of the Idols*, trans. R. J. Hollingdale (London: Penguin Books, 1968), 81.

14. Nietzsche, *Beyond Good and Evil*, trans. Walter Kaufmann (New York: Vintage Books, 1966), 27.

15. Nietzsche, *The Twilight of the Idols*, 29. The subtitle of the book is *"or How to Philosophize with a Hammer."*

16. For example, reflecting on an earlier commentary of his, Nietzsche writes, "In the above-mentioned work, on which I was then engaged, I made opportune and inopportune reference to the propositions of that book, not in order to refute them—what have I to do with refutations!—but, as becomes a positive spirit, to replace the improbable with the more probable, possibly one error with another" (Nietzsche, *On the Genealogy of Morals*, trans. Walter Kaufmann and R. J. Hollingdale [New York: Vintage Books, 1967], 18).

17. Though it is outside the scope of this work, it is perhaps helpful to contextualize Nietzsche's response to the threat of nihilism or, more generally, that of suffering, by contrasting it to that of Arthur Schopenhauer. Paul Tillich locates Nietzsche in the philosophical tradition of "voluntarism," that is, theories that emphasize the primacy of will or other nonrational factors (e.g., love, as in the Christian tradition) over the intellect (*A History of Christian Thought*, ed. Carl Braaten [New York: Simon & Schuster, 1967], 487–503). Nietzsche's predecessor,

Schopenhauer, articulated a voluntaristic view, seeing all of nature as an expression (an "objectification") of a blind Will, forever seeking yet never realizing satisfaction of its cravings. This Schopenhauerian Will was to be understood not as a purposeful, conscious being but rather as a morally ambiguous, conflictual force. Schopenhauer's moral response to this world of "Will and Idea," formulated when Buddhism was first being introduced to the West, was one of self-negation. Schopenhauer sought *release* from the incessant, insatiable cravings of the Will (and personal will). In this life it is only art, and particularly music, that provides glimpses of the eternal and affords us brief respites from the toils of willfulness. While Nietzsche agreed (in a general sense) with Schopenhauer's view that the world is an expression of Will, his ethical response was the polar opposite. Rather than seek *release* from the will, Nietzsche urged us to *express* this will in a process of "self-overcoming." Rather than *negate* the self, Nietzsche urged us to *affirm* the self.

18. Nietzsche, *On the Genealogy of Morals*, 20.

19. Nietzsche, *Anti-Christ*, trans. R. J. Hollingdale (London: Penguin Books, 1968), 137.

20. Nietzsche, *Gay Science*, 169.

21. Ibid., 168.

22. Ibid., 307.

23. Ibid.

24. Nietzsche, *Beyond Good and Evil*, 204.

25. Ibid., 207.

26. Nietzsche, *On the Genealogy of Morals*, 26.

27. Ibid., 34.

28. Walter Kaufmann, *Nietzsche*, 178–87, esp. 184.

29. Nietzsche, *Gay Science*, 79.

30. Nietzsche, *Beyond Good and Evil*, 29.

31. Ibid., 11.

32. Ibid.

33. Nietzsche, *Gay Science*, 177.

34. Ibid., 176–77.

35. Nietzsche, *Beyond Good and Evil*, 29.

36. Nietzsche, *Twilight of the Idols*, 45.

37. Ibid.

38. Ibid., 46.

39. Ibid.

40. Ibid., 47.

41. Ibid., 44.

42. Nietzsche, *Beyond Good and Evil*, 24.

43. Ibid.

44. Nietzsche, *On the Genealogy of Morals*, 45.

45. Ibid.

46. Nietzsche, *The Will to Power* (pp. 1–2), quoted in Kaufmann, *Nietzsche*, 122.

47. Kaufmann, *Nietzsche*, 100.

48. Quoted in Frederick Copleston, *A History of Philosophy*, vol. 7 (New York: Image Books, 1965), 403.

49. Kaufmann, *Nietzsche*, 113.

50. Ibid., 179.

51. Quoted in Kaufmann, *Nietzsche*, 179. And further, "Nietzsche approached the conception of a will to power from two distinct points of view. First, he thought of it as a craving for worldly success, which he repudiated as harmful to man's interest in perfecting himself. Secondly, he thought of the will to power as a psychological drive in terms of which many diverse phenomena could be explained; e.g., gratitude, pity, and self-abasement" (ibid., 185).

52. Quoted in Kaufmann, *Nietzsche*, 183.

53. Kaufmann, *Nietzsche*, 192.

54. Ibid., 216.

55. Nietzsche, *Beyond Good and Evil*, 31.

56. Ibid., 47–48.

57. Ibid.

58. Quoted in Kaufmann, *Nietzsche*, 310.

59. Kaufmann discusses at length the integral role of sublimation, as necessary counterpart of Nietzsche's central concept of "will to power," and in contrast to the dynamic of repression (*Nietzsche*, 211–56).

60. Ibid., 236. Kaufmann describes the process in this manner: "Sublimation is possible only because there is a basic force (the will to power) which is defined in terms of an objective (power) which remains the same throughout all 'metamorphoses.' This essential objective is preserved no less than is the energy, while the immediate objective is canceled; and the lifting up consists in the attainment of greater power" (ibid., 230).

61. Nietzsche, *On the Genealogy of Morals*, 96.

62. In fact, as with all concepts that connote a "thing," Nietzsche was critical of the notion of the will as a singular faculty of effective causal animation. For example, we read, "Willing seems to me to be above all something *complicated*, something that is a unit only as a word— and it is precisely in this one word that the popular prejudice lurks, which has defeated the always inadequate caution of philosophers....But

now let us notice what is strangest about the will—this manifold thing for which the people have only one word: inasmuch as in the given circumstances we are at the same time the commanding *and* obeying parties...[yet] we are accustomed to disregard this duality, and to deceive ourselves about it by means of the synthetic concept 'I,' a whole series of erroneous conclusions, and consequently of false evaluations of the will itself, has become attached to the act of willing—to such a degree that he who wills believes sincerely that willing *suffices* for action" (Nietzsche, *Beyond Good and Evil*, 25–26).

63. Kaufmann, *Nietzsche*, 229.
64. Ibid., 229–30.
65. Nietzsche, *On the Genealogy of Morals*, 79.
66. Kaufmann, *Nietzsche*, 242.
67. Nietzsche, *On the Genealogy of Morals*, 45.
68. Ibid., 17 (emphasis in original).
69. Quoted in Kaufmann, *Nietzsche*, 200.
70. Nietzsche, *On the Genealogy of Morals*, 57–58.
71. Ibid., 58.
72. Ibid., 60.
73. Ibid., 62.
74. Ibid., 84.
75. Ibid., 87: "The *instinct for freedom* (in my language: the will to power)."
76. Ibid., 84.
77. Ibid., 85.
78. Nietzsche, *On the Genealogy of Morals*, 84–85. And, in even more graphic language, Nietzsche wrote: "This animal that rubbed itself raw against the bars of its cage as one tried to 'tame' it; this deprived creature, racked with homesickness for the wild, who had to turn itself into an adventure, a torture chamber, an uncertain and dangerous wilderness—this fool, this yearning and desperate prisoner became the inventor of the 'bad conscience'" (ibid., 85).
79. Ibid., 87.
80. Ibid., 88.
81. Ibid., 85.
82. Ibid., 178.
83. Ibid., 87–88.
84. Nietzsche, *Gay Science*, 307.
85. Nietzsche, *Beyond Good and Evil*, 44.
86. Nietzsche, *Twilight of the Idols*, 66.
87. Nietzsche, *Gay Science*, 307, and idem, *Beyond Good and Evil*, 45.

88. Nietzsche, *Anti-Christ*, 127.

89. Kaufmann, *Nietzsche*, 100.

90. Paul Tillich made the following observations about forms of knowledge and their characteristics that will provide some of the terminology in my discussion. "Knowing is a form of union. But the union of knowledge is a peculiar one; it is a union through separation. Detachment is the condition of cognitive union." Tillich distinguished two basic types of knowing: "controlling" and "receiving." Controlling reason is "predominantly determined by the element of detachment. It unites subject and object for the sake of the control of the object by the subject. It transforms the object into a completely conditioned and calculable 'thing.'" In the realm of applied technology "controlling knowledge is verified by the success of controlling actions. The technical use of scientific knowledge is its greatest and most impressive verification." Yet in the realm of human relationships, according to Tillich, it is not detachment that yields understanding, but rather union. This is because humans, as personal subjects, "resist objectification" if they are to be truly understood. "Without union there is no cognitive approach to man. In contrast to controlling knowledge this cognitive attitude can be called 'receiving knowledge.'" Unlike controlling reason, "emotion is the vehicle" for receiving reason. Whereas controlling reason is verified *experimentally*, receiving reason is verified *experientially*. By this Tillich meant that verification of one's truth claims can occur empirically as with controlling knowledge, or it "can occur within the life process itself. The verifying experiences of a nonexperimental character are truer to life, though less exact and definite" (Tillich, *Systematic Theology*, vol. 1 [Chicago: University of Chicago Press, 1951], 94–102).

91. Neal Weiner addresses this issue in the following manner: "The problem is thus to explain the unavailability of this demonstration [i.e., a rational demonstration of usefully specific ethical truths that is convincing to all normally well-educated people of the same culture] while not undermining the sense of rationality that enables us to maintain the interpersonal and intercultural validity of ethical truth" (*Harmony of the Soul*, 158).

92. C. G. Jung, *Psychology and Western Religion*, trans. R. F. C. Hull (Princeton: Princeton University Press, 1984), 255–65 (1956).

93. Ibid.

94. "I take my stand on Kant, which means that an assertion doesn't posit its object" (Carl G. Jung, *Letters*, vol. 1, *1906–1950*, ed. Gerhard Adler in collaboration with Aniela Jaffé, trans. R. F. C. Hull [Princeton: Princeton University Press, 1973], 294 [1946]).

95. Jung, *Psychology and Western Religion*, 260 (1956).

96. Jung, *Letters*, 1:556 (1950).

97. Jung, *Psychology and Western Religion*, 259 (1956).

98. "When I use the word 'feeling' in contrast to 'thinking,' I refer to a judgment of value—for instance, agreeable or disagreeable, good or bad, and so on. Feeling according to this definition is not an emotion (which, as the word conveys, is involuntary). *Feeling* as I mean it is (like thinking) a *rational* (i.e., ordering) function, whereas intuition is an *irrational* (i.e., perceiving) function" (Carl G. Jung et al., *Man and His Symbols* [New York: Doubleday, 1964], 61).

99. Carl G. Jung, *The Collected Works of C. G. Jung*, vol. 16, *The Practice of Psychotherapy*, trans. R. F. C. Hull (Princeton: Princeton University Press, 1955), 279–80 (1943).

100. Ibid., 279.

101. "*Caput draconis* = 'head of the dragon,' an alchemical concept symbolizing the union of highest and lowest" (editors' note in Jung, *Letters*, 1:408 [1946]).

102. Carl G. Jung, *The Collected Works of C. G. Jung*, vol. 10, *Civilization in Transition*, trans. R. F. C. Hull (Princeton: Princeton University Press, 1964), 440–414 (1958).

103. Jung, *Collected Works*, 16:123 (1951).

104. Jung et al., *Man and His Symbols*, 92.

105. Jung, *Psychology and Western Religion*, 258.

106. Jung, *Collected Works*, 10:454 (1958).

107. Carl G. Jung, *The Collected Works of C. G. Jung*, vol. 4, *Freud and Psychoanalysis*, trans. R. F. C. Hull (Princeton: Princeton University Press, 1961), 334 (1929).

108. Ibid.

109. Carl G. Jung, *The Collected Works of C. G. Jung*, vol. 18, *The Symbolic Life: Miscellaneous Writings*, trans. R. F. C. Hull (Princeton: Princeton University Press, 1950), 618 (1949).

110. Jung, *Psychology and Western Religion*, 265 (1957).

111. Jung, *Collected Works*, 10:459 (1959) (emphasis in original).

112. Ibid., 445.

113. Jung, *Psychology and Western Religion*, 261(1956).

114. Carl G. Jung, *Letters*, vol. 2, *1951–1961*, ed. Gerhard Adler in collaboration with Aniela Jaffé; trans. R. F. C. Hull (Princeton: Princeton University Press, 1973), particularly 43, 61, 101–2, 367–68, 370–78 (1952–57).

Chapter 7

1. "Martin Buber published an article entitled "Religion und modernes Denken," *Merkur* [Stuttgart] 6, no. 2 (Feb. 1952), in which he labeled Jung's religious position as "Gnosticism" (editor's note in Carl G. Jung, *Letters*, vol. 2, *1951–1961*, ed. Gerhard Adler in collaboration with Aniela Jaffé; trans. R. F. C. Hull [Princeton: Princeton University Press, 1973], 43 [1952]).

2. Originally published as a book, *Antwort auf Hiob* (Zurich, 1952); the English translation contained in *The Collected Works of C. G. Jung*, vol. 11, *Psychology and Religion*, trans. R. F. C. Hull (Princeton: Princeton University Press, 1958), 355–470, was first published in England in 1954. It was reprinted by the Pastoral Psychology Book Club, Great Neck, New York, in 1956. Jung, *Collected Works*, 11:355.

3. Hans Jonas, *The Gnostic Religion: The Message of the Alien God and the Beginnings of Christianity* (Boston: Beacon Press, 1958), 32.

4. Ibid.

5. Mircea Eliade, *A History of Religious Ideas*, vol. 2, *From Guatama Buddha to the Triumph of Christianity*, trans. Willard R. Trask (Chicago: University of Chicago Press, 1982), 368–74.

6. Ibid., 372.

7. Jonas, *Gnostic Religion*, 42–47.

8. Carl G. Jung, *The Collected Works of C. G. Jung*, vol. 18, *The Symbolic Life: Miscellaneous Writings*, trans. R. F. C. Hull (Princeton: Princeton University Press, 1950), 730 (1957).

9. Ibid., 664 (1952).

10. "This [encounter with alchemy via Richard Wilhelm sending Jung a copy of the Chinese alchemical text, *The Secret of the Golden Flower*] was a momentous discovery: I had stumbled upon the historical counterpart of my psychology of the unconscious. The possibility of a comparison with alchemy, and the uninterrupted intellectual chain back to Gnosticism, gave substance to my psychology" (Carl G. Jung, *Memories, Dreams, Reflections*, recorded and ed. by Aniela Jaffé; trans. Richard and Clara Winston [New York: Vintage Books, 1961], 204–5).

11. "Creative illness" was a term employed by Henri F. Ellenberger to describe "mental illness" that yields a positive transformation of the personality and is the experiential source of subsequent creative output based on the personal "vision" gained through the illness (Henri F. Ellenberger, *The Discovery of the Unconscious: The History and Evolution of Dynamic Psychiatry* [New York: Basic Books, 1970], 216, 672–73).

12. Reprinted in Jung, *Memories, Dreams, Reflections*, 378–90.

13. Jung, *Letters*, 2:571 (1960).

14. Ibid., 2:381 (1957).

15. Ibid., 237–38 (1955).

16. Ibid., 486 (1959).

17. Ibid., 592 (1960).

18. Elaine Pagels, *The Gnostic Gospels* (New York: Vintage Books, 1979), 146.

19. Jung, *Letters*, 2:583 (1960).

20. Jung, *Collected Works*, 18:663 (1952). Also, "I make no metaphysical assertions and even in my heart I am no Neo-Manichean; on the contrary I am deeply convinced of the unity of the self, as demonstrated by the mandala symbolism" (Carl G. Jung, *Letters*, vol. 1, *1906–1950*, ed. Gerhard Adler in collaboration with Aniela Jaffé, trans. R. F. C. Hull [Princeton: Princeton University Press, 1973], 541 [1949]).

21. Jung, *Collected Works*, 18:664–65 (1952); originally published as "A Reply to Martin Buber," in *Merkur* [Stuttgart], 6, no. 5 (May 1952).

22. "Your alternative is either 'metaphysical God' or Brother Klaus' 'own unconscious.'"(Jung, *Letters*, 1:408 [1946]).

23. Jung, *Letters*, 2:245 (1955) (emphasis in original).

24. Ibid., 368 (1957).

25. Carl G. Jung, *Jung Speaking*, ed. William McGuire and R. F. C. Hull (Princeton: Princeton University Press, 1977), 360 (1958).

26. Jung, *Letters*, 2:545 (1959).

27. Ibid.

28. Carl G. Jung, *The Collected Works*, vol. 15, *The Spirit in Man, Art, and Literature*, trans. R. F. C. Hull (Princeton: Princeton University Press, 1966), 104 (1930).

29. Ibid.

30. Carl G. Jung, *The Collected Works*, vol. 10, *Civilization in Transition*, trans. R. F. C. Hull (Princeton: Princeton University Press, 1964), 461 (1959).

31. "Our moral freedom reaches as far as our consciousness, and thus our liberation from compulsion and captivity" (Jung, *Letters*, 2:547 [1959]).

32. Jung, *Letters*, 1:556 (1950).

33. Jung, *Letters*, 2:485 (1959).

34. Ibid., 312 (1956).

35. Ibid., 435 (1958).

36. Jung, *Collected Works*, 18:720 (1957). Jung used the term "beyond good and evil" not in the sense of amoral, or moral relativity, but rather in an epistemological sense of "we pass no moral judgment"

(ibid.). Jung was likewise critical of certain gnostic texts that, despite their context of a world-negating theology, were pollyannish: "Sayings like 'Heaven above, Heaven Below, Stars above, Stars below, All that is above, All that is below, Grasp this, and Rejoice,' are too optimistic and superficial; they forget the moral torment occasioned by the opposites, and the importance of ethical values" (Carl G. Jung, *The Collected Works of C. G. Jung*, vol. 16, *The Practice of Psychotherapy*, trans. R. F. C. Hull [Princeton: Princeton University Press, 1955], 189 [1946]).

37. Jung, *Letters*, 2:495 (1959).

38. Ibid., 311 (1956).

39. Jung, *Collected Works*, 18:720 (1957).

40. Jung, *Letters*, 2:316 (1956).

41. Carl G. Jung, *Psychology and Western Religion*, trans. R. F. C. Hull (Princeton: Princeton University Press, 1984), 261 (1956).

BIBLIOGRAPHY

Barrett, William. *Death of the Soul: From Descartes to the Computer*. Garden City, NY: Anchor Press, 1986.

Becker, Ernest. *The Denial of Death*. New York: Free Press, 1973.

Berger, Peter. *The Sacred Canopy: Elements of a Sociological Theory of Religion*. Garden City, NY: Doubleday, 1967.

Blake, William. *The Essential Blake*. Edited by Stanley Kunitz. New York: Ecco Press, 1987.

Browning, Don S. *Religious Thought and the Modern Psychologies: A Critical Conversation in the Theology of Culture*. Philadelphia: Fortress Press, 1987.

Buber, Martin. *I and Thou*. Translated by Walter Kaufmann. New York: Charles Scribner's Sons, 1970.

Copleston, Frederick, S.J. *A History of Philosophy*, vols. 1–3. New York: Image Books, 1946, 1950, 1953.

———. *A History of Philosophy*, vols. 4–6. New York: Image Books, 1960, 1959, 1960.

———. *A History of Philosophy*, vols. 7–9. New York: Image Books, 1965, 1966, 1977.

Crosby, Donald A. *The Specter of the Absurd: Sources and Criticisms of Modern Nihilism*. Albany: State University of New York Press, 1988.

Edinger, Edward F. *Ego and Archetype: Individuation and the Religious Function of the Psyche*. New York: Penguin Books, 1972.

Eliade, Mircea. *A History of Religious Ideas*, vol. 2, *From Guatama Buddha to the Triumph of Christianity*. Translated by Willard R. Trask. Chicago: University of Chicago Press, 1982.

———. *The Myth of the Eternal Return*. Translated by Willard R. Trask. Princeton: Princeton University Press, 1954.

Ellenberger, Henri F. *The Discovery of the Unconscious: The History and Evolution of Dynamic Psychiatry*. New York: Basic Books, 1970.

Erikson, Erik H. *The Life Cycle Completed*. New York: W. W. Norton, 1982.

———. *Young Man Luther: A Study in Psychoanalysis and History*. New York: W. W. Norton, 1958.

Flax, Jane. *Thinking Fragments: Psychoanalysis, Feminism, and Postmodernism in the Contemporary West*. Berkeley: University of California Press, 1990.

Flew, Antony. *A Dictionary of Philosophy*. New York: St. Martin's Press, 1979.

Frankean, William K. *Ethics*. Englewood Cliffs, New Jersey: Prentice Hall, 1973.

Frankl, Victor. *Man's Search For Meaning*. New York: Washington Square Press, 1959.

Freud, Sigmund. *An Autobiographical Study*. Translated and edited by James Strachey. New York: W. W. Norton, 1952.

———. *Beyond the Pleasure Principle*. Translated and edited by James Strachey. New York: W. W. Norton, 1961.

———. *Character and Culture*. Edited by Philip Rieff. New York: Collier Books, 1963.

———. *Civilization and Its Discontents*. Translated and edited by James Strachey. New York: W. W. Norton, 1961.

———. *The Ego and the Id*. Translated by Joan Riviere; revised and edited by James Strachey. New York: W. W. Norton, 1960.

———. *The Future of an Illusion*. Translated and edited by James Strachey. New York: W. W. Norton, 1961.

———. *New Introductory Lectures on Psycho-Analysis*. Translated and edited by James Strachey. New York: W. W. Norton, 1965.

———. *An Outline of Psycho-Analysis*. Translated and edited by James Strachey. New York: W. W. Norton, 1949.

———. *Three Essays on the Theory of Sexuality*. Translated and newly edited by James Strachey. New York: Basic Books, 1962.

———. *Totem and Taboo*. Translated by James Strachey. New York: W. W. Norton, 1950.

Freud, Sigmund, and C. G. Jung. *The Freud/Jung Letters*. Edited by William McGuire. Translated by Ralph Manheim and R. F. C. Hull. Cambridge, MA: Harvard University Press, 1988.

Gay, Peter. *Freud: A Life for Our Time*. New York: Anchor Books, 1988.

Hannah, Barbara. *Jung, His Life and Work: A Biographical Memoir*. New York: G. P. Putnam's Sons, 1976.

Harvey, Van A. *A Handbook of Theological Terms*. New York: Collier Books, 1964.

Heisig, James. *Imago Dei: A Study of C. G. Jung's Psychology of Religion*. Lewisburg, PA: Bucknell University Press, 1979.

Hick, John. *Evil and the God of Love*. San Francisco: Harper & Row, 1966.

———. *God Has Many Names*. Philadelphia: Westminster Press, 1980.

Hillman, James. *Re-Visioning Psychology*. New York: HarperPerennial, 1975.

Homans, Peter. *Jung in Context: Modernity and the Making of a Psychology*. Chicago: University of Chicago Press, 1979.

Jaffé, Aniela. *The Myth of Meaning in the Work of C. G. Jung*. Translated by R. F. C. Hull. New York: Penguin Books, 1971.

Johnson, Mark. *Moral Imagination: Implications of Cognitive Sciences for Ethics*. Chicago: University of Chicago Press, 1993.

Jonas, Hans. *The Gnostic Religion: The Message of the Alien God and the Beginnings of Christianity*. Boston: Beacon Press, 1958.

Jung, Carl G. *The Collected Works of C. G. Jung*. Volume 3, *Psychogenesis of Mental Disease*. Translated by R. F. C. Hull. Princeton: Princeton University Press, 1960.

———. *The Collected Works of C. G. Jung*. Volume 4, *Freud and Psychoanalysis*. Translated by R. F. C. Hull. Princeton: Princeton University Press, 1961.

———. *The Collected Works of C. G. Jung*. Volume 5, *Symbols of Transformation*. Translated by R. F. C. Hull. Princeton: Princeton University Press, 1956.

———. *The Collected Works of C. G. Jung*. Volume 6, *Psychological Types*. A Revision by R. F. C. Hull of the Translation by H. G. Baynes. Princeton: Princeton University Press, 1971.

———. *The Collected Works of C. G. Jung*. Volume 7, *Two Essays on Analytical Psychology*. Translated by R. F. C. Hull. Princeton: Princeton University Press, 1953.

———. *The Collected Works of C. G. Jung*. Volume 8, *The Structure and Dynamics of the Psyche*. Translated by R. F. C. Hull. Princeton: Princeton University Press, 1960.

———. *The Collected Works of C. G. Jung*. Volume 9, part i, *The Archetypes and the Collective Unconscious*. Translated by R. F. C. Hull. Princeton: Princeton University Press, 1959.

———. *The Collected Works of C. G. Jung*. Volume 9, part ii, *Aion*. Translated by R. F. C. Hull. Princeton: Princeton University Press, 1959.

———. *The Collected Works of C. G. Jung*. Volume 10, *Civilization in Transition*. Translated by R. F. C. Hull. Princeton: Princeton University Press, 1964.

———. *The Collected Works of C. G. Jung.* Volume 11, *Psychology and Religion: West and East.* Translated by R. F. C. Hull. Princeton: Princeton University Press, 1958.

———. *The Collected Works of C. G. Jung.* Volume 12, *Psychology and Alchemy.* Translated by R. F. C. Hull. Princeton: Princeton University Press, 1953.

———. *The Collected Works of C. G. Jung.* Volume 13, *Alchemical Studies.* Translated by R. F. C. Hull. Princeton: Princeton University Press, 1967.

———. *The Collected Works of C. G. Jung.* Volume 14, *Mysterium Coniunctionis.* Translated by R. F. C. Hull. Princeton: Princeton University Press, 1963.

———. *The Collected Works of C. G. Jung.* Volume 15, *The Spirit in Man, Art, and Literature.* Translated by R. F. C. Hull. Princeton: Princeton University Press, 1966.

———. *The Collected Works of C. G. Jung.* Volume 16, *The Practice of Psychotherapy.* Translated by R. F. C. Hull. Princeton: Princeton University Press, 1955.

———. *The Collected Works of C. G. Jung.* Volume 17, *The Development of Personality.* Translated by R. F. C. Hull. Princeton: Princeton University Press, 1954.

———. *The Collected Works of C. G. Jung.* Volume 18, *The Symbolic Life: Miscellaneous Writings.* Translated by R. F. C. Hull. Princeton: Princeton University Press, 1950.

———. *The Collected Works of C. G. Jung.* Supplementary Volume A, *Zofingia Lectures.* Translated by Jan van Heurck. Princeton: Princeton University Press, 1983.

———. *C.G. Jung Speaking.* Edited by William McGuire and R. F. C. Hull. Princeton: Princeton University Press, 1977.

———. *Letters.* Volume 1, *1906–1950.* Edited by Gerhard Adler in collaboration with Aniela Jaffé. Translated by R. F. C. Hull. Princeton: Princeton University Press, 1973.

———. *Letters.* Volume 2, *1951–1961.* Edited by Gerhard Adler in collaboration with Aniela Jaffé. Translated by R. F. C. Hull. Princeton: Princeton University Press, 1973.

———. *Memories, Dreams, Reflections.* Recorded and edited by Aniela Jaffé. Translated by Richard and Clara Winston. New York: Vintage Books, 1961.

———. *Psychology and Western Religion.* Translated by R. F. C. Hull. Princeton: Princeton University Press, 1984.

Jung, Carl G., M.-L. von Franz, Joseph L. Henderson, Jolande Jacobi, and Aniela Jaffé. *Man and His Symbols.* New York: Doubleday, 1964.

Kant, Immanuel. *Critique of Practical Reason.* Translated by Lewis White Beck. New York: Macmillan, 1956.

———. *Critique of Pure Reason.* Translated by Norman Kemp Smith. New York: St. Martin's Press, 1929.

Kaufmann, Walter. *Discovering the Mind,* vol. 3. New York: McGraw-Hill, 1980.

———. *Nietzsche: Philosopher, Psychologist, Antichrist.* Princeton: Princeton University Press, 1950.

Kohák, Erazim. *The Embers and the Stars: A Philosophical Inquiry into the Moral Sense of Nature.* Chicago: University of Chicago Press, 1984.

Koyré, Alexandre. *From the Closed World to the Infinite Universe.* Baltimore: John Hopkins University Press, 1957.

Lasch, Christopher. *The Culture of Narcissism: American Life in an Age of Diminishing Expectations.* New York: W. W. Norton, 1979.

Locke, John. *An Essay Concerning Human Understanding.* New York: Penguin Books, 1964.

Maddi, Salvatore R. *Personality Theories: A Comparative Analysis.* Pacific Grove, CA: Brooks/Cole Publishing, 1989.

Nelson, Benjamin. *On the Roads to Modernity: Conscience, Science, and Civilizations: Selected Writings.* Edited by Toby E. Huff. Totowa, NJ: Rowman & Littlefield, 1981.

Neumann, Erich. *Depth Psychology and a New Ethic.* Translated by Eugene Rolfe. Boston: Shambhala, 1990.

Nietzsche, Friedrich. *Anti-Christ.* Translated by R. J. Hollingdale. London: Penguin Books, 1968.

———. *Beyond Good and Evil.* Translated by Walter Kaufmann. New York: Vintage Books, 1966.

———. *Ecce Homo.* Translated and edited by Walter Kaufmann. New York: Vintage Books, 1967.

———. *The Gay Science.* Translated by Walter Kaufmann. New York: Vintage Books, 1974.

———. *On the Genealogy of Morals.* Translated by Walter Kaufmann and R. J. Hollingdale. New York: Vintage Books, 1967.

———. *The Twilight of the Idols.* Translated by R. J. Hollingdale. London: Penguin Books, 1968.

Nussbaum, Martha C. *The Fragility of Goodness: Luck and Ethics in Greek Tragedy and Philosophy.* Cambridge: Cambridge University Press, 1986.

Olney, James. *The Rhizome and the Flower: The Perennial Philosophy, Yeats and Jung*. Berkeley: University of California Press, 1980.

Otto, Rudolf. *The Idea of the Holy*. Translated by John W. Harvey. London: Oxford University Press, 1923.

Pagels, Elaine. *The Gnostic Gospels*. New York: Vintage Books, 1979.

Progoff, Ira. *Jung's Psychology and its Social Meaning*. New York: Dialogue House Library, 1953.

Ricoeur, Paul. *The Symbolism of Evil*. Boston: Beacon Press, 1967.

Rieff, Philip. *The Triumph of the Therapeutic: Uses of Faith after Freud*. Chicago: University of Chicago Press, 1966.

Singer, June. *Seeing Through the Visible World: Jung, Gnosis, and Chaos*. San Francisco: Harper & Row, 1990.

Stein, Murray. *Solar Conscience, Lunar Conscience: An Essay on the Psychological Foundations of Morality, Lawfulness, and the Sense of Justice*. Wilmette, IL: Chiron Publications, 1993.

Stevens, Anthony. *Archetypes: A Natural History of the Self*. New York: Quill, 1983.

———. *On Jung*. London: Routledge, 1990.

Storr, Anthony. *Freud*. Oxford: Oxford University Press, 1989.

Storr, Anthony, ed. *The Essential Jung*. Princeton: Princeton University Press, 1983.

Taylor, Charles. *Hegel and Modern Society*. Cambridge: Cambridge University Press, 1979.

———. *Sources of the Self: The Making of the Modern Identity*. Cambridge, MA: Harvard University Press, 1989.

Thoreau, Henry David. *Walden and Other Writings*. Edited by Joseph Wood Krutch. Toronto: Bantam Books, 1962.

Tillich, Paul. *The Courage to Be*. New Haven: Yale University Press, 1952.

———. *A History of Christian Thought*. Edited by Carl E. Braaten. New York: Simon & Schuster, 1967.

———. *The Meaning of Health*. Edited by Perry LeFevre. Chicago: Exploration Press, 1984.

———. *Systematic Theology*, vol. 1. Chicago: University of Chicago Press, 1951.

———. *Theology of Culture*. Edited by Robert C. Kimball. London: Oxford University Press, 1959.

von Franz, Marie-Louise. *C. G. Jung*. Translated by William H. Kennedy. Toronto: Inner City Books, 1998.

Waugh, Patricia, ed. *Postmodernism*. London: Edward Arnold, 1992.

Wehr, Demaris S. *Jung & Feminism*. Boston: Beacon Press, 1987.

Weiner, Neal O. *The Harmony of the Soul: Mental Health and Moral Virtue Reconsidered*. Albany: State University of New York Press, 1993.

Whitehead, Alfred N. *Process and Reality: An Essay in Cosmology*. Gifford Lectures 1927–28. Edited by David Ray Griffin and Donald W. Sherburne. New York: Free Press, 1929.

Wright, Robert. *The Moral Animal: Evolutionary Psychology and Everyday Life*. New York: Vintage Books, 1994.

INDEX

Adaptation: neurosis understood in terms of, 70, 73–74, 79–82

Archetypes: affirm the individual, though "universal," 58; described, 159–60; expression of instincts, 159, 164, 166

Attitude: described, 72–73; importance of, as root problem of psychopathology, 72

Body: both body and mind (soma and psyche) as foundations of Jung's conception of psyche, 155; consciousness, 58; unity with mind, 46–49

Collective: basic conflict with the individual, 99; collective unconscious, distinct from personal unconscious, 160; as conservative, 116; dangerous to both individual and group adaptation, 117–18; described, 99; moral decline of, 115; motives for identification with, 108–10; positive aspects of, 95–96, 110, 114; transformation within as likely ephemeral, 113–14

Conflict (and harmony): adaptation, 86; and Jung, 56–60; problem described, 51–52; relationship to conscience, 52–56

Conscience: agency, form of knowledge, and dialectic, 18–19; ambivalent, 24; both conflict and means of resolution, 227; Court of, 8; critiques of, 124–26; desire, risk, and grace, complementing guilt, authority, and law, 4; effect upon understanding of individuation, 225–28; encounter with ontological foundations of reality, 231; ethical conscience described, 21, 169–71, 173–74; "ethical" conscience as yielding moral truth, 211; etymology of, 5; expressing psychic substratum possessing ontological and epistemological significance, 207; fallibility of, 11, 55, 176; good and evil, 229–31; historical development of concept and practice, 8–10; how psychoanalytic practice enables positive revisioning of, 150, 152–54; I–Thou relationship, 174; instance of transcendent function, 158; "it is" becomes "I ought" and *id* becomes *thou*, by way of, 232; Jung's distinction of "moral" and "ethical" conscience, 21; Jung's psychology of religion, 228–31; Jung's theory of, in distinction to Freud, 168–71; leads from ethical to religious, providing ultimate rationale for individuation, 228; means of "divine service," 24; means of relating instincts and ego, 209; "moral" and "ethical" forms, 169–71, 173–74; most definitive of

285